SOCIAL SECURITY:
NEW ISSUES AND DEVELOPMENTS

SOCIAL SECURITY:
NEW ISSUES AND DEVELOPMENTS

PAUL O. DEAVEN AND WILLIAM H. ANDREWS
EDITORS

Nova Science Publishers, Inc.
New York

LIBRARY OF CONGRESS CATALOGING-IN-PUBLICATION DATA
Social security : new issues and developments / Paul O. Deaven and William H. Andrews (editors).
     p. cm.
 ISBN 978-1-60456-243-9 (hardcover)
 1. Social security--United States. 2. Retirement income--Government policy--United States. 3. Old age pensions--Government policy--United States. 4. Pension trusts--Government policy--United States. I. Deaven, Paul O. II. Andrews, William H.
HD7125.S59928   2007
368.4'300973--dc22   2007047821

Published by Nova Science Publishers, Inc. ✤ *New York*

CONTENTS

PREFACE

Social Security, in the United States, currently refers to the Federal Old-Age, Survivors, and Disability Insurance (OASDI) program.

The original Social Security Act[1] and the current version of the Act, as amended encompass several social welfare or social insurance programs. The larger and better known initiatives of the program are:

- Federal Old-Age, Survivors, and Disability Insurance
- Unemployment Insurance
- Temporary Assistance to Needy Families
- Health Insurance for Aged and Disabled (Medicare)
- Grants to States for Medical Assistance Programs (Medicaid)
- State Children's Health Insurance Program (SCHIP)
- Supplemental Security Income (SSI)

Social Security in the United States is a social insurance program funded through dedicated payroll taxes called Federal Insurance Contributions Act (FICA). The term, in everyday speech, is used only to refer to the benefits for retirement, disability, survivorship, and death, which are the four main benefits provided by traditional private-sector pension plans. By dollars paid, the U.S. Social Security program is the largest government program in the world.

Largely because of solvency questions ranging from immediate crisis to large projected future shortfalls, reform of the Social Security system has been a major political issue for more than three decades.

This new book presents the latest issues and developments related to this program.

Chapter 1 - Policymakers have debated creating a system of individual accounts (IAs) as part of Social Security for many years. President Bush included a call for individual accounts in his 2005 State of the Union address, and several members of Congress have introduced bills in the 109th Congress that include IAs. However, throughout this debate, very little attention has been paid to the practical issues of program design and implementation — issues that could have a significant impact on the cost of the program, the level of participation by workers, the fees levied on accounts, and, ultimately, the assets available at retirement.

This chapter describes policymakers' administrative and structural choices regarding the collection and investment of assets in a system of individual accounts. The choices are many.

It would need to be determined who would be eligible to participate in IAs, how individuals would enroll, how participants would make their contributions, and how much would be collected from them. Workers would need to be educated about enrollment in the new program, the investment choices they face, and the implications for their final benefits. It must also be established how records would be kept, what services would be provided to account holders, and how errors would be corrected. Other choices surround how assets would be invested and whether there would be any restrictions on fees. In each of these areas, this chapter briefly summarizes the options available within a system of IAs, the potential implications of particular policy choices and, when appropriate, current Social Security and pension policy.

The consequences of inadequate system design have become clear in other countries that have adopted IAs. In Australia, a public campaign had to be designed to locate the owners of 3 million lost accounts. In Great Britain, unscrupulous financial advisers persuaded thousands of investors to leave state pension funds, to their disadvantage, in a widely reported "mis-selling" scandal. To provide insights, this chapter also gives examples of problems that other countries have faced when implementing IAs.

A system of IAs could involve millions of Americans, billions of dollars, and could have a broad impact on the American economy. If workers contributed 2% of their current taxable earnings, the accounts could grow to as much as 10% of GDP in 10 years and to 25% of GDP in 20 years. A contribution rate of 5% could accumulate more equities in IAs in 11 years than are currently held by all mutual funds combined. Thus, the stakes are high and there is a compelling need for thorough planning and administration.

Chapter 2 - The Old-Age, Survivors, and Disability Insurance (OASDI) program, commonly referred to as Social Security, is facing a long-term financial deficit. In response to this challenge, President Bush made Social Security reform the key focus of his 2005 domestic social policy agenda. On February 2, 2005, the President laid out specifications for a system of voluntary individual accounts to be phased-in as part of a reformed Social Security system. Administration officials concede that the individual accounts themselves do not alleviate the solvency problem. The individual account proposal would likely make the solvency problem worse over the next 75 years. The President stated that these accounts are just one piece of a comprehensive Social Security reform package and that additional measures will be needed to achieve long-term solvency.

Under the President's 2005 individual account proposal, individuals born prior to 1950 would have experienced no change in their Social Security benefits. Individuals born in 1950 and later would have had the option to participate in Social Security individual accounts (IAs). Workers who chose to participate in IAs would not have been permitted to opt-out of the IA system. Workers would have been allowed to divert up to 4% of their payroll taxes to IAs, subject to a dollar limit that increased over time. But on average people would have had to earn at least 3.3% per year after inflation to break even. This would have occurred because, in addition to administrative costs, their traditional benefits would have been reduced or "offset" by the amount of their contributions, plus 3% a year in interest. The proposal did not include a "minimum benefit" guarantee to ensure that participants would receive a total benefit at least equal to the poverty threshold.

Analyzing the President's 2005 IA proposal using assumptions on investment returns and administrative costs provided by the Social Security Administration, CRS found that the total of the reduced Social Security benefit *plus* the annuity that would have been available using the actual IA balance would have exceeded Social Security current-law promised benefits if the account earned the 4.6% annual real rate of return projected by the Social Security actuaries. However, if the account earned the 2.7% risk-adjusted annual real rate of return projected by the actuaries, workers would have faced a slight reduction in overall Social Security income relative to current law. Younger workers and those with higher lifetime earnings would have benefitted the most from IAs. Younger workers would have been able to contribute to their IA throughout their careers and would have had higher contributions as a result of continued wage growth. Higher earners would have benefitted from being able to accrue larger account balances as the dollar cap on contributions increased.

This chapter is based on the President's 2005 IA proposal. The version portrayed in his FY2007 budget submission is not significantly different from his 2005 proposal. The main substantive difference is that the average interest that a worker would need to earn to break even would be reduced to 2.7% from 3%. Thus, if the account earned the 2.7% risk-adjusted annual rate of return, the worker would experience no reduction in overall Social Security income relative to current law.

Chapter 3 - Over the past few years, there has been intense debate about Social Security reform in the United States. A number of options, ranging from changing the benefit formula to adding individual accounts, has been discussed. The policy debate takes place against the backdrop of an aging population, rising longevity, and relatively low fertility rates, which pose long-range financial challenges to the Social Security system. According to the 2007 Social Security Trustees Report's intermediate assumptions, the Social Security trust funds are projected to experience cash-flow deficits in 2017 and to become exhausted in 2041.

As policymakers consider how to address Social Security's financing challenges, efforts of Social Security reform across the world have gained attention. One of the most oft-cited international cases of reform is Chile. Chile initiated sweeping retirement reforms in 1981 that replaced a state-run, pay-as-you-go defined benefit retirement system with a private, mandatory system of individual retirement accounts where benefits are dependent on the account balance. As a pioneer of individual retirement accounts, Chile has become a case study of pension reform around the world. Although Chile's experience is not directly comparable to the situation in the United States because of large differences between the countries, knowledge of the case may be useful for American policymakers.

This CRS report focuses on the Chilean individual retirement accounts system. It begins with a description of the U.S. Social Security policy debate, along with a brief comparison of Chile and the United States. Next, the report explains what Chile's individual retirement accounts system is and how it works. The pension reform bill sent to the Chilean Congress for debate in 2007 is also discussed. The report does not address other components of Chile's social security system, such as maternity, work injury, and unemployment.

The final section provides an assessment of Chile's now 26-year-old individual retirement accounts system. Pension reforms have contributed to the rapid growth in the Chilean economy over the past two decades and returns on pension fund investments have been greater than expected. Administrative costs, however, have been high and participation rates have been modest at best. There is concern that the system does not cover the entire labor force and provides inadequate benefits to low income workers.

Chapter 4 - One issue that never seems far from the minds of policymakers is Social Security. At the heart of the issue is the large shortfall of projected revenues needed to meet the mounting costs of the system. For the moment, the amount of Social Security tax receipts exceeds the amount of benefits being paid out. The Social Security trustees estimate that, beginning in 2017, the amount of benefits being paid out will exceed tax collections. According to the trustees' best estimate, the trust fund will be exhausted in the year 2040.

Some have argued that because the Social Security trust fund is intended to meet rising future costs of the program, its surplus should not be counted as contributing to official measures of the budget surplus. With regard to current saving, however, it makes no difference whether the surplus is credited to the trust fund or simply seen as financing current federal government outlays (including Social Security benefits). Off-budget surpluses contribute to national saving in exactly the same way as on-budget surpluses do. The additional saving they represent adds to the national saving rate and allows current investment spending to be higher than it would otherwise be.

With respect to household saving for retirement, how much is "enough" may be a subjective matter. But, one standard might be whether accumulated wealth is sufficient to avoid a decline in living standards upon retirement. A number of studies have found, however, that Americans may not tend to save enough to avoid such a decline in their living standard.

Social Security may affect saving in several ways. It may reduce household saving as participants pay some of their Social Security contributions by reducing what they otherwise would have set aside. It reduces the risk associated with retirement planning and so may free participants to cut precautionary saving. It may, however, encourage additional saving by making it possible to retire earlier, thus giving participants a longer period of retirement to plan for. To the extent that Social Security involves a transfer of income from workers to retirees, it tends to reduce household saving by shifting resources from potentially high savers to those who save less.

Proposed reforms have different effects on saving. Those that would move toward a more fully funded system would be likely to increase national saving, investment, and the size of the economy in the future. Reforms that would partially "privatize" using individual accounts, might tend to reduce national saving, unless contributions to those accounts were mandatory. Those that invested Social Security funds in private sector assets would be unlikely to have any effect on national saving.

Chapter 5 - Generally, the goal of disability insurance is to replace a portion of a worker's income should illness or disability prevent him or her from working. Individuals may receive disability benefits from either federal or state governments, or from private insurers. This chapter presents information on two components of federal disability benefits, those provided through the Social Security Disability Insurance (SSDI) and the Supplemental Security Income (SSI) programs. The SSDI program is an insured program that provides benefits to individuals who have paid into the system and meet certain minimum work requirements. The SSI program, in contrast, is a means-tested program that does not have work or contribution requirements, but restricts benefits to those who meet asset and resource limitations.

The SSDI program was enacted in 1956 and provides benefits to insured disabled workers under the full retirement age (and to their spouses, surviving disabled spouses, and children) in amounts related to the disabled worker's former earnings in covered employment. The SSI program, which went into effect in 1974, is a needs-based program that provides a flat cash benefit assuring a minimum cash income to aged, blind and disabled individuals who have very limited income and assets.

To receive disability benefits under either program, individuals must meet strict medical requirements. For both SSDI and SSI disability benefits, "disability" is defined as the inability to engage in substantial gainful activity (SGA) by reason of a medically determinable physical or mental impairment expected to result in death or last at least 12 months. Generally, the worker must be unable to do any kind of work that exists in the national economy, taking into account age, education, and work experience.

Both programs are administered through the Social Security Administration (SSA) and therefore have similar application and disability determination processes. Although SSDI and SSI are federal programs, both federal and state offices are used to determine eligibility for disability benefits. SSA determines whether someone is disabled according to a five-step process, called the sequential evaluation process, where SSA is required to look at all the pertinent facts of a particular case. Current work activity, severity of impairment, and vocational factors are assessed in that order. An applicant may be denied benefits at any step in the sequential process even if the applicant may meet a later criterion.

The SSDI program is funded through the Social Security payroll tax and revenues generated by the taxation of Social Security benefits, portions of which are credited to a separate Disability Insurance (DI) trust fund. In contrast, the SSI program is funded through appropriations from general revenues.

Generally, the goal of disability insurance is to replace a portion of a worker's income should illness or disability prevent him or her from working. Individuals may receive disability benefits from either federal or state governments, or from private insurers.

This chapter presents information on two components of federal disability benefits, those provided through the Social Security Disability Insurance (SSDI) and the Supplemental Security Income (SSI) programs.[1] The SSDI program is an insured program that provides benefits to individuals who have paid into the system and meet certain minimum work requirements. The SSI program, in contrast, is a means-tested program that does not have work or contribution requirements, but individuals must meet the asset and resource limitations. To receive disability benefits under either program, individuals must meet strict medical requirements.

Chapter 6 - Supplemental Security Income (SSI) is a major benefit program for low-income persons with disabilities and senior citizens. As a means tested program, SSI places income and resource limits on individuals and married couples for the purposes of determining their eligibility and level of benefits. To become and remain eligible to receive SSI benefits, single individuals may not have countable resources valued at more than $2,000 and married couples may not have countable resources valued at more than $3,000. Although a person's home and car are excluded from these calculations, most other assets owned by a person or married couple are counted and in most cases, the assets of both partners in a marriage are considered shared and equally available to both the husband and the wife.

A person's countable income must be below SSI program guidelines to qualify for benefits and a person's monthly benefit level is reduced by a portion of his or her earned and unearned income. The income of a person ineligible for SSI can be considered when calculating the benefit amount of that person's spouse. A complicated process of deeming is used to determine how much of the ineligible person's income is to be considered when calculating his or her spouse's monthly SSI benefits.

In some cases marriage may result in a person being denied SSI benefits or seeing his or her SSI benefit level reduced because of the increase in family income or assets that results from the marriage. This can occur if an SSI beneficiary marries another SSI beneficiary or a person not in the SSI program. This potential effect of marriage on the SSI eligibility and benefits of SSI beneficiaries has been called a "marriage penalty" by the National Council on Disability.

This chapter provides an overview of the potential effect of a marriage to another SSI recipient or an ineligible person on an individual's eligibility for and level of SSI benefits. Examples of cases in which a marriage can reduce a person's SSI benefits are provided. To date, no legislation has been introduced in the 110th Congress that would change the way marriage can affect SSI eligibility and benefits.

This chapter provides an overview of the potential effects of marriage on Supplemental Security Income (SSI) eligibility and benefits. It includes an overview of the SSI program, information on the SSI resource limits, and a discussion of how the marriage of an SSI beneficiary to either another beneficiary or an ineligible person can affect his or her eligibility for benefits or monthly benefit level. In some cases, marriage may result in a person being denied SSI benefits or having his or her monthly SSI benefit level reduced. This situation has been called a "marriage penalty" by the National Council on Disability.[1]

Chapter 7 - On April 2, 2003, the House of Representatives passed H.R. 743 (the *Social Security Protection Act of 2003*, H.Rept. 108-46), as amended, by a vote of 396-28. A substitute amendment offered by Rep. Green of Texas was defeated by a 196-228 vote. One month earlier, H.R. 743 was considered by the House under suspension of the rules, and it failed to receive the two-thirds majority vote required for passage. H.R. 743 closely resembles H.R. 4070 from the 107th Congress. H.R. 4070, which passed the House unanimously and the Senate with amendment under unanimous consent, did not receive final passage before the 107th Congress adjourned. H.R. 743 is a bipartisan measure that would impose stricter standards on individuals and organizations serving as representative payees for Social Security and Supplemental Security Income (SSI) recipients; make non-governmental representative payees liable for "misused" funds and subject them to civil monetary penalties; tighten restrictions on attorneys representing Social Security and SSI disability claimants; limit assessments on attorney fee payments; prohibit fugitive felons from receiving Social Security benefits; modify the *"last day rule"* under the Government Pension Offset; and make other changes designed to reduce Social Security fraud and abuse. The Congressional Budget Office estimates that the measure would result in net savings of $655 million over 10 years.

On February 12, 2003, Rep. E. Clay Shaw, Chairman of the House Ways and Means Subcommittee on Social Security, introduced H.R. 743, the *Social Security Protection Act of 2003* (H.Rept. 108-46).[1] H.R. 743 closely resembles H.R. 4070 from the 107th Congress, which was passed by the House by a vote of 425-0 in June 2002. A substitute amendment to H.R. 4070 (S.Amdt. 4967) was passed by the Senate under unanimous consent in November 2002. The measure did not receive final action in the House before the 107th Congress adjourned.[2] On February 27, 2003, the House Ways and Means Subcommittee on Social Security held a hearing on the bill. On March 5, 2003, the House considered H.R. 743, as amended by the Chairman, under suspension of the rules (debate was limited to 40 minutes, floor amendments were not allowed and a two-thirds majority vote was required for passage).[3] Following debate in which many Members expressed strong opposition to a provision that would modify the *"last day rule"* under the Government Pension Offset (described below), the measure failed by a vote of 249-180.[4]

On March 13, 2003, the House Ways and Means Committee held a markup on H.R. 743, as amended. Rep. Jefferson offered an amendment that would incorporate H.R. 887 into the bill. Under H.R. 887, sponsored by Rep. Jefferson and co-sponsored by 109 Members, individuals whose combined monthly income from a noncovered pension and a Social Security spousal benefit is $2,000 or less would be exempt from the Government Pension Offset (GPO). In addition, the Jefferson amendment would hold the Social Security trust funds harmless (i.e., the increased cost to the Social Security system as a result of the change would be paid from general revenues). At the markup, Rep. Jefferson stated that the proposal would cost an estimated $19 billion over 10 years.[5] The Jefferson amendment was defeated by a vote of 14-21. Rep. Stark offered an amendment that would reduce the GPO from two-thirds to one-third of the government pension.[6] As under the Jefferson amendment, the increased cost to the Social Security system would be paid from general revenues. The Stark amendment was defeated by a vote of 15-22. H.R. 743, as amended, was approved by the Committee by a vote of 35-2.

On April 2, 2003, the House considered H.R. 743, as amended, for a second time. The measure was considered under a rule (H.Res. 168, H.Rept. 108-54) that provided for one hour of debate on the measure and 40 minutes of debate on a substitute amendment by Rep. Green of Texas. The Green amendment would strike from the bill the provision that would modify the GPO *"last day rule"* (section 418, described below). It would make no other changes to the measure. The Green amendment failed by a vote of 196-228, mostly along party lines. A motion by Rep. Green to recommit the bill to the House Ways and Means Committee with instructions to report the measure back to the House with an amendment addressing the concerns of federal, state and local government employees with respect to the GPO also failed by a vote of 203-220. H.R. 743, as amended, was then passed by the House by a vote of 396-28. The major provisions of H.R. 743, amended, as passed by the House are described below. The Congressional Budget Office estimates that the measure would result in net savings of $655 million over 10 years (fiscal years 2004-2013).

Chapter 8 - Some Social Security beneficiaries who were born from 1917 to 1921 — the so-called *notch babies* — believe they are not receiving fair Social Security benefits.[1] The notch issue resulted from legislative changes to Social Security during the 1970s. The 1972 Amendments to the Social Security Act first established cost-of-living adjustments (COLAs) for Social Security benefits. This change was intended to adjust benefits for inflation automatically, but an error in the formula caused benefits to rise substantially faster than inflation. Congress corrected the error in the 1977 Amendments. However, benefits for beneficiaries born from 1910 to 1916 were calculated using the flawed formula, giving them unintended windfall benefits. The notch babies, born from 1917 to 1921, became eligible for benefits during the period in which the corrected formula was phased in. Some feel it is unfair that their benefits are lower than those who received the windfall benefits. The term "notch" comes from graphs of benefit levels over time; there is a v-shaped dip for those born from 1917 to 1921, during the transition to the corrected formula.

A number of legislative attempts have been made over the years to give notch babies additional benefits, but none have been successful. A congressionally mandated commission studied the issue and concluded in its 1994 report that "benefits paid to those in the 'Notch' years are equitable, and no remedial legislation is in order." This CRS report will be updated as events warrant.

In: Social Security: New Issues and Developments   ISBN: 978-1-60456-243-9
Editors: P. O. Deaven, W. H. Andrews, pp. 1-42   © 2008 Nova Science Publishers, Inc.

Chapter 1

THE STRUCTURE OF SOCIAL SECURITY INDIVIDUAL ACCOUNT CONTRIBUTIONS AND INVESTMENTS: CHOICES AND IMPLICATIONS*

Debra B. Whitman

ABSTRACT

Policymakers have debated creating a system of individual accounts (IAs) as part of Social Security for many years. President Bush included a call for individual accounts in his 2005 State of the Union address, and several members of Congress have introduced bills in the 109th Congress that include IAs. However, throughout this debate, very little attention has been paid to the practical issues of program design and implementation — issues that could have a significant impact on the cost of the program, the level of participation by workers, the fees levied on accounts, and, ultimately, the assets available at retirement.

This chapter describes policymakers' administrative and structural choices regarding the collection and investment of assets in a system of individual accounts. The choices are many. It would need to be determined who would be eligible to participate in IAs, how individuals would enroll, how participants would make their contributions, and how much would be collected from them. Workers would need to be educated about enrollment in the new program, the investment choices they face, and the implications for their final benefits. It must also be established how records would be kept, what services would be provided to account holders, and how errors would be corrected. Other choices surround how assets would be invested and whether there would be any restrictions on fees. In each of these areas, this chapter briefly summarizes the options available within a system of IAs, the potential implications of particular policy choices and, when appropriate, current Social Security and pension policy.

The consequences of inadequate system design have become clear in other countries that have adopted IAs. In Australia, a public campaign had to be designed to locate the owners of 3 million lost accounts. In Great Britain, unscrupulous financial advisers persuaded thousands of investors to leave state pension funds, to their disadvantage, in a

---

* Excerpted from CRS Report RL33398, dated May 1, 2006.

widely reported "mis-selling" scandal. To provide insights, this chapter also gives examples of problems that other countries have faced when implementing IAs.

A system of IAs could involve millions of Americans, billions of dollars, and could have a broad impact on the American economy. If workers contributed 2% of their current taxable earnings, the accounts could grow to as much as 10% of GDP in 10 years and to 25% of GDP in 20 years. A contribution rate of 5% could accumulate more equities in IAs in 11 years than are currently held by all mutual funds combined. Thus, the stakes are high and there is a compelling need for thorough planning and administration.

Much of the debate surrounding the creation of individual accounts (IAs) as part of Social Security has focused on the fiscal implications of funding accounts and the risks and rewards of investing in equities. Rarely debated, however, are the structural and administrative choices surrounding the design of IAs. Arguably, these choices would have a more significant impact on the number of people who choose to participate in a system of IAs and the benefits that seniors receive during retirement than on the fiscal and budgetary issues that fill the newspapers.

This chapter focuses on policymakers' administrative and structural choices regarding the collection and investment of IA assets. The choices are many. It would need to be determined who would be eligible to participate in IAs, how individuals would enroll, how participants would make their contributions, and how much would be collected from them. Workers would need to be educated about enrollment in the new program, the investment choices they face, and the implications for their final benefits. It must also be established how records would be kept once contributions are collected, what services would be provided to account holders, and how assets would be invested. In each of these areas, this chapter briefly summarizes the options available within a system of IAs, the potential implications of particular policy choices and, when appropriate, current Social Security and pension policy.

Although there are clearly interactions between the collection and investment of assets and the payout of accounts (including early withdrawals), this chapter does not address the choices policymakers have regarding how IA benefits should be paid or how IAs might interact with current Social Security benefits.[1] The one exception is in describing how couples could share accounts. For completeness, a discussion of the option to share account withdrawals at retirement is included in this chapter.

Table 1 (below) lists the specific questions addressed in this chapter.

Table 1. Individual Account Contribution and Investment Choices

Issues	Choices To Be Made
Eligibility	▪ Would workers of all ages be eligible to participate? ▪ Would individuals who work in jobs that are not currently covered by Social Security be eligible to participate?
Participation and enrollment	▪ Would participation in the program be voluntary or mandatory? ▪ If participation is voluntary, could contributors move in and out of the program over time? ▪ How would participants enroll in IAs?
Participation incentives	▪ Would there be any tax incentives to encourage participation? ▪ Would the government provide other targeted incentives to participate? ▪ Would IAs affect a participant's eligibility for needs-based programs?

Table 1. (Continued)

Issues	Choices To Be Made
Contribution amounts	<ul><li>How much would participants contribute to their IAs?</li><li>Would there be limits on total contributions?</li><li>Could nonworkers contribute?</li><li>Would couples share accounts?</li></ul>
Collection of contributions	<ul><li>How would participants' contributions be collected?</li><li>If contributions are collected by the government, would they be collected as part of a worker's payroll tax or income tax?</li><li>Would employers face new record-keeping requirements?</li></ul>
Education	<ul><li>What types of education would be provided?</li><li>Who would provide workers with information about participating and investing in IAs?</li><li>Who would provide participants with investment advice?</li></ul>
Administrative and record-keeping issues	<ul><li>Who would be responsible for the administrative and record-keeping tasks for IAs?</li><li>What type of administrative and record-keeping services would be provided?</li><li>Who would be responsible for finding and correcting errors?</li></ul>
Investment of account assets	<ul><li>Who would invest IA assets?</li><li>Would accounts be insured?</li><li>Would there be multiple investment choices?</li><li>Would participants have access to "lifecycle" funds?</li><li>What would the default investment portfolio be?</li></ul>
Fees	<ul><li>Would there be limits on the amount and structure of administrative fees?</li><li>Would the government provide a subsidy to cover the start-up costs or administrative fees?</li></ul>

Source: The Congressional Research Service (CRS).

One recurring choice is whether the administrative functions should be managed by the government or private entities. For example, policymakers would need to establish who would be responsible for providing participants with information on how to enroll, who would be responsible for maintaining account records, and who would be responsible for investing account assets. In each of these choices, the government could assume these responsibilities, or these tasks could be contracted out to a single or diverse set of private entities. Although policymakers may have ideological preferences for one management system or another, this chapter will highlight the practical implications of each choice.

The administrative choices described in this chapter are relevant regardless of whether the IAs are designed to be in addition to Social Security — often referred to as add-on accounts — or to divert payroll tax from Social Security — often referred to as carve-out accounts. Depending on the type of account policymakers might choose, some choices would be more straightforward. For example, in a carve-out system of IAs, it would be straightforward to use the current payroll tax system to collect contributions.

Administrative and structural design is critical to a well-functioning system of IAs. The consequences of inadequate system design have become clear in other countries. In Australia, a public campaign had to be designed to locate the owners of 3 million lost accounts. In Great Britain, unscrupulous financial advisers persuaded thousands of investors to leave state pension funds, to their disadvantage, in a widely reported "mis-selling" scandal. These international experiences can provide valuable lessons for American policymakers. Thus, this chapter includes examples of the choices and difficulties other countries have faced while implementing their own systems of IAs.

If IA legislation were to move through Congress, the structural and administrative choices surrounding the collection and investment of account assets would need to be addressed. These issues would affect the cost of the program, the fees levied on accounts, and, ultimately, the assets available at retirement. In the 109th Congress, and in several previous sessions, there have been numerous proposals to include IAs as part of Social Security.[2] To varying degrees, these legislative proposals have addressed the choices raised in this chapter. However, many questions remain unanswered. Although many of these decisions may seem mundane, no effective system can be designed without addressing them.

ELIGIBILITY

Would Workers of All Ages Be Eligible to Participate?

Under current law, employers are allowed to exclude some workers from employer-sponsored retirement plans based on their age or work status.[3] Policymakers need to decide whether workers who are at the end or at the very beginning of their careers would be eligible to participate in IAs. Workers near retirement age may not have time to collect significant account balances. Very young workers may not have the financial sophistication to make decisions about whether to participate and how to invest their funds. Alternatively, legislators may wish to follow the model of Social Security, which receives contributions (i.e., payroll taxes) from all workers in jobs that are covered by Social Security.

Would Individuals Who Work in Jobs that Are Not Currently Covered by Social Security Be Eligible to Participate?

Currently 96% of all workers are covered by Social Security. However, approximately 28% of state and local government workers, as well as some federal employees (i.e., those covered under the Civil Service Retirement System), are exempt from paying taxes into Social Security.[4] These workers are covered only by their public retirement pension program, unless they worked at some point during their careers in jobs that were covered by Social Security. Allowing workers who are not participating in Social Security to participate in IAs would provide consistent coverage of workers who move between covered and uncovered employment. However, this policy may require additional contributions for those workers who do not currently pay Social Security payroll taxes.[5]

PARTICIPATION AND ENROLLMENT

Would Participation in the Program Be Voluntary or Mandatory?

Once it has been determined which workers would be eligible to participate in IAs, it would have to be decided whether those workers would be required to participate or whether they could choose whether (or not) to join.[6] A voluntary program would allow individuals to choose to participate based on their own calculations or impressions of the costs and benefits of an IA. The number of individuals who chose to participate in a voluntary program would likely depend on the extent of public education, the ease of enrollment, individuals' perceptions of risk, and whether or not there are any financial advantages to participating. On the other hand, a mandatory program, which would require all eligible individuals to participate, may help reduce administrative expenses by spreading fixed costs across a larger number of participants. However, a mandatory program would not allow Americans to make independent personal choices about whether it was in their financial interest to participate.

If Participation Is Voluntary, Could Contributors Move in and out of the Program over Time?

If individuals are allowed to move in and out of the program during their working years, they would accrue lower account balances because they would not consistently make contributions. In addition, allowing changes without penalties could encourage risky behavior by participants who invest their accounts in high-risk investments and opt out if their investments do poorly.[7] Allowing a single decision point would also help to reduce administrative costs, reduce the ability of participants to try to time the market, and may help simplify benefit payments if there are interactions between the accounts and Social Security.

How Would Participants Enroll in IAs?

The mechanism by which workers enroll in IAs would have an important impact on participation. Choices for enrolling participants include registering through employers; registering through the income tax system; or applying directly through the mail, by phone, via the Internet, or at a Social Security branch office. Each option has benefits and drawbacks. Enrollment through employers would capture the current working population but would require additional paperwork for employers and could lead to confusion on the part of individuals who hold multiple jobs simultaneously or who change jobs and are inconsistent in their enrollment elections. Employer-based enrollment must also include provisions for the 16 million Americans who are self-employed.[8] Enrollment on income tax forms would reduce the burden on employers but would not address the 18 million households that do not file income tax forms.[9] Enrollment through other mechanisms would require contacting and processing the enrollments of roughly 163 million current workers and continued outreach and enrollment of new entrants to the workforce.

Another enrollment option is to assume that every worker wishes to participate but allow those who do not the option of dropping out. Workers would need to be notified in advance of their automatic enrollment and given adequate opportunity to opt out.[10] Recent research on §401(k) plans has shown the rate of participation increases substantially when workers are automatically enrolled.[11] However, even with the ability to opt out, automatic enrollment is likely to induce many individuals to participate, regardless of whether IAs would actually be financially advantageous.

PARTICIPATION INCENTIVES

Would There Be Any Tax Incentives to Encourage Participation?

The current tax code provides a variety of tax preferences for the deposits, earnings, and withdrawals of various retirement savings programs. Policymakers may wish to consider similar preferences for IAs. In general, the tax treatment of IAs would have an important impact on program cost, individual participation, account balances, and, ultimately, benefits. The importance of these incentives would vary across the population, depending on how they are designed.

One key choice would be whether the incentives are offered as tax credits or tax deductions. Tax credits reduce the amount of income tax an individual must pay.[12] A tax credit is more valuable than a tax deduction of an equal amount because the credit results in a reduction in tax owed rather than a reduction in taxable income.[13] Tax deductions, which lower taxable income, would provide larger incentives for high-income participants than for those with lower taxable income.[14]

What Tax Advantages Are Provided to Other Forms of Retirement Savings?

The current tax code contains a variety of tax preferences for the deposits, earnings, and withdrawals of retirement savings programs such as Social Security, IRAs, Roth IRAs, and employer-sponsored pensions.

- Employers and employees each contribute 6.2% of covered wages, up to a ceiling for Social Security (Old-Age Survivors Disability Insurance), although the tax treatment of contributions differs. Employees must pay income taxes on their own contributions but not on their employer's contributions. Self-employed workers pay the full 12.4% on 92.35% of net self-employment earnings, but they receive special income tax credits. Social Security benefits are not taxed for low-income beneficiaries, but high-income beneficiaries are taxed on 50% to 85% of their benefits (depending on their total income).
- Traditional IRAs and employer-based retirement plans (e.g., §401(k) plans) allow participants to deduct contributions from their income for tax purposes and defer taxes on all earnings until funds are withdrawn, at which point they are taxed as ordinary income.
- Roth IRAs and "Roth 401(k)s" allow taxpayers to make contributions from their after-tax earnings or savings, but all account accumulations and withdrawals are tax-exempt.
- Employers also receive tax incentives for private pensions. Employer contributions to pension plans are treated as tax deductible business expenses by the IRS.

Would the Government Provide Other Targeted Incentives to Participate?

To encourage participation in IAs, policymakers could provide financial incentives to all participants or to certain groups, such as low earners.[15] Many employers, including the federal government, match their workers' contributions to defined contribution pension programs — such as §401(k) plans — up to a set threshold.[16] Matching participants' contributions could provide a financial incentive to all individuals to participate, but would likely provide a larger transfer to high earners than low earners. Alternatively, policymakers could design a system of progressive matching that would provide larger transfers to low earners, mimicking the structure of the Social Security program, in which low earners receive a relatively higher replacement rate than high earners. Finally, a match could be provided only to participants who earn below a given threshold.

Would IAs Affect a Participant's Eligibility for Needs-Based Programs?

Some needs-based benefit programs — Supplemental Security Income (SSI), food stamps, Medicaid, State Children's Health Insurance Program (SCHIP) — take into consideration both an individual's income and available resources to determine eligibility.[17] Assets accumulated in defined contribution retirement plans —§401(k)s, IRAs, the federal Thrift Savings Program — are considered resources in some of these programs.[18] These assets must generally be withdrawn (regardless of tax penalties) and spent down to an amount below the program's resource limit before a low-income individual can qualify for the needs-based benefit, creating a disincentive for low-income workers to save for retirement in these plans. Amounts in defined benefit pension plans, however, are excluded from the resource tests in these programs. Withdrawals from defined contribution pension plans (whether taken while working or retired) and income from defined benefit pension plans are counted toward the income limits of needs-based programs.

Policymakers could decide whether assets in an IA would be considered when calculating an individual's eligibility for needs-based programs both before and after retirement age.

- Before Retirement Age. If IA assets are accessible before retirement age, many low-income participants may be forced to liquidate their IAs to qualify for needs-based programs, unless the accounts were explicitly excluded from resource calculations. On the other hand, if assets are considered inaccessible or if IA accumulations were excluded from resource calculations, eligibility for needs-tested benefits would not be affected. However, in some programs, this would create an inequity across retirement savings vehicles, with savings in IAs having preferential treatment to savings in defined contribution retirement plans.
- After Retirement. IAs could affect both income and resource eligibility. First, account withdrawals, including annuity payments, would likely be considered towards a program's income limits. Second, unless they are specifically excluded, post-retirement account assets would likely be considered toward a needs-based program's resource limits, forcing low-income retirees to exhaust their IAs to qualify for assistance. However, if such an exclusion were to be applied only to IAs, it could result in inequitable treatment of individuals with other types of retirement savings.

CONTRIBUTION AMOUNTS

How Much Would Participants Contribute to Their IAs?

The amount that participants contribute to IAs would have an important effect on the cost and size of an IA system. Budgetary pressures could compel policymakers to consider limiting the amount participants may contribute to their IAs, regardless of whether funds come from current payroll taxes or from other sources. In a system of "carve-out" accounts (in which a share of payroll taxes is diverted from the Social Security Trust Funds), the higher the contribution limit, the larger the Social Security shortfall. Depending on the tax treatment of account contributions, there could also be significant budgetary implications of accounts funded outside the current payroll tax system.

In general, the amount that participants contribute to their IAs would directly affect the funds available at retirement. The Congressional Research Service (CRS) estimates that an average-wage worker who contributed 1% of his or her salary over a 40-year career would have an IA balance of $34,429 at retirement, whereas a 5% contribution would yield $178,924.[19]

Would There Be Limits on Total Contributions?

Contribution limits can be established to limit the cost of the programs and, depending on the structure, the level of benefits for some individuals. Contribution limits could be set as a share of earnings, which would allow higher-earning participants to make relatively larger contributions and accrue higher account balances than low-earning participants. Alternatively, a ceiling could be set as a limit to the amount of earnings used to assess contributions. These ceilings are commonly found in other countries as a way to limit the amount that high-earning individuals contribute to their pension system.[20] These contribution limits would primarily affect the relative contributions of higher-earning participants who would not be able to contribute the same share of earnings as low-earning participants. Finally, contribution limits could be a set dollar amount, as is done for §401(k) plans and IRAs.

Alternatively, policymakers could choose not to limit contributions; they could even try to encourage additional retirement savings by allowing IA participants to make contributions over and above any standard contribution rate. Once the administrative structure is established, participants may view making additional contributions to IAs as a low-cost way to increase their savings for retirement. This may be particularly true for individuals who do not have access to employer-sponsored retirement accounts. However, depending on the tax treatment and design of accounts, allowing unlimited contributions could weaken current employer-based retirement savings plans and may not increase net savings because individuals may simply substitute one form of retirement savings for another, especially if IAs receive tax preferences or other incentives.

What Are the Contribution Limits in Current Retirement Savings Programs?

Many current retirement savings programs, including Social Security, have limits on the amount that individuals contribute.

- In 2006, the maximum taxable earnings subject to the 5.3% tax an individual pays for the Old-Age Survivors portion of Social Security is $94,200, so the

> maximum contribution is $4,992.60 for an employee (or $9,985.20 for both the employer and employee contribution).
> - For an IRA (both traditional and Roth) in 2006, the maximum contribution is $4,000 per year for those younger than 50 and $5,000 for those 50 and older.
> - In tax-deferred retirement savings such as the Thrift Savings Program and §401(k) plans, individual contributions are limited to $15,000 in 2006. Participants age 50 or older can make additional "catch-up" deferrals of up to $5,000. The combined employer and employee contribution is limited to $44,000.

Could Nonworkers Contribute?

Another important policy choice would be whether to allow nonworkers to contribute to an IA, as is done in some other countries. In Italy, non-working people, including children, are allowed to participate in an IA. Allowing nonworkers to contribute would help ensure that account balances meet some standard of adequacy at retirement. Whether it is to provide family care-giving, to attend school, or due to job loss or disability, time out of the work force — especially at a young age —would significantly reduce a participant's account accumulation. For example, when an average-earning female is out of the workforce and not contributing to an IA for five years, she would accumulate 16%-18% less than if she had not taken any time out.[21] Generally, the younger a person is while out of the workforce, the smaller the account balance would be at retirement, as the participant would lose both contributions and compounded interest on those contributions. The ability to pay into accounts for non-working individuals — either by the individuals, their spouses, or other approved parties, such as parents — would help ensure that participants who leave the workforce for an extended period of time would have adequate income during retirement. However, collecting contributions from nonworkers may be administratively burdensome, as nonworkers would not be able to use existing wage reporting systems.

Would Couples Share Accounts?

In a simple IA system, assets would be collected from an individual and used to fund his or her own retirement. This contrasts with Social Security, which provides benefits to the worker as well as the worker's current and former spouses based on a worker's past earnings.[22] If policymakers choose to mimic this feature and allow married couples to share accounts or share in the benefits from those accounts, a system that transfers assets within couples would need to be established. However, there is at least one characteristic of Social Security that is impossible to mimic in IAs without additional federal contributions.[23] Any transfer of assets between husbands and wives would reduce the payout for the primary account holder. This contrasts with Social Security, in which a worker's benefits are not reduced if a current spouse, or even three ex-spouses, also receive benefits based on his or her earnings.

Transfers of assets between husbands and wives in a system of IAs could be done several ways: contributions could be split at the time of deposit, accounts could be split at the time of divorce, or individuals could be required to purchase joint and survivor annuities at retirement. Whichever policy is chosen to share assets, it would need to contain provisions for divorce, as there is a high probability that by the time a participant reaches retirement age, he or she would have been divorced at some point in his or her life.[24]

Split Account Deposits

Accounts could be split at the time of deposit so that contributions and investment earnings accumulated during marriage are split evenly. Each spouse would retain any contributions and investment earnings accumulated while single or from previous marriages. There are some advantages and disadvantages to this approach. One advantage of contribution splitting is that, unlike with Social Security, women or men who divorce after fewer than 10 years of marriage would receive payments based on their former spouse's earnings. Participants may also prefer this option. Some one-earner couples may wish to divide contributions to allow a stay-at-home spouse to accumulate IA assets. Some two-earner couples may wish to split contributions between two accounts, as it would allow couples with different salaries to accrue similar account balances. Splitting contributions also may have disadvantages. Depending on how account fees are structured, two-earner couples may wish to consolidate their accounts into one account to reduce the impact of a flat-dollar fee, or to take advantage of lower fees with higher account balances (such as those currently offered by many banks). Splitting contributions would also add a significant administrative burden by requiring the collection of timely and accurate reports of each participant's marital status. Because marriage is a state-defined legal status, a new national reporting system would have to be created to track marriages, divorces, and possibly participants' joint preferences on contribution sharing.[25]

Split Accounts at Divorce

Another way to transfer assets between couples would be to split contributions and interest earned during a marriage at the time of divorce. Policymakers could choose to model the rights of former spouses in IAs on Social Security law, on state family law, on laws used for other retirement plans, or to establish a new federal policy. Roughly 1 million women age 62 or over receive Social Security benefits based, either in part or in whole, on the work record of an ex-spouse.[26] To receive spousal benefits in Social Security, a divorcee's former marriage must have lasted at least 10 years. If IAs are legally considered property, then state family laws could be used to determine distributions between couples during marriage, divorce, and/or when an account holder dies. However, this would lead to inequities across states and confusion for couples who moved across state lines during their marriage.[27] In addition, many people who get divorced are unable to afford an attorney and may not fully pursue their rights to claim their spouse's IA assets. Alternatively, policymakers may wish to use rules currently governing pensions or §401(k)s to define the rights of spouses.[28] Finally, policymakers may choose to explicitly establish uniform federal spousal rights for IAs.[29]

Split Accounts at Retirement

Finally, couples could share account distributions at retirement, either directly or by purchasing joint and survivor life annuities. Account balances could be divided between married couples when either spouse retires. As with contribution splitting at the time of deposit, administrative issues surrounding the tracking of marriages over a lifetime would be an obstacle in ensuring that assets are properly credited to former spouses. Another way to share IAs at retirement would be to require the purchase of joint and survivor life annuities. A life annuity is an insurance product that promises payment for as long as the annuitant lives. Married participants could be required to purchase joint-life annuities for themselves and their current (or former) spouses. However, this would lower the payments a participant receives from his or her own IA. Joint-life annuities provide significantly lower payments than single annuities and are sensitive to the ages of both spouses. Also, it would be complicated to structure annuities for divorced and remarried participants or participants who divorce after they have purchased an annuity.

COLLECTION OF CONTRIBUTIONS

How Would Participants' Contributions Be Collected?[30]

Policymakers could choose to designate whether contributions would be collected by the government, by employers, or whether individual participants would be responsible for sending in their contributions directly. All of these models exist currently for the various forms of retirement savings. Social Security contributions are withheld by employers and collected by government as a payroll tax. Contributions to employer-sponsored pensions are collected by employers and invested either directly by the company or forwarded to private fund managers. Finally, individuals who set aside funds for retirement in savings accounts or IRAs generally must take responsibility for opening their own accounts and making deposits.

While each of these options is possible for a system of IAs, in general, the more decentralized the system of collection, the higher the administrative costs. A centralized system in which the government collects contributions from employers may also provide a more consistent record of deposits, which may be necessary if there are any interactions between IAs and Social Security benefits.

If Contributions Are Collected by the Government, Would They Be Collected as Part of a Worker's Payroll Tax or Income Tax?

One way to collect IA contributions would be through a payroll tax, which is how funds are collected for the current Social Security system. Under current law, covered employers and employees each contribute 6.2% of payroll for Old-Age Survivors and Disability Insurance (OASDI) and 1.45% for the Hospital Insurance (HI) part of Medicare. Self-employed individuals pay the full 15.3% but receive certain tax credits. High earners and their employers do not pay OASDI taxes on earnings greater than $94,200, but there is no such limit for HI tax.[31] If contributions are collected through the payroll tax system, policymakers would have to decide whether tax rates would be the same for participants and nonparticipants, whether the current cap on taxable earnings would apply, and whether the contribution would be withdrawn from the employer or employee share (or both). Tax treatment differs between the employers' and employees' contributions. Employees pay income tax on their share of the payroll tax, but not on the employers' share.

IA contributions could also be collected through the income tax system. Unlike with the payroll tax, the income tax form has the advantage of collecting information about a participant's total income from multiple jobs as well as non-wage income. Many tax filers also provide family information, such as their household income, marital status, and the existence of dependent children. A system of IAs that incorporates links among family members, provides participation incentives such as matching contributions based on earnings, or calculates rates of withdrawal based upon total retirement income may require this detailed information about participants. An additional mechanism for collecting contributions would also need to be implemented for workers who choose not to file income tax returns because their incomes are below the applicable filing thresholds. These workers could be required to file forms with an IRS service center or other centralized collection agency, although the additional filing burden would likely reduce participation among these workers.

Would Employers Face New Record-Keeping Requirements?[32]

Policymakers may choose to rely on the current payroll tax reporting system for employers or to develop new requirements for IAs. Relying on the current system could lead to long delays — estimated at 15 months on average — between the time when contributions would be deducted from participants' paychecks and when they would be credited to their IAs.[33] Under current law, employers are required to report individual tax contributions once per year. The current reporting system is also error-prone because the majority of small employers submit their reports on paper.[34] Long delays in reporting would cause participants to lose interest on their contributions.[35] To reduce delays, employers could be required to report and deposit IA contributions more frequently or to submit IA contributions electronically.[36] However, reporting contributions more frequently would impose additional costs on employers, particularly small employers or those without sophisticated salary-administration systems.[37]

EDUCATION

What Types of Education Would Be Provided?

Successful implementation of a system of IAs would benefit from an American public informed about its choices and the implications for its future retirement income. However, the type of financial education needed would vary significantly between those who choose to participate and those who do not, and between those who have a limited understanding of their financial options and sophisticated investors who regularly make decisions about their retirement savings and investments. Public education needs would also increase with the complexity of the program.

Information About Participation and Investment Options

All Americans would need basic information on who is eligible and how to participate in IAs. Individuals would need information on how to enroll and disenroll, how much they could contribute, how contributions would be collected, and whether they would receive any financial incentives for participating. Individuals would also need to be educated about the benefits and tradeoffs of participating in IAs so they could make informed choices about whether or not to join the system. In particular, participants would need to understand how participation in IAs could affect their Social Security benefits. Information may also need to be provided to all employers to describe any changes made to current withholding and reporting requirements for workers who participate in IAs.

Those individuals who choose to participate in a system of IAs would need to understand the types of investment options that would be available to them and the structure of any administrative fees that may exist. Unless this information is standardized and clearly presented, the average worker may find it too complicated or time-consuming to compare fees and performance across multiple investment vehicles. Even then, if the number of choices becomes too high, participants may feel overwhelmed. In 2004, new entrants to the Swedish personal account system faced 664 investment fund choices. Fewer than 10% of these new participants made an active investment choice, while the other 90% ended up in the default fund.[38]

Financial Education

IA participants would need at least a basic level of financial literacy to make informed investment choices. Athough it has been estimated that nearly one-half of all American households own a mutual fund,[39] a universal system of IAs would add millions of new investors who may not have any previous experience with financial institutions.[40] Participants would benefit from understanding historical investment returns, the behavior of various asset classes, the financial mathematics of compounding, the principle of portfolio diversification, the relationship between risk and return, the implication of fees, and the impact of inflation.[41] To plan for an adequate retirement income, participants would need to have a realistic estimate of their final account balances based on their earnings and rates of contribution. They would also need to understand that the number of years remaining until retirement should be a factor in determining the appropriate level of risk in their portfolio. In addition, participants should be educated about annuities, scheduled withdrawals, and other ways account balances can be used to provide income after they retire. Investment education may boost participation in IAs. In §401(k) plans, investor education has been shown to improve both participation and the savings rate.[42]

Financial Advice

Many participants may wish to have more personalized advice on how to invest their accounts. Although financial *education* can be generic and provided to all participants, financial *advice* would be targeted to an individual participant or group of participants to help them make the proper choice among investment options. Ideally, financial advisers would provide assistance with a participant's IA asset allocation while considering that individual's (and his or her spouse's) current and expected future financial status, including private pension coverage, the type and amount of investments in other savings accounts, preferences toward risk, and expected retirement date and life span. This type of detailed assistance can be expensive, because the advisers would need a high level of training and consultations may take several hours. As participants age or face major life events, such as a disability or the death of a spouse, they may need to reassess their financial plan and require additional advice.

Who Would Provide Workers with Information About Participating and Investing in IAs?

Traditionally, the federal government has been responsible for providing the public with basic information regarding changes to a public program.[43] One advantage of the government providing the public with information about IAs would be that it would increase consistency and allow a single point of contact. The educational outreach could rely on existing public outreach, such as the annual Social Security Statement[44] or one of the several existing federal programs aimed at increasing financial literacy.

The cost of a federally managed public education campaign would depend on the complexity of the IA program and the types of media used for outreach.[45] These costs could be charged to participants as part of their administrative fees or passed on to taxpayers through general revenue financing.

There are also a wide range of financial education programs currently available to the public, including programs through nonprofits, schools, employers, financial institutions, and community-based organizations.[46] Policymakers could rely on these current systems to provide information about the IAs or develop new systems and resources specifically targeted to informing the public about participating and investing in the program.

Existing Federal Programs Aimed at Improving Financial Literacy

There are a number of existing federal programs aimed at improving financial literacy. The "Savings Are Vital to Everyone's Retirement (SAVER) Act of 1997"(P.L. 105-92) directed the Secretary of Labor to provide education and outreach to promote retirement savings. The act also required that National Summits on Retirement Savings be convened in 1998, 2001, and 2005 (held in March 2006). Past summits have produced reports to highlight major findings and recommendations.

Established in 2002 and located within the Department of the Treasury, the Office of Financial Education promotes access to financial education tools that encourage personal financial management, planning, and saving. The office also has responsibility for coordinating the Financial Literacy and Education Commission, which was established as part of the Fair and Accurate Credit Transactions (FACT) Act of 2003 (P.L. 108-159). Charged with improving the financial literacy and education of people throughout the United States, the commission is chaired by the Secretary of Treasury and composed of representatives from 20 federal departments, agencies, and commissions. The commission has established a website ([http://www.mymoney.gov]) and a toll-free telephone number (1-888-mymoney) to coordinate the presentation of educational materials from across the spectrum of federal agencies that deal with financial issues and markets.

Congress recently required the Office of Personnel Management (OPM) to develop a retirement financial literacy and educational strategy for federal employees as part of the Thrift Savings Plan Open Elections Act of 2004 (P.L. 108-469). OPM is required to educate federal employees on the need for retirement savings and investment and on how to calculate the retirement investment needed to meet their retirement goals. They must also provide information and counseling on the benefits the federal government provides and on how to plan for retirement.

Other federal programs are also directed at improving American's financial education. The Excellence in Economics Education (EEE) program was established as part of the No Child Left Behind Act (P.L. 107-110) to promote economic and financial literacy of all students in kindergarten through grade 12. The Federal Deposit Insurance Corporation (FDIC) has created the Money Smart program as a model for banks and other organizations interested in sponsoring financial education workshops, and the Federal Reserve has hosted a variety of personal financial education programs. The U.S. Department of Housing and Urban Development (HUD) provides free counseling to address homelessness, buying or renting a home, and mortgage delinquency.

Sources: Dept. of Labor, Saver Summit: [http://www.saversummit.dol.gov/1997 saveract. html]. Department of the Treasury, Office of Financial Education: [http://www.treas.gov/offices/ domestic-finance/financial-institution/fin-education/]; Office of Personnel Management, Retirement Financial Literacy and Education Strategy: [http://www.opm.gov/benefits/ literacy_ education.asp]; Department of Education, Excellence in Economics Education Program: [http://www.ed.gov/programs/econeducation/index.html]; Federal Deposit Insurance Corporation, Money Smart Program: [http://www.fdic.gov/consumers/consumer/ moneysmart/ overview.html]; U.S. Department of Housing and Urban Development (HUD); and Housing Counseling [http://www.hud.gov/offices/hsg/ sfh/hcc/hcc_ home.cfm].

Alternatively, private investment managers or sales agents could be given the responsibility of educating the public about the IA program and the available investment options. Private investment managers could include financial education in their individual marketing materials or, to avoid conflicts of interest, be required to contribute to independent financial literacy campaigns. Alternatively, sales agents who represent one or multiple investment managers could be given the responsibility to provide the public with investment education. The costs of education, like the costs of advertising, could be incorporated into the management fees charged to participants. Government oversight would likely be necessary to ensure that education materials meet basic standards for accuracy and protect the public interest.[47]

Some countries that have implemented IAs have used a mixed public and private campaign to promote financial literacy and provide information on participation and investment options. For example, in Sweden, information about all private investment fund managers and investment options is consolidated by the government into a single catalog, which is mailed annually to participants. A major media campaign by both the government and private investment funds helped provide Swedes with information about their new IA system and facilitate a high level of active participation. Unfortunately, attempts to limit costs have led to a substantial decline over time in the resources dedicated to Swedish investor education.[48] This may be why a recent survey found that 52% of Swedes felt they have far from sufficient knowledge needed to handle their pensions.[49]

To be most effective, information materials would have to be delivered in a variety of formats. Due to the diversity of the population, there is no one-size-fits-all approach to delivering financial information.[50] Although the Internet has been shown to be the most popular source for personal financial information, many individuals do not have regular Internet access. Those individuals likely to be most in need of financial education — females, minorities, older individuals, and less educated individuals — report that they prefer learning in a communal environment, such as a seminar.[51] In addition, targeted educational strategies would need to be developed for individuals with limited education or low levels of literacy, with limited language ability or proficiency, or with special needs.

Individuals with Special Needs

Using survey data, CRS estimates that in 2001, more than 1% of the non-institutionalized population age 18-64 (2 million individuals) and 8% of those age 65 and older (more than 2.5 million individuals) had difficulty keeping track of money or bills due to a physical or mental health condition. Financial education programs could be designed to specifically target these individuals to help them make wise decisions in a system of IAs.

However, some of these individuals, particularly those with cognitive impairments or cognitive disabilities, may never be able to make independent and informed choices about whether to participate and invest in an IA. Unless an individual, institution, or organization is specifically designated to make investment decisions on their behalf, individuals with special needs would likely follow the defaults of the system. They would participate only if the system is set as opt-out, would contribute at the default rate and into the default investment fund, and follow the default payout option.

Nearly 2 million adult OASDI beneficiaries currently have a designated individual, institution, or organization that is allowed to make financial decisions on their behalf. Under current law, if a Social Security beneficiary cannot independently manage or direct the management of his or her money, a "representative payee" is given the task of receiving the Social Security benefits and paying for the beneficiary's current needs. Representative payees receive no compensation and are personally liable for reimbursement of misused funds.

Under current law, if the OASDI beneficiary's benefits are greater than his or her current needs, representative payees are responsible for conserving or investing the excess funds. Investments by representative payees of conserved funds are limited by state law. Most states have adopted the Uniform Prudent Investor Act (UPIA) within their laws or have state laws that parallel those of the UPIA. The UPIA provides investment rules for trustees and fiduciaries, including representative payees, that protect the OASDI beneficiary's assets while providing the prospect of a better income. In most states, no specific type of investments is required or restricted. Policymakers would have to determine whether individuals who have cognitive disabilities or impairments or who require representative payees would be eligible to participate in a system of IAs and, if so, how participation and investment decisions would be made on their behalf.

A comprehensive system of IAs would require policies that accommodate individuals with special needs, including those with cognitive impairments or disabilities. These individuals may continue to have some paid employment or may develop impairments later in life after they have made contributions to an IA. These issues will have to be examined in relation to current federal and state laws and existing federal programs including the Social Security Disability Insurance program.

Source: CRS analysis of the 2001 Panel of the Survey of Income and Program Participation. State laws for investments of representative payees' conserved funds: [http://policy.ssa.gov/ poms.nsf/lnx/0200603040].

Who Would Provide Participants with Investment Advice?

Currently a wide variety of financial specialists — stockbrokers, financial planners, registered investment advisers, life insurance salespeople — provide investment advice. These professionals face differing educational and certification requirements, as well as different federal and state regulations.[52]

As described above, individualized investment advice can be costly. The structure of advisory fees may affect both the type of investment advice offered and the population who receives it.[53] If advisers are compensated for their services by the participants with a flat fee, the fees may consume a large share of contributions of low earners. Alternatively, if advisers fees are paid as a proportion of account assets, there would be financial incentives to provide detailed advice only to individuals with high earnings or account assets. Under current law, advisers are generally restricted from charging "performance fees" — compensation tied to capital gains or asset appreciation.[54] Policymakers would need to determine whether IA investment advisers would face any additional fee restrictions or reporting requirements.[55]

The provision of investment advice may also carry responsibility. Policymakers would need to determine whether IA investment advisers would face personal liability for providing advice that is against the interests of their clients. Under current law, registered investment advisers are considered fiduciaries and are required to act in their clients' best interests. To protect workers against potential conflicts of interest, firms that offer §401(k) investment funds to a company's workers are banned (under the Employee Retirement Income Security Act) from providing direct financial advice to those workers.[56] Many American employers also currently shy away from providing direct investment advice for their employees who participate in private pensions because they could be perceived as acting as a fiduciary and potentially incur personal liabilities.[57] Under a system of IAs, the potential liability for providing poor investment advice could be huge. In the UK system of IAs, the widely reported "mis-selling" scandal led to billions of dollar payments by investment advisers to nearly 2 million Britains who were sold personal pensions when they would have been financially better off at retirement in their employers' pension scheme.[58]

ADMINISTRATIVE AND RECORD-KEEPING ISSUES

Who Would Be Responsible for the Administrative and Record-Keeping Tasks for IAs?

Maintaining account records, responding to participant questions, and tracking account balances and transactions are just a few of the administrative tasks that would be required under a system of IAs. Policymakers could chose to designate these responsibilities to the government, private entities, or employers.

One option would be to administer accounts through a highly centralized government administrative structure. If there were linkages between IAs and current Social Security benefits, this function could be included within or in tandem with the Social Security Administration. Having the government provide administrative services for IAs could facilitate efficiencies by relying on existing systems for collecting data, centralizing processing, and providing economies of scale. However, it could require a significant new bureaucracy.

Record keeping could also be centralized under a single, private entity. This centralized clearinghouse could assume record-keeping responsibilities similar to how the federal government's Thrift Savings Plan (TSP) uses the National Finance Center to process records for all federal employees.[59] The advantage of either a public or private centralized system is that personal information about participants could be kept confidential even if funds are eventually transferred to private fund managers. It would also reduce the burden on employers and participants, who would only have to deal with a single entity.

The private sector could also manage IAs through a decentralized structure run similar to the current system of IRAs. Participants would deal directly with financial institutions to make contributions, investment allocations, and possibly to withdraw their benefits. Although competition among providers could help lower administrative costs, generally the more decentralized the system, the higher the costs due to economies of scale.

The final administrative option would be to give employers the responsibility of setting up pension funds for each of their employees, a model that is currently used in most employer-sponsored pensions. Similarly in Australia, some 8,000 organizations manage pension funds. Some of these are associated with large Australian companies; others are set up by financial institutions and allow small employers to band together; finally, some funds are industry-wide organizations generally jointly organized by union and employer representatives.[60] Administrative costs would be likely be higher under this option, as costs would be incurred each time a worker changes jobs and a new account must be established.

What Type of Administrative and Record-Keeping Services Would Be Provided?

Regardless of the choice of who provides the administrative function, there are a host of options regarding the types of services that could be provided. On one extreme, participants could receive an annual statement of account balance by mail, receive customer service only by telephone during regular work hours, and have the ability to change asset allocations only once per year. At the other end of the spectrum, a high-service system could provide IA participants with personalized participant education, round-the-clock Internet and telephone-based self-management, immediate access to account information updated daily, and the unlimited ability to change allocations. Participants could also receive personalized "wake-up calls" — notices that the value of their portfolio fell below a comparative benchmark — to supplement their regular statements and warn of investment performance below a comparative index. In general, providing participants with additional services and account access would raise the administrative costs and therefore decrease IA account balances over time.[61]

Who Would Be Responsible for Finding and Correcting Errors?

IAs would require a system of checks and balances to find and ultimately correct errors. Errors can be the mistake of the participant, the employer, the record keeper, the investment fund manager, or the government. In some cases, accounts may be lost due to changes in name or address, the death of the worker, or participant errors. In the United States, the Social Security Administration is unable to process approximately 1% of all contributions due to mismatches between workers' names and Social Security numbers.[62] Similar mismatches within a system of IAs could mean that billions of dollars would not be credited to participants' accounts. In Australia, the government is trying to locate the owners of 3 million lost personal accounts, representing up to one in three workers and worth $5.7 billion (in U.S. dollars).[63] Errors may also be caused by an employer and may result from negligence, business closure, or even fraud.[64] Errors that are thought to involve fraud could result in costly litigation. Sixteen years after Chile adopted a system of IAs, some 150,000 cases involving alleged problems with employers remitting pension contributions were pending in Chilean courts.[65]

In the current Social Security system, workers are largely sheltered from any negative consequence of an administrative or contribution error. To protect workers from errors made by their employers, SSA posts earnings credits to participants' records even if their employers have failed to send the attendant taxes, as long as the worker supplies proof of earnings (such as a copy of the worker's W-2 tax form).[66] Resolving errors in a system of IAs would likely be costly both for the entity charged with correcting them and for the participants who may lose contributions or interest on any funds in dispute.[67] Policymakers could decide whether these costs would be borne by workers or the government, or whether a separate insurance system should be established.

INVESTMENT OF ACCOUNT ASSETS

Who Would Invest IA Assets?

Policymakers would need to determine who would have the responsibility for investing account contributions and accumulations. This responsibility could be given to a government entity, a centralized investment board, or to private fund managers. The implications of each choice are described below.

Government Management

One option would be to have all IA assets invested by a single government entity. This would likely lead to lower administrative costs due to economies of scale and reduced transaction costs. The government could determine the asset allocation of the collectively invested funds, or individual IA participants could choose an asset portfolio and the government would invest funds to meet aggregate totals.

A common concern raised with regard to a government-managed fund is that it may be susceptible to political interference — such as choosing or limiting specific investments based on political criteria or trying to influence the private market through the use of proxy voting rights. Political interference or controls on investments can decrease returns. In the United States, one study found that pension funds directly managed by state and local governments experienced average returns of 1.5% less per year than comparable private pension plans.[68] In Sweden, public pension funds are estimated to have earned 3.2% less per year from 1960 to 1975 due to interference by the Central Bank.[69] To reduce fears that government-controlled investment would lead to political interference in private business, some countries with publicly managed IAs have imposed concentration limits, delegated voting rights to independent fund managers, or put caps on the voting power of the fund.[70]

Centralized Investment Board

One way to protect funds from political interference but retain economies of scale would be to use a centralized investment board to manage IA assets. The investment board could be designed to insulate investment decisions from political motives by restricting investments to index funds or other benchmarks, creating strict conditions on the voting rights associated with the ownership of securities, isolating the board's budget from the appropriations process, and creating other barriers to maintain independence.

Two examples of a centralized investment board within the federal government currently exist: the Thrift Savings Program (TSP) and the National Railroad Retirement Investment Trust (NRRIT). Since 1986, federal employees have had the choice of contributing a share of their salary into the TSP retirement savings program. These contributions, along with a government match, are centrally invested in funds managed by the Federal Retirement Thrift Investment Board. Since 2002, the federal government has been acquiring corporate stocks, bonds, and other assets to provide revenue for a federal entitlement program, Railroad Retirement. An independent entity, the NRRIT board, manages and invests the assets of the Railroad Retirement program with the assistance of independent advisers and investment managers.

As in the case of government-managed investments, investments in a centralized investment board can be centrally managed or participant-directed. For example, the NRRIT board collectively invests the total assets of the trust and uses active investment management strategies to increase portfolio returns. In contrast, individual TSP participants direct the investment of their contributions in a limited set of index funds. While it is possible to structure a centralized program to allow participants choice between funds, this approach does not provide participants with a choice between providers.

Centralized Investment Management: The National Railroad Retirement Investment Trust and the Federal Retirement Thrift Investment Board

The Railroad Retirement Board (RRB) is an independent agency in the executive branch of the federal government. The RRB's primary function is to administer comprehensive retirement-survivor and unemployment-sickness benefit programs for the nation's railroad workers and their families. Railroad retirement benefits are a federal entitlement and are protected by statute.

Revenues in excess of railroad retirement-survivor benefits and administrative expenses are invested to provide additional trust fund income. Historically, the RRB was required to invest excess assets in interest-bearing U.S. government or U.S. government-guaranteed securities. In 2001, as part of the Railroad Retirement and Survivors' Improvement Act (P.L. 107-90), Congress created a new entity, the National Railroad Retirement Investment Trust (NRRIT), which is allowed to invest in non-Treasury securities such as publicly traded stocks in private companies. As of September 30, 2005, the market value of NRRIT-managed assets was $27.7 billion.

The NRRIT was designed to insulate investment decisions from political interference. The NRRIT is not considered a government agency and is separate from the RRB. Congress directed that the NRRIT be managed by an independent board of trustees, jointly chosen by railroad employers and employees. The members of the board are not considered officers or employees of the U.S. government and are not subject to congressional confirmation. Trustees and fund managers are required to vote proxies solely in the interest of the RRB. To ensure accountability, the board of trustees is subject to reporting and fiduciary standards similar to the ERISA standards. All individual trustees must be bonded to protect the NRRIT against fraud and have the option of being insured.

The Federal Retirement Thrift Investment Board is an independent agency of the executive branch that sets policies for investment of the Thrift Savings Program (TSP) assets and administers the TSP. The board consists of five part-time board members appointed by the President and an executive director selected by the rest of the board. The executive director and members of the board are fiduciaries of the fund and are required to act prudently and solely in the interest of TSP participants and beneficiaries.

To protect the TSP from political interference, the board is exempt from the normal budget and appropriations process and the legislative and budget clearance process of the Office of Management and Budget. In addition, voting rights associated with the ownership of securities in the TSP may not be exercised by the board, other government agencies, the executive director, federal employees, Members of Congress, former federal employees, or former Members of Congress. Further, the board does not select specific investments; rather, it selects appropriate indices for investment funds and contracts with Barclays Global Investors to manage fund assets. Finally, proxy voting rights are exercised by the fund manager, Barclays, who is required to vote all shares to provide the maximum financial benefits to TSP participants. As of December 31, 2005, TSP managed assets totaling $173 billion.

Sources: National   Railroad   Retirement   Investment   Trust [http://www.rrb.gov/mep/nrrit.asp]; Federal Retirement Thrift Investment Board [http://www.frtib.gov].

Private Fund Managers

A more decentralized option would be to allow participants to contract with private fund managers to manage their account assets. This structure is currently used for retirement savings accounts such as §401(k) plans, where many employers contract with private money managers to invest the retirement savings of their employees, or IRAs, where individuals contract with private fund managers to invest their personal retirement savings.

Policymakers could establish the conditions under which fund managers were allowed to participate. Policymakers could consider whether private fund managers should follow any licensing and registration requirements.[71] Current securities law and regulations would need to be reviewed to ensure they are adequate to protect the range of investors participating in IAs and the size of the account assets. Policymakers could also determine which fund manager could invest the assets of accounts in which the participant does not actively choose a fund manager. This default may randomly assign participants with fund managers — similar to the way elderly Medicaid recipients were randomly assigned to a Medicare Part D prescription drug provider — or a single fund manager could be chosen as the default provider. Finally, policymakers could determine whether there would be a limit on the number of fund managers that are allowed to participate, either nationally or by state, and what criteria would be used to choose among eligible fund managers.[72] Too stringent limits could result in a very small number of firms with few incentives to compete by offering lower prices or better services. Alternatively, if the number of investment managers is unrestricted, participants may be faced with the responsibility of choosing from hundreds or even thousands of fund managers who each offer a range of investment options. A choice of this magnitude would likely reduce the probability that an individual would participate in the system and, for those who do participate, would likely lead many to invest their accounts in the default fund manager (if one is designated).

Countries that have private fund managers also typically have private sales agents that represent one or more fund managers. These agents generally receive a commission for enrolling participants into a particular fund and may provide information about fund options and some form of financial education and advice to potential participants. Many countries have found it necessary to regulate both the qualifications of sales agents and the types of information they provide to potential participants.[73] Other countries with sales agents have regulated the ability of individuals to move between funds to reduce the incentives for sales agents to generate commissions by switching participants between funds.[74]

Mixed Administration

A mixed administrative structure is also possible. Participants could be required to invest their assets in a centrally managed fund until they obtain a threshold balance in their account, at which point they could move their funds to a private fund manager. This type of system could take advantage of economies of scale to reduce administrative costs for small accounts. However, this design would set up a two-tiered system in which participants with larger account balances — primarily those with high incomes or older participants who have accumulated balances over a longer period of time — would have more choices than those with smaller account balances.

Implications

When choosing the responsible party for investing IA assets, it is important to be cognizant of how large these funds could become as a share of the economy. If workers contributed 2% of their current taxable earnings, CRS estimates that the accounts could grow to as much as 10% of the country's total economic output (GDP) in 10 years and to 25% of GDP in 20 years.[75] A 5% contribution rate could amass assets of as much as 25% of GDP in 10 years and could surpass 62% of GDP in 20 years. In three years, a 5% contribution could accumulate more assets in IAs than the total current holdings of the largest mutual fund manager.[76] And in just 11 years, IA assets could surpass the combined total currently invested by mutual funds in the U.S. equity market.

The decision regarding who should be responsible for investing IA assets has broad implications for the cost of the program, the administrative system, and possibly the diversity of choice of investment options. In justifying the decision to use a centralized investment structure for the Thrift Savings Plan, Congress stated:

> As an alternative the committee considered permitting any qualified institution to offer employees specific investment vehicles. However, the committee rejected that approach for a number of reasons. First, there are literally thousands of qualified institutions who would bombard employees with promotions for their services. The committee concluded that employees would not favor such an approach. Second, few, if any, private employers offer such an arrangement. Third, even qualified institutions go bankrupt occasionally and a substantial portion of an employee's retirement benefit could be wiped out. This is in contrast to the diversified fund approach which could easily survive a few bankruptcies. Fourth, it would be difficult to administer. Fifth, this 'retail' or 'voucher' approach would give up the economic advantage of this group's wholesale purchasing power derived from its large size, so that employees acting individually would get less for their money.[77]

Would Accounts Be Insured?

IA participants would be exposed to the risk that their accounts could lose value due to the failure of the institution that holds their deposits or due to market volatility.[78] To maintain investor confidence and protect participants' assets, policymakers may wish to consider a system to insure participants against these risks. However, providing protection may have the unintended effect of encouraging risky investment behavior by participants who may seek out risky private fund managers or high-return, high-risk investments because they have nothing to lose.

Currently, investors receive some protection from the risk that they will lose their deposits if the institution in which they have entrusted their savings fails. Investors who make deposits in financial instructions, such as banks, credit unions, or with securities firms, are insured — up to a set limit — if those institutions close due to bankruptcy or other financial difficulty and customer assets are missing.[79]

Assets in defined benefit pension plans — and not defined contribution plans, such as §401(k)s — are insured if their plan terminates without enough assets to pay benefits owed to each participant.[80] The cost of these guarantees in times of financial trouble has been significant.[81] Policymakers would need to determine whether IA deposits would receive protection from these existing institutions, whether a new system of protection would be established, or whether participants would bear the full risk.

Although investors in many cases are currently protected against loss due to the collapse of the institution that holds their deposits, there are no similar protections against losses due to market volatility.[82] Individual investors bear the sole burden if the value of their portfolios plummet.[83] Concern over the impact of market volatility on retirement income has caused countries such as Japan, Argentina, Chile, and Poland to adopt "guarantees" for their defined contribution pension accumulations.[84] Guarantees fall into two basic categories, *minimum rate of return* guarantees and *minimum benefit* guarantees, and can be designed to protect against loss, promise a minimum rate of return, or ensure plan participants that the benefits they receive upon retirement would be at a minimum level irrespective of the accounts' actual performance.[85] These guarantees are expensive and are highly sensitive to the type of guarantee offered, the structure of the participants' portfolio, and the number of years the portfolio would be invested.[86] The Congressional Budget Office (CBO) recently estimated the cost of guaranteeing that IA participants would receive at least the current level of scheduled Social Security benefits.[87] CBO estimates that there is a 1 in 10 chance that such a guarantee could cost as much as $1.9 trillion over 75 years, whereas a guarantee of at least 80% of scheduled benefits could cost $400 billion.

Key issues in designing any insurance system would be how the protection is funded and what liability the government would assume.[88] Guarantees could be provided by the private market, and IA participants could bear the costs directly through higher fees, allowing investors who have a low tolerance for risk to pay directly for their enhanced security. Insurance costs would generally rise with the size of the portfolio, so that fees would be more expensive for high earners or older participants with larger accounts. Alternatively, the government could assume responsibility for any liabilities. This would force non-participants to help subsidize the premiums of account participants. However, depending on the size of the accounts and the types of risks that are insured, the federal government may be the only entity with enough resources to provide financial backing.

Regardless of the funding source, if IAs were to be insured, they would have to face strong regulations on the types of portfolios offered and the institutions that invest them. The cost of insuring unregulated accounts is likely prohibitive. Some countries have found that strict regulations have helped their systems' viability. However, other countries have found that there may be unintended consequences to specific regulations designed to protect investors from risk. For example, in Chile, regulations that attempted to reduce risk have resulted in reducing meaningful investment choice for participants.[89] In Poland, investment funds are required to meet performance targets or else to make up the shortfall. Because the performance targets are calculated quarterly, investment mangers focus on short-term goals rather than a long-term investment strategy.[90]

Would There Be Multiple Investment Choices?

As mentioned above, collectively managed assets could also be collectively invested, leaving participants with no choice in how to invest their contributions. Alternatively, participants could be offered a choice in the way their accounts are invested. In deciding how many investments to offer, policymakers face a tradeoff between offering a variety of investment choices, reducing risk, and keeping administrative costs low.[91]

One option would be to follow the same rules governing private defined contribution retirement plans and require that participants be given at least enough choice so as to allow them to diversify their portfolio.[92] Alternatively, investment choices could be limited to a set choice of stock index funds and bond funds similar to the Federal employees' Thrift Savings Program (TSP). If policymakers wish to limit the number of funds, the investment criteria may have to be carefully defined to achieve an adequate level of choice for asset diversification while insulating the selection process from political interference.[93]

What Are the Investment Choices in the Thrift Savings Program?

Thrift Savings Program (TSP) participants can choose to allocate all or part of their accounts to any of five funds.

- There are two fixed income funds. The "G Fund" consists of short-term, nonmarketable U.S. Treasury Securities. The "F Fund" is invested in the Lehman Brothers Aggregate bond index.
- There are three stock funds. The "C Fund" is a large-company domestic stock fund that tracks the Standard and Poor's 500 stock index. The medium and small company "S Fund" tracks the Wilshire 4500 stock index. The International Stock Index Investment "I Fund" tracks the returns of the Morgan Stanley Capital International EAFE (Europe, Australasia, Far East) stock index.

In August 2005, the TSP also began to offer five lifecycle "L Funds." Each fund provides a different mix of the fixed income and stock investments and is geared toward employees with a particular retirement date.

Source: For more recent information on the TSP, see CRS Report RL30387, *Federal Employees' Retirement System: The Role of the Thrift Savings Plan*, by Patrick J. Purcell.

At the other extreme, IA investment choices could be unlimited and include any type of financial asset. However, this would likely raise administrative expenses and could subject participants to extremely high-risk assets. In addition, when presented by an unlimited and possibly confusing array of investment options, participants may find that they lack the expertise or the interest to choose a well-diversified portfolio.[94]

A related issue is whether to allow IA fund options in which investments are chosen based on social, ethical, or environmental criteria. U.S. 401(k) plans are increasingly adding socially responsible investment funds to their portfolio options.[95] Some countries have developed policies on "responsible investing" that set standards for the types of investments used in their publicly managed pension funds.[96]

Policymakers could decide if criteria other than an investment's projected risk and return could be used to select IA investment options.

Would Participants Have Access to "Lifecycle" Funds?

Financial advisers nearly universally recommend investors follow a strategy of holding a mixed portfolio of stocks and bonds and rebalancing the portfolio's allocations over time as asset prices change, and also reallocating between assets as an individual ages, to reduce the level of risk as the person nears retirement. However, in practice, few investors rebalance their portfolios. Therefore, in addition to funds of pure stocks and bonds, policymakers could decide to require that participants are offered funds that combine stocks and bonds in ways to reduce risk while allowing participants exposure to higher returns.[97]

To address this behavior, a financial product that automatically reallocates investment funds is becoming a more popular offering in private pensions. These so-called "lifecycle funds" are balanced portfolios with varying risk and reward characteristics. There are two types of lifecycle funds: targeted-maturity and static-allocation. In the first, targeted-maturity funds, the proportion of stock in a portfolio falls over time to provide a level of risk appropriate to the participant's age. A targeted-maturity lifecycle fund, however, can expose younger investors to more risk than they might prefer or expose older investors to less risk and lower returns than they need to adequately provide retirement income. An alternative investment structure is the static-allocation lifecycle fund, which is consistently rebalanced to maintain a fixed ratio of stocks and bonds over a career based on the participant's preference for risk. However, unless participants reallocate their investments as they age, static-allocation lifecycle funds may expose participants to more risk than is appropriate.

Lifecycle funds have become increasingly popular among defined contribution pension plan sponsors and participants.[98] Five months after they began, more than 220,000 (out of 3.5 million) TSP participants had already shifted their investments or contributions into the new lifecycle "L" funds as of December 31, 2005. These funds offer participants, even those with little or no investment knowledge, the ability to broadly diversify their accounts and follow an appropriate asset allocation strategy.

In designing a system of IAs, policymakers could determine whether these types of funds would be available to IA participants.

What Would the Default Investment Portfolio Be?

It would have to be determined how to invest the assets of workers who fail to make an active choice of where to allocate their IA contributions. The default option could allocate all nonresponsive participants' assets into a particular fund, such as a bond index fund, or allocate them across the range of funds to ensure diversification.

In choosing default funds, retirement fund managers often pick investments that provide the lowest risk and therefore also provide the lowest expected rate of return. For example, in the Thrift Savings Program, all contributions are invested in the government securities "G Fund" until the participant designates an alternative contribution allocation. Studies of investment behavior show that there is a great deal of inertia in investment and allocation choices.[99] Thus, the choice of a default may be a key decision, because many workers may remain in the default fund until they retire.

FEES

Would There Be Limits on the Amount and Structure of Administrative Fees?

The amount and structure of management fees would have a significant impact on participants' flexibility and on their final account balances. Although a 1% fee may sound modest, compounded each year it would reduce the ending account balance by 22% over a 40-year period.[100] Experience in other countries has shown the impact of high fees. In Chile, fees consumed 33% of the individual account contributions of a worker earning the minimum wage and 28% of the contributions of an average worker who retired in 2000 and participated in the plan since its inception in the 1980s.[101]

While the level of fees would have a large effect on account balances, the structure of fees — whether they are proportional or flat-dollar — would also play an important role.[102] Proportional fees are assessed as a set share of account assets, deposits, or a percentage of the fund's annual yield. These fees can be charged on contributions at the time of deposit, periodically on assets during the life of the account (such as quarterly or annually), or at the time of withdrawal. Under a system of proportional fees, private fund managers would have financial incentives to discriminate against small account holders because providers would receive more revenue from high-income participants or individuals with large accounts. As the costs of account management are generally unrelated to the size of an individual's account, fund managers may prefer to charge flat-dollar fees. With a flat-dollar fee structure, all accounts are charged the same amount, and private fund managers would not have the same financial incentives to treat small and large investors differently. However, these fees act like a regressive tax that consumes a larger share of small accounts than larger accounts.

Add-on fees or loads such as those charged to mutual fund investors could also have an important impact on participants' flexibility and choice. For example, back-end load fees — which provide a commission at the time of sale — could be set to discourage participants from switching between private fund managers. Although UK workers are allowed to move between account managers annually, it was reported in 1999 that many managers set penalties for moving that reduced the average pension by 27%.[103] Private fund managers could also impose transaction fees, which could discourage participants from switching investments or rebalancing their portfolios, or encourage fund managers to actively manage or "churn" accounts to increase revenue.

How High Are the Administrative Fees Estimated To Be in IAs?

The administrative costs of a system of IAs would depend on many of the choices raised in this chapter. Specifically, administrative costs would vary depending on the size and structure of the accounts, on whether the accounts are administered centrally or through a decentralized system of private fund managers, on the level of services and education provided to account holders, and on the degree of choice participants have among investment options. The amount individual participants would pay would also depend on the amount of government subsidy (if any) and the structure of the fees.

Recognizing these uncertainties and that costs would be higher in the early years of plan implementation, several government agencies have attempted to quantify the administrative costs of a system of IAs. There is a large range of estimates. In a 2001 report by the Social Security Administration, analysts estimated that a centralized program of IAs would require startup costs from $1.2 billion to $2.3 billion and ongoing costs of between 0.95% and 4% of IA assets, which would decline over time. In their analysis of a specific IA proposal, CBO estimated that the total administrative costs would be roughly $27 billion over the first 10 years, an amount that includes $1.5 billion in start-up costs and ongoing annual charges of between $7 and $17 per account, depending on the investment options. A Government Accountability Office study estimated that fees could range between 0.1% and 3.0% of assets per year, depending on the structure of the system.

To put these estimates in context, the Federal Thrift Savings Plan currently charges administrative fees of less than 0.1% of account assets, or roughly $25 per year per participant. However, this charge does not include the costs to federal agencies of collecting contributions and educating their workers about participation and investment options. In the private market, one study of fees estimated that the dollar-weighted average annual fee in 2003 on retail equity mutual funds was 1.25% of account balances, whereas the fees charged on bond mutual funds were 0.88% and on money market funds 0.33%.

Sources: CBO "Analysis of H.R. 3304, Growing Real Ownership for Workers Act of 2005," Letter to the Honorable Max Baucus, September 2005 at [http://www.cbo.gov/ftpdocs/ 66xx/doc6645/09-13-BaucusLetter.pdf]. CBO "Administrative Costs of Private Accounts in Social Security," March 2004 at [http://www.cbo.gov/ftpdocs/52xx/doc5277/Report.pdf]. GAO "Social Security Reform: Administrative Costs for Individual Accounts Depend on System Design" GAO/HEHS- 99-131 June, 1999, at [http://www.gao.gov/archive/ 1999/he99131.pdf]. Investment Company Institute, "Total Shareholder Cost of Mutual Funds, 2003" *Fundamentals,* vol. 13, no. 5, 2004, at [http://www.ici.org/stats/res/fm-v13n5.pdf]. Lawrence E. Hart, Mark Kearney, Carol Musil, and Kelly Olsen "SSA's Estimates of Administrative Costs Under a Centralized Program of Individual Accounts," January 2001, at [http://www.ssa.gov/policy/ docs/research/rr2000-01rev.pdf].

Small accounts present a unique set of issues. There are roughly 30 million workers (roughly 18% of the total workforce) in this country earning less than $5,000 per year.[104] Under an IA plan with a contribution rate of 2%, each of these workers would annually contribute less than $100. If fees are structured as a share of contributions or account assets, private fund managers may find that it is not cost effective to manage such small accounts. Alternatively, if fees are set at a flat rate for all participants, the fees could consume a large share of small account assets.

In setting up a system of IAs, policymakers may choose to set restrictions on the level or structure of administrative fees. Currently, private pension funds do not have explicit restrictions on fees other than broad "prudence" or "reasonableness" standards. However, many countries with IAs have set limits on the structure of charges, and some have established ceilings for asset-based charges.[105] While many countries have been successful at reducing costs, they have largely done so by restricting individual choice and competition among pension fund administrators.[106] Limiting fees would likely reduce marketing, education, and the range of choice and services provided to account holders (unless these activities are subsidized by the federal government).[107] Whether or not limits are set on the level or structure of fees, consistent reporting and disclosure standards should be established to allow participants to easily compare and understand fees and their impact on account balances.

Would the Government Provide a Subsidy to Cover the Startup Costs or Administrative Fees?

Policymakers may choose to finance startup costs or administrative costs through general revenue, either for all accounts during the start of the system or for some IA participants such as those with small accounts or low earnings.[108] This would effectively increase the rate of return on assets in those accounts. However, it would reduce incentives for investors to seek low-cost providers. This policy may also raise concerns about equity, because nonparticipants would be forced to pay some of the costs of IAs.

CONCLUSION

A system of individual accounts within Social Security could involve millions of Americans, billions of dollars, and could have a broad impact on the American economy. Thus, if IAs were to be adopted, the stakes are high to design a well-functioning system to administer the collection and investment of account assets.

Each choice also involves a cost. Although competition may help to drive down costs, in general, the more decentralized the system, the higher the administrative costs. Costs would also be higher for options that provide participants with more services — such as account management options, multiple investment choices, and personalized financial advice. Even small costs can have a significant impact on the retirement income of participants. Over a 40 year period, a 1% administrative fee can reduce final account balances by 22%.

Program design is important. Some countries have faced major problems with retirement accounts due to inadequate planning and insufficient regulation. Most recently, we have seen in this country the importance of adequate planning in the difficulties some beneficiaries have reported during the implementation of the new Medicare Part D prescription drug benefit. One lesson to be learned from these experiences is that major policy changes require insight and foresight.

More research is needed on the implications of IA program design. Although this chapter highlights the broad implications of basic IA collection and investment options, more thorough analysis is needed, especially in regard to the interaction among options. Seemingly unimportant details may have large impacts, and policymakers should be made aware of the implications when considering IA proposals.

REFERENCES

[1]   For a thorough resource on this topic, see Virginia P. Reno, Michael J. Graetz, Kenneth S. Apfel, Joni Lavery, and Catherine Hill (eds.), (2005). *Uncharted Waters: Paying Benefits from Individual Accounts in Federal Retirement Policy, Study Panel Final Report*, Washington, DC, National Academy of Social Insurance, January, at [http://www.nasi.org/ usr_doc/Uncharted_Waters_Report.pdf]. (Hereafter cited as NASI, *Uncharted Waters.*)

[2]   For details on these proposals, see CRS Issue Brief IB98048, *Social Security Reform*, by Dawn Nuschler.

[3]   The Employee Retirement Income Security Act (ERISA, P.L. 93-406) allows employers to exclude from their retirement plans workers who are younger than 21 years old, who work fewer than 1,000 hours per year, or who have worked for less than one year.

[4]   For a complete list of workers who do not participate in Social Security, see CRS Report 94-28, *Social Security and Medicare Taxes and Premiums: Fact Sheet*, by Dawn Nuschler.

[5]   Policymakers also may consider whether IA contributions for noncovered workers would count toward current offsets (i.e., the Windfall Elimination Provision and the Government Pension Offset) to their Social Security benefits. (For a description of these offsets, see CRS Report 98-35, *Social Security: The Windfall Elimination Provision (WEP)*, and CRS Report RL32453, *Social Security: The Government Pension Offset (GPO)*, both by Laura Haltzel.)

[6]   Another option is to initially have a system in which some individuals are required to participate, but participation is voluntary for another group, while some other individuals are prohibited from joining. This type of system existed in Poland when the country started a private account system in 1999. At that time, all citizens younger than 30 were required to participate, Poles age 30 to 50 could choose to join the system, and those older than 50 were prohibited from participating. (OECD, *Pensions at a Glance: Public Policies Across OECD Countries*, 2005, p. 153.)

[7]   American Academy of Actuaries Issue Brief, "Social Security Reform: Voluntary or Mandatory Individual Accounts?," September 2002, at [http://www.actuary.org/pdf/ socialsecurity/accounts_sept02.pdf].

[8]   Social Security Administration, Annual Statistical Supplement, 2005, at [http://www.ssa.gov/policy/docs/statcomps/supplement/2005/4b.html#table4.b1]. The Congressional Research Service (CRS) estimate is adjusted to include workers not covered by Social Security.

[9]   An estimated 18 million households, or 12% of all tax units, do not file an annual tax return, often because they do not owe taxes or are ineligible for any tax credits. Ninety-seven percent of nonfilers have income below $10,000 per year. (*NASI, Uncharted Waters* p. 41.)

[10]   The Internal Revenue Service (IRS) has issued several rulings in recent years to clarify that employers are permitted to enroll employees in §401(k) and §403(b) plans automatically through payroll deduction, provided that the employee is notified in

advance and has the option to drop out of the plan. For more details, see CRS Report RS21954, *Automatic Enrollment in Section 401(k) Plans*, by Patrick Purcell.

[11] Studies indicate that automatic enrollment in §401(k)s boosts the participation rate from a national average of about 75% of eligible employees to between 85% to 95%. (See William Gale, J. Mark Iwry, and Peter R. Orzag, *The Automatic 401(k): A Simple Way to Strengthen Retirement Savings*, the Retirement Security Project No. 2005-1, at [http://www.brookings.edu/views/papers/20050228_401k.pdf].)

[12] Tax credits can be non-refundable or refundable. Non-refundable tax credits reduce the amount of tax owed, but would not provide any benefits for those low-income participants without a tax liability. In contrast, refundable tax credits either reduce the amount of tax owed or provide cash back to participants whose credit exceeds their tax liability. Such credits would have the largest impact on low-income participants, many of whom do not pay income tax.

[13] For example, a $300 deduction would reduce the taxes of a married couple in the 25% marginal tax bracket by $75 and by $30 if the couple were in the 10% bracket. A $300 tax credit would reduce the taxes by $300, regardless of the participant's tax bracket.

[14] For example, a taxpaying married couple with $6,000 in deductible contributions saves $1,500 in tax if they are in the 25% marginal tax bracket, but only $600 if they are in the 10% bracket.

[15] The characteristics of "low earners" would have to be carefully defined when targeting financial matches. Workers may have low earnings either because they have low wages or because they work for short periods of time. Workers with low wages may work multiple jobs, and their total earnings may not be low. Over an individual's lifetime, he or she could experience periods of both low earnings and high earnings. For example, a college student who works at summer jobs may fall below a set threshold but then rise above it when she graduates and take a full time job. It is also important to recognize that low earners may not have low incomes. Low earners may receive income from other sources, such as assets, or from other family members.

[16] In the Thrift Savings Program (TSP), federal agencies contribute an amount equal to 1% of the base pay for each employee covered by the Federal Employees Retirement System (FERS) whether or not the employee chooses to contribute anything to the plan. In addition, employee contributions up to 5% of pay are matched by the federal government (dollar for dollar on the first 3% and $.50 on the dollar for the next 2%).

[17] A list of needs-based programs can be found in CRS Report RL32233, *Cash and Noncash Benefits for Persons with Limited Income: Eligibility Rules, Recipient and Expenditure Data, FY2002-FY2004*, by the Knowledge Services Group.

[18] Resource limits vary by program and often by state. For example, food stamp rules count some defined contribution retirement savings plans — IRAs and Keoghs — as an asset but exclude others — §401(k) plans and Federal Employees Thrift Savings Plans. For a comprehensive discussion of how retirement accounts are treated in means tested programs see Zoë Neuberger, Robert Greenstein, and Eileen P. Sweeney, "Protecting Low-Income Families' Retirement Savings: How Retirement Accounts are Treated in Means-Tested Programs and Steps to Remove Barriers to Retirement Savings," The Retirement Security Project, June 2005 at [http://www.cbpp.org/6-21-05socsec.pdf]. For a description of defined contribution and defined benefit pension plans, see CRS

Report RL30122, *Pension Sponsorship and Participation: Summary of Recent Trends*, by Patrick Purcell.

[19] The Congressional Research Service (CRS) estimates are for illustrative purposes only and are expressed in real 2005 dollars. The estimates are based on an individual who earns the economy-wide average annual wage (projected using the intermediate assumptions of the 2004 Social Security Trustee's Report), who makes contributions for 40 years (2010-2049), who earns a 3% real annual return on account assets (the projected rate of return to government bonds and the risk-adjusted rate of return used by the SSA Actuaries), and for whom no administrative fees are charged.

[20] The average earnings ceiling on public pension contributions in 19 Organization for Economic Co-operation and Development (OECD) member countries is 183% of average economy-wide earnings. OECD, *Pensions at a Glance: Public Policies Across OECD Countries*, 2005, p. 33.

[21] Employee Benefits Research Institute (EBRI) "The Impact of Workers' Earnings Profiles on Individual Account Accumulations" *EBRI Notes*, vol. 21 no. 10, October 2000, at [http://www.ebri.org/pdf/notespdf/1000notes.pdf].

[22] About 14 million individuals receive Social Security benefits based at least in part on a current or former spouses' work record. In Social Security, the current or former age-eligible wife or husband of a retired or disabled worker is eligible to receive retirement benefits of an amount equal to 50% of the worker's benefit, and an elderly widow or widower is eligible to receive an amount up to 100% of the worker's benefit (providing no early retirement reductions apply). These benefits are available to an unmarried, divorced spouse only if their marriage lasted at least 10 years.

[23] Other features of the current Social Security system that would be difficult to replicate include survivor and disability benefits for young workers who have small accounts, spousal benefits for spouses who retire before the worker gains access to his or her account, and the generally progressive structure of the benefit formula.

[24] In 2001, 41% of men and 39% of women age 50 to 59 had been divorced sometime in their lifetime. (Rose Kreider, "Number, Timing, and Duration of Marriages and Divorces: 2001" U.S. Census Bureau Household Economics Studies, February 2005, p. 6, at [http://www.census.gov/prod/2005pubs/p70-97.pdf].)

[25] No consistent national reporting system to track marriages and divorces currently exists. IRS records for taxpayers may not be an accurate record of marital status for that tax year, as there are certain circumstances in which legally married couples could file as unmarried (e.g., single or head of household). The Social Security Administration also does not collect information on a worker's marital history until the time at which he or she applies for benefits.

[26] *NASI, Uncharted Waters* p. 119.

[27] Distributions would be dependent on whether the couple resides in one of the nine community property states — which treat all property acquired during a marriage to be held jointly by the spouses — or in a common law state — where property belongs exclusively to the spouse who holds title. Movements between states could result in mixed property.

[28] In an employer-provided defined benefit pension, the default payout to a married worker must be a joint and survivor annuity and spouses must consent to a lower payout and any loans. Accounts established under §401(k) provide few rights for spouses. Only

if the §401(k) plan offers annuities *and* the worker chooses one is spousal consent required to choose a payment other than an joint and survivor annuity. Laws governing pensions and retirement savings accounts do not automatically provide divorcees with access to these accounts, requiring state courts to determine the distribution of funds as a part of divorce settlements.

[29] For a thorough list of options see *NASI, Uncharted Waters,* p. 127.

[30] Rather than directly collecting IA contributions, policymakers could also choose to fund IAs with general revenue.

[31] See CRS Report RL32896, *Social Security: Raising or Eliminating the Taxable Earnings Base,* by Debra Whitman.

[32] For a more thorough discussion of these issues, see CRS Report RL32756, *Social Security Individual Accounts and Employer-Sponsored Pensions,* by Patrick J. Purcell.

[33] President's Commission to Strengthen Social Security, *Strengthening Social Security and Creating Personal Wealth for All Americans,* December 2001, p. 47.

[34] In 2003, 72% of all employers submitted reports to SSA on paper. (See CRS Report RL32756, *Social Security Individual Accounts and Employer-Sponsored Pensions,* by Patrick J. Purcell.)

[35] For example, assuming identical annual rates of return at 7%, a deposit of $100 a month ($1,200 per year) after 40 years would yield $254,166 if funds were deposited annually, $260,966 if deposited quarterly, and $262,481 if deposited monthly. Smaller accounts would lose less interest. For a $300 annual deposit, the difference between annual and monthly deposits over 40 years would only be $2,080. (Kelly Olsen and Dallas Salisbury "Individual Social Security Accounts: Issues in Assessing Administrative Feasibility and Costs" in *Beyond Ideology: Are Individual Social Security Accounts Feasible?* Edited by Dallas Salisbury, Employee Benefits Research Institute, Washington, DC, 1999, p. 20) and (Fred T. Goldberg and Michael J. Graetz, "A Practical and Workable System of Personal Retirement Accounts, in *Administrative Aspects of Investment-Based Social Security Reform,* John B. Shoven ed., University of Chicago Press, Chicago, 2000, p. 19).

[36] Policymakers could choose to follow the depository requirements of §401(k) plans in which contributions must be credited to individuals' §401(k) accounts on the earliest date that they can reasonably be segregated from the employer's general assets, but in no event later than 15 days following the month in which a contribution was received by an employer. (As set in Department of Labor regulation 29 CFR § 2510.3-102, at [http://www.dol.gov/ ebsa/regs/fedreg/proposed/97_7709.htm].

[37] Prior to 1978, employers were required to report W-2 information along with their quarterly wage and tax statements. It has been estimated that the change from quarterly to annual reporting has saved small businesses close to $1 billion per year. (Kelly Olsen and Dallas Salisbury "Individual Social Security Accounts: Administrative Issues" EBRI Issue Brief Number 236, Special Report 40, September 2001, p. 18, at [http://www.ebri.org/pdf/ briefspdf/0901ib.pdf].)

[38] One explanation is that many of the new entrants were very young workers. (Weaver, R. Kent, "Social Security Smorgasbord? Lessons from Sweden's Individual Pension Accounts," Brookings Policy Brief #140, June 2005 at [http://www.brookings.edu/ comm/policybriefs/pb140.pdf].)

[39] Investment Company Institute, "U.S. Household Ownership of Mutual Funds in 2005," Fundamentals, vol. 14 no. 5, October 2005, at [http://www.ici.org/shareholders/ us/fm-v14n5.pdf].

[40] Roughly 10% to 20% of the population does not have a checking account or a savings account with a bank or credit union.(*NASI, Uncharted Waters*, p. 10.)

[41] The impact of inflation is a crucial but misunderstood concept for retirement planning. Inflation has averaged 3% per year over the last 75 years, implying that expenses have doubled every 25 years. If this trend continues, a 40-year-old would need twice his or her current income just to maintain the same standard of living in retirement at age 65 and four times his or her current income to maintain that standard at age 90. One survey found that nearly two-thirds of American adults and students did not know that money loses its value in times of inflation. Elizabeth Bell and Robert I. Lerman "Can Financial Literacy Enhance Asset Building," Urban Institute Opportunity and Ownership Project, No. 6, September 2005 at [http://www.urban.org/UploadedPDF/ 311224_ financial_ literacy.pdf].

[42] Steven Nyce, "The Importance of Financial Communication for Participation Rates and Contribution Levels in §401(k) Plans," Benefits Quarterly, vol. 21, Issue 2, April 2005.

[43] For example, in 1965, a massive outreach effort was conducted to get older individuals to sign up for the newly enacted Medicare program. The effort consisted of mailings, a media campaign, and targeted door-to-door outreach targeting individuals age 65 and older that cost $7.2 million (roughly $44 million in today's dollars). More recently, the Centers for Medicare and Medicaid Services spent $253 million and the Social Security Administration spent $347 million in FY2005 for education and outreach for the temporary Medicare-approved discount card and the new Medicare Part D prescription drug program. Even with the extensive public education campaign, the Inspector General found that 37% of beneficiaries needed additional help with the process of signing up after they decided to enroll in the discount card program. Sources: CRS Report RL32828, *Beneficiary Information and Decision Supports for the Medicare-Endorsed Prescription Drug Discount Card*, by Diane Justice; CRS conversation with CMS budget analyst on Jan. 6, 2005; and Department of Health and Human Services, Office of the Inspector General, "Temporary Medicare-Approved Drug Card: Beneficiaries' Awareness and Use of Information Resources," October 2005, at [http://oig.hhs.gov/oei/reports/oei-05-04-00200.pdf].

[44] The Social Security Statement is an easy-to-read statement of past earnings and expected future benefits which is mailed annually to workers and former workers age 25 and older. [http://www.ssa.gov/mystatement/].

[45] A 2001 study by the Social Security Administration estimated that start-up costs for a public information campaign for a centrally administered system of IAs would be $60-$225 million and that ongoing costs would be $5 million per year. (Lawrence E. Hart, Mark Kearney, Carol Musil, and Kelly Olsen "SSA's Estimates of Administrative Costs Under a Centralized Program of Individual Accounts" January 2001, p. 29, at [http://www.ssa.gov/ policy/docs/research/rr2000-01rev.pdf], hereafter cited as Hart et al., "SSA's Estimates of Administrative Costs.")

[46] Burhouse, Susan, Donna Gambrell, and Angelisa Harris, "Delivery Systems for Financial Education in Theory and Practice," FYI, Federal Deposit Insurance

Corporation, Sept. 22, 2004, at [http://www.fdic.gov/bank/analytical/fyi/ 2004/ 092204fyi.html].

[47] The Centers for Medicare and Medicaid Services (CMS) issued extensive guidelines for private firms in their marketing of the Medicare Part D prescription drug benefit. [http://www.cms.hhs.gov/pdps/PrtDPlnMrktngGdlns.asp].

[48] Statement of Julia Lynn Coronado, Testimony Before the Subcommittee on Social Security of the House Committee on Ways and Means, June 2005, "Sweden's Public Pension Reform: Lessons for the United States, at [http://waysandmeans.house.gov/ hearings.asp?formmode=view and id=2800].

[49] Swedish Premium Pensions Committee, 2005 Report to Minister Sven-Erik Osterberg, "Difficult Waters? Premium Pension Savings on Course," at [http://www.sweden.gov.se/ content/1/c6/05/22/65/077d40e8.pdf].

[50] To inform the public about the prescription drug discount card, CMS relied on a variety of education and outreach efforts, including media advertising, direct mail, Medicare's website and toll-free help line, one-on-one counseling, and partnerships with community organizations. (Government Accountability Office Report 06-139R "Medicare: CMS's Beneficiary Education and Outreach Effort for the Medicare Prescription Drug Discount Card and Transitional Assistance Program," Memorandum to Henry Waxman, at [http://www.gao.gov/new.items/d06139r.pdf].)

[51] Jeanne M. Hogarth and Marianne A. Hilgert, "Financial Knowledge, Experience and Learning Preferences: Preliminary Results from a New Survey on Financial Literacy," Consumer Interest Annual 48 (2002), p. 6, at [http://www.consumerinterests.org/files/ public/FinancialLiteracy-02.pdf].

[52] People or firms that get paid to give advice about investing in securities generally must register with either the Securities and Exchange Commission (SEC) or the state securities agency where they have their principal place of business. The SEC regulates larger investment advisers, whereas the states regulate investment advisers with less than $25 million in assets under management who do not advise a mutual fund. Stockbrokers who provide advice that is "solely incidental to" their business as brokers are not required to register as advisers. Currently, there are approximately 8,100 SEC-registered investment advisers and approximately 15,000 investment advisers registered in one or more states. (Investment Advisers Registration Depository at [http://www.iard.com/regulatory.asp].)

[53] To provide at least a limited level of advice at a reasonable cost, the UK has implemented a two-tiered system. "Full advice" is provided by professionals with financial planning qualifications. Salespeople providing "basic advice," which is heavily prescribed and limited to a specific range of products, are not required to hold formal qualifications. (Financial Services Authority, "A Basic Advice Scheme for the Sale of Stakeholder Products," June 2004, at [http://www.fsa.gov.uk/ pubs/cp/cp04_11.pdf].)

[54] These restrictions are designed to limit the incentives for investment advisers to take undue risks while managing their clients' assets. However, investment advisers are allowed to charge performance fees to registered mutual funds, persons with assets exceeding $1 million, or sophisticated investor pools.

[55] In the UK, financial advisers were recently required to standardize the information about their services into two documents. The first provides the consumer with

information about the type of advice and the range of products offered. The second document tells the consumer about the amount and existence of commissions of fees and provides information on how these fees compare to market averages. (Financial Services Authority, "New rules from the FSA on financial advice: Bringing more choice for consumers," August 2005, at [http://www.fsa.gov.uk/ consumer/ 10_WHATS_NEW/FIRMS/new_advice_rules.html]).

[56] Jennifer Levitz, "Congress Is Split on 401(k) Advisers — Lawmakers May Loosen Restrictions but Worry Over Conflicts of Interest," *Wall Street Journal*, Jan. 31, 2006, p. D2.

[57] A fiduciary who breaches any of the responsibilities imposed by the Employee Retirement Income Security Act (ERISA) is, under § 409, personally liable to make good to the plan any losses resulting from each such breach. (See CRS Report RL31248, *Enron: Selected Securities, Accounting, and Pension Laws Possibly Implicated in its Collapse*, by Michael V. Seitzinger, Marie B. Morris, and Mark Jickling.)

[58] UK investment advisers paid billions of pounds in fines and compensation for allegedly providing poor advice to more than 1.7 million investors to leave state pension funds and participate in personal accounts. As of 2002, the mis-selling scandal was reported to have cost insurers and financial advisers at least £11.8 billion ($20.5 billion in 2004 dollars) in compensation payments to investors and nearly £10 million ($17.5 million) in fines. (Financial Services Authority press release, "11.8 Billion Compensation for Pensions and FSAVC Reviews," June 27, 2002, at [http://www.fsa.gov.uk/Pages/ Library/ Communication/PR/2002/070.shtml], and BBC News, "Pension Scandals Cost £11.8 Billion," June 27, 2002, at [http://news.bbc.co.uk/1/hi/business/2070271.stm]).

[59] The National Finance Center (NFC) of the Department of Agriculture is the record-keeper for the Thrift Savings Program for federal departments and agencies. The NFC performs detailed record keeping of participant account balances and responds to telephone and written inquiries from participants. The NFC's fees to the TSP for these services for FY2005 were approximately $30 million. (Deloitte Independent Auditors Report of the Thrift Savings Fund, dated Mar. 4, 2005, at [http://www.tsp.gov/forms/financial-stmt.pdf].)

[60] Lawrence H. Thompson "Administering Individual Accounts in Social Security: The Role of Values and Objectives in Shaping Options," Occasional Paper Number 1, The Retirement Project, The Urban Institute, Washington, 1999, p. 10-11, at [http://www.urban.org/UploadedPDF/retire_1.pdf], hereafter cited as Thompson, "Administering Individual Accounts in Social Security."

[61] One study by the SSA estimates that the ongoing costs of a centrally administered high-service IA program similar to the one described above, but without the "wake-up calls," would be $1.3 billion and require 12,470 additional full-time employees, whereas a system with basic services would cost $440 million and require an additional 4,965 full-time employees (Hart et al., "SSA's Estimates of Administrative Costs" p. 24).

[62] SSA places wage items that fail to match name and Social Security number records into its Earnings Suspense File (ESF). As of October 2004, the ESF had accumulated about $463 billion in wages and 246 million wage items for Tax Years 1937 through 2002. (Social Security Administration, Office of the Inspector General, "Social Security Number Misuse in the Service, Restaurant, and Agricultural Industries," April 2005,

Audit Report#: A-08-05-25023, at [http://www.ssa.gov/oig/ADOBEPDF/A-08-05-25023.pdf]).

[63] One reason for the lost accounts is that employers choose the financial intermediary for their employees. Thus, when a worker changes jobs, they may lose track of previous accounts. See [http://www.unclaimedsuper.com.au].

[64] Approximately 10% of U.S. employers reporting wages to SSA go out of business each year. (Kelly Olsen and Dallas Salisbury "Individual Social Security Accounts: Administrative Issues," EBRI Issue Brief Number 236, Special Report 40, September 2001, p. 31, at [http://www.ebri.org/pdf/briefspdf/0901ib.pdf]).

[65] Thompson, "Administering Individual Accounts in Social Security," p. 27. In 1999, Chile had roughly 6 million participants in its pension system. (Carmelo Mesa-Lago, "Structural Reform of Social Security Pensions in Latin America: Models, Characteristics, Results and Conclusions," International Social Security Review, vol. 54, no. 4, September 2001, pp. 67-92(26), at [http://www.ingentaconnect.com/ content/ bpl/issr/2001/ 00000054/00000004/art00105].)

[66] The SSA does not investigate errors of less than one earning credit ($920 in 2005). It has been estimated that if no errors were allowed, up to 15% of all employers would need to be contacted annually to correct errors (Hart et al., "SSA's Estimates of Administrative Costs," p. 27).

[67] According to the Government Accountability Office (GAO), in 1998, nearly 2 million businesses owed $49 billion in unpaid payroll taxes. GAO concluded that most unpaid payroll taxes are not fully collectable and that there is often no recovery potential because many of the businesses are insolvent, defunct, or otherwise unable to pay. GAO Report GAO/AIMD/GGD-99-211, "Unpaid Payroll Taxes; Billions in Delinquent Taxes and Penalty Assessments Are Owed," August 1999, at [http://www.gao.gov/ archive/1999/ a299211.pdf]. The Federal Retirement Thrift Investment Board requires federal agencies to repay both principal and interest earnings to employees' Thrift Savings Plan accounts that were lost as a result of an agency's error (5 §U.S.C. 8432a).

[68] E. P. Davis, Pension Funds, Retirement-Income Security and Capital Markets, an International Perspective, Oxford University Press, 1995. Other studies have shown that socially and politically targeted investments at the state and local level have been rare and the impact on investment returns have been insignificant. (Alicia H. Munnell and Annika Sunden, "Investment Practices of State and Local Pension Funds: Implications for Social Security Reform," in Pensions in the Public Sector, Olivia S. Mitchell and Edwin C. Hustead, eds., Pension Research Council and University of Pennsylvania Press, 2001.)

[69] Thompson, "Administering Individual Accounts in Social Security," p. 6.

[70] Robert Holzmann, Richard Hinz, and World Bank staff, Old-Age Income Support in the 21st Century: An International Perspective on Pension Systems and Reform, World Bank, Washington, DC, 2005.

[71] For a discussion of these issues, see Fred T. Goldberg and Michael J. Graetz, "A Practical and Workable System of Personal Retirement Accounts," in Administrative Aspects of Investment-Based Social Security Reform, John B. Shoven, ed., University of Chicago Press, Chicago, 2000, p. 19.

[72] Participants in individual accounts in Sweden must currently choose from more than 700 mutual funds. A recent government report that evaluated the pension system

recommends lowering the number of choices to between 100 and 200 by requiring a fund to achieve a set share of the market or be eliminated. (Swedish Premium Pensions Committee, 2005 Report to Minister Sven-Erik Osterberg, "Difficult Waters? Premium Pension Savings on Course," at [http://www.sweden.gov.se/content/1/c6/ 05/22/65/ 077d40e8.pdf].)

[73] In Poland 450,000 agents — representing roughly 1% of the total population — were registered to sell pension funds in 1999. The large number was likely due to the limited number of requirements for becoming an agent (no criminal record, being of legal age, and paying a $25 registration fee) and may have led to questionable practices to lure workers to particular funds. (Barbara E. Kritzer, "Social Security Reform in Central and Eastern Europe: Variations on a Latin American Theme," *Social Security Bulletin*, vol. 64, no. 4, June 2003, at [http://www.ssa.gov/policy/docs/ssb/v64n4/v64n4p16.pdf].)

[74] In Chile, there was more than 1 sales agent per 200 customers and roughly half of the participants switched providers in 1995. This high turnover was associated with large administrative costs, and the Chilean authorities responded by imposing restrictions on switching between funds. (Solange Berstein and Alejandro Micco, "Turnover and Regulation in the Chilean Pension Fund Industry," Central Bank of Chile Working Paper No. 180, September 2002, at [http://www.bcentral.cl/esp/estpub/estudios/ dtbc/ pdf/ dtbc180.pdf].)

[75] CRS estimates are for illustrative purposes only and assume that IA contributions are taken as a share of the Social Security wage base (as projected by the SSA Actuaries), began in 2005, were invested solely in equities which grew at a constant real annual rate of 6.5% (the equity rate used by SSA Actuaries when projecting solvency proposals), no administrative fees were charged, and no withdrawals were taken. Actual account accumulations may be smaller (if withdrawals were taken, administrative charges were paid, or investment returns were less than 6.5%) or larger (if investment returns were more than 6.5% or workers who are not currently covered by Social Security were allowed to participate).

[76] In 2005, the mutual fund industry had $3.9 trillion in assets invested in domestic equities. The largest fund group was Vanguard, with $788 billion in assets (of all types). (Financial Research Corporation, "November 2005 Estimated Mutual Fund Net Flows," Dec. 27, 2005, at [http://www.frcnet.com].)

[77] Conference Report 99-606 to accompany H.R. 2672, Federal Employees Retirement System Act of 1986.

[78] Other risks, such as inflation, could also affect account values.

[79] Banks and thrift intuition deposits are insured up to $100,000 against institutional collapse by the Federal Deposit Insurance Corporation. The National Credit Union Share Insurance Fund insures customers' credit union "shares" up to $100,000. Investors in stocks, bonds, and mutual funds held at securities firms are insured up to $500,000 (of which $100,000 may be cash) against institutional collapse by the Securities Investor Protection Corporation. Depending on the size of the accounts, these limits may be too low to offer IA participants adequate levels of protection. For more details, see CRS Report RS21987, *When Financial Businesses Fail: Protection for Account Holders*, by William D. Jackson.

[80] This insurance is provided through the Pension Benefit Guarantee Corporation. The maximum pension guarantee is $47,659 a year for plans that terminate in 2006. For

more information, see CRS Report 95-118, *Pension Benefit Guaranty Corporation: A Fact Sheet*, by Paul J. Graney.

[81] For example, in the 1980s, the total cost to taxpayers of the savings and loan crisis was $132 billion. The current liabilities to the Pension Benefit Guarantee Corporation are estimated to be $87 billion over the next 10 years. (U.S. General Accounting Office, GAO-AIMD-96-123 Financial Audit: Resolution Trust Corporations 1995 and 1994 Financial Statements (1996), p. 15, at [http://www.gao.gov/archive/1996/ai96123.pdf], and Congressional Budget Office, "The Risk Exposure of the Pension Benefit Guaranty Corporation," September 2005, at [http://www.cbo.gov/ftpdocs/66xx/doc6646/09-15-PBGC.pdf].)

[82] Federal employees have access to an investment vehicle that provides a guarantee of principal (a *minimum rate of return* guarantee of at least 0%). The Thrift Savings Program G Fund is invested in short-term U.S. Treasury securities specially issued to the TSP. Payment of principal and interest is guaranteed by the U.S. government. Thus, there is no "credit risk" for assets in the G Fund. However, the guarantee does not protect participants from inflation risk.

[83] IA participants could lose money in their accounts due to poor investment performance. In the first year of the Swedish system, the 10 worst performing funds lost, on average, 77% of their value. While it was unlikely that Swedish participants put their entire contributions into these funds, there were no legal constraints on doing so. (Weaver, R. Kent, "Social Security Smorgasbord? Lessons from Sweden's Individual Pension Accounts," Brookings Policy Brief #140, June 2005, at [http://www.brookings.edu/comm/policybriefs/pb140.pdf].)

[84] John A. Turner and David M. Rajnes, "Relative Rate of Return Guarantees for Social Security Defined Contribution Plans: What Do They Accomplish?" The Pensions Institute of Birkbeck College, University of London, Discussion Paper PI-0202, March 2002.

[85] Marie-Eve Lachance and Olivia S. Mitchell, "Understanding Individual Account Guarantees," pp. 159-186, in *The Pension Challenge: Risk Transfers and Retirement Income Security*, Oxford University Press, December 2003.

[86] For a portfolio invested half in equities and half in bonds over a 40-year career, the cost of providing a *rate of return* guarantee of at least the 10-year Treasury bond return or a *minimum benefit* guarantee of at least the current Social Security scheduled benefit would be 16% of total contributions or 0.65% of assets annually. (Ibid.)

[87] Congressional Budget Office, "Evaluating Benefit Guarantees in Social Security," Background Paper, March 2006, at [http://www.cbo.gov/ftpdocs/70xx/doc7058/03-07-SS_Guarantees.pdf].

[88] For more details on the current system of deposit insurance, see CRS Report RL31552, *Deposit Insurance: The Government's Role and Its Implications for Funding*, by Gillian Garcia, William D. Jackson, and Barbara Miles.

[89] Chile measures a fund manager's performance against the returns of other funds. This has caused most funds to hold very similar portfolios. (Statement of Barbara Bovbjerg, Government Accountability Office "Social Security Reform: Preliminary Lessons from Other Countries' Experiences," Testimony Before the Subcommittee on Social Security, Committee on Ways and Means, House of Representatives, June 16, 2005, at [http://www.gao.gov/new.items/d05810t.pdf].)

[90] Dariusz Stanko, "Polish Pension Funds, Does the System Work? Cost, Efficiency and Performance Measurement Issues," The Pensions Institute, Working Paper, January 2003, at [http://www.pensions-institute.org/workingpapers/wp0302.pdf/].

[91] Regardless of the absolute number of funds IA participants are offered, a determination would be needed if funds could be actively managed or must follow a set investment index. In general, actively managed funds have higher administrative costs than index funds. Policymakers could also establish diversification requirements for the funds. Specifically, they could decide if funds would be required to reflect the performance of a large number of companies, or invested across all major commercial sectors, or be concentrated in a single firm or industry.

[92] For example, section §404(c) of ERISA relieves the sponsor of an individual-account plan, such as a §401(k) plan, of responsibility for investment losses if the plan allows the participant to exercise control over the assets in his or her account and provides the participants with a broad range of investment choices. Federal regulations require these plans to offer participants at least three investment alternatives, not including the employer's own securities, that have materially different risk and return characteristics. One study found that the median number of investment options in §401(k) plans was eight and approximately 12% of §401(k) offer four or fewer investment choices, and approximately 11% offer 13 or more alternatives. (Edwin J. Elton, Martin J. Gruber, and Christopher R. Blake, "The Adequacy of Investment Choices Offered by 401K Plans," *Journal of Public Economics*, March 2004, at [http://papers.ssrn.com/sol3/papers.cfm?abstract_id=567122].)

[93] Many countries have used political criteria for determining investment options. For example, some countries have tried to promote domestic capital market growth by limiting the share of account assets that can be invested internationally.

[94] Having too many investment choices may also reduce the number of people who choose to participate in IAs. Recent research has shown that the likelihood of an individual to participate in a §401(k) diminishes by about 2% for every 10 additional options. (Iyengar, Sheena S., Jiang, W., and Huberman, G., "How Much Choice is Too Much: Determinants of Individual Contributions in 401K Retirement Plans," in Mitchell, O. S. and Utkus, S., eds., *Pension Design and Structure: New Lessons from Behavioral Finance*, Oxford: Oxford University Press, 2004, pp. 83-97.)

[95] William Baue, "Socially Responsible Investment Through 401k Plans Comes of Age," Oct. 10, 2003, at [http://www.socialfunds.com/news/article.cgi/article1239.html].

[96] Canada has a policy of responsibly investing their centrally-managed pension assets that includes a "commitment to engage with companies to encourage improved performance and disclosure of environmental, social and governance (ESG) factors." [http://www.cppib.ca/info/faqs/index.html#SIP].

[97] Although a portfolio with a mix of stocks and bonds would reduce the variation in potential account outcomes, it would also lower the long-run return. The size of annual pensions for a worker who invested half of his or her contributions in stocks and the other half in bonds would typically be about one-third lower than for a worker who invested solely in equities. (Gary Burtless, "How Would Financial Risk Affect Retirement Income Under Individual Accounts?" October 2000, Center for Retirement Research an Issue in Brief #5, at [http://www.bc.edu/centers/crr/ib_5.shtml].)

[98] Assets in lifecycle funds totaled $103 billion in 2004, up from $69 billion in 2003 and $44 billion in 2002. (Investment Company Institute, 2005, "Mutual Funds and the U.S. Retirement Market in 2004," *Fundamentals*, vol. 14, no. 4, Washington DC, Investment Company Institute, at [http://www.ici.org].)

[99] John Beshears, James J. Choi, David Laibson, and Bridgette C. Madrian, "The Importance of Default Options for Retirement Savings Outcomes: Evidence from the United States," National Bureau of Economic Research Working Paper 12009, January 2006, at [http://www.nber.org/papers/W12009].

[100] Calculation by CRS assuming a $1,000 annual deposit and a constant annual return of 7%.

[101] Indermit S. Gill, Truman Packard and Juan Yermo, *Keeping the Promise of Social Security in Latin America*, The World Bank, 2005, p. 148. Text uses revised estimates.

[102] Account holders could also be charged a mix of flat and proportional fees.

[103] Kelly Olsen and Dallas Salisbury "Individual Social Security Accounts: Administrative Issues," EBRI Issue Brief Number 236, Special Report 40, September 2001, p. 153, at [http://www.ebri.org/pdf/briefspdf/0901ib.pdf].

[104] Preliminary data for 2003; number represents wage and salary and self employed workers covered by Social Security. (Social Security Administration, Annual Statistical Supplement, 2005, at [http://www.ssa.gov/policy/docs/statcomps/supplement/2005/4b.html#table4.b1]).

[105] Robert Holzman and Richard Hinz, *Old-Age Income Support in the Twenty-First Century: An International Perspective on Pension Systems and Reform*, The World Bank, 2005, p. 121.

[106] Indermit S. Gill, Truman Packard and Juan Yermo, *Keeping the Promise of Social Security in Latin America*, The World Bank, 2005, p. 233.

[107] In practice, it would be difficult to set an appropriate limit on fees. A limit that is too high would be ineffectual, whereas one too low might prevent fund managers from covering their costs. In other countries, ceilings have become a "de facto minimum as well as a legal maximum" so that virtually all funds charge the maximum rate. (Edward Whitehouse "Administrative Charges for Funded Pensions: Comparison and Assessment of 13 Countries," in *Insurance and Private Pension Compendium for Emerging Economies*, Book 2 Part 1:6)b, Organization for Economic Co-operation and Development, 2001, at [http://www.oecd.org/dataoecd/8/20/1816104.pdf].)

[108] Another way to subsidize the account fees would be to adjust the "offset" or reduction in Social Security benefits by the administrative costs that are charged to the individuals' accounts. In effect, the administrative costs are then paid by the Social Security Trust Funds.

In: Social Security: New Issues and Developments
Editors: P. O. Deaven, W. H. Andrews, pp. 43-72

ISBN: 978-1-60456-243-9
© 2008 Nova Science Publishers, Inc.

Chapter 2

SOCIAL SECURITY REFORM: PRESIDENT BUSH'S 2005 INDIVIDUAL ACCOUNT PROPOSAL*

Laura Haltzel

ABSTRACT

The Old-Age, Survivors, and Disability Insurance (OASDI) program, commonly referred to as Social Security, is facing a long-term financial deficit. In response to this challenge, President Bush made Social Security reform the key focus of his 2005 domestic social policy agenda. On February 2, 2005, the President laid out specifications for a system of voluntary individual accounts to be phased-in as part of a reformed Social Security system. Administration officials concede that the individual accounts themselves do not alleviate the solvency problem. The individual account proposal would likely make the solvency problem worse over the next 75 years. The President stated that these accounts are just one piece of a comprehensive Social Security reform package and that additional measures will be needed to achieve long-term solvency.

Under the President's 2005 individual account proposal, individuals born prior to 1950 would have experienced no change in their Social Security benefits. Individuals born in 1950 and later would have had the option to participate in Social Security individual accounts (IAs). Workers who chose to participate in IAs would not have been permitted to opt-out of the IA system. Workers would have been allowed to divert up to 4% of their payroll taxes to IAs, subject to a dollar limit that increased over time. But on average people would have had to earn at least 3.3% per year after inflation to break even. This would have occurred because, in addition to administrative costs, their traditional benefits would have been reduced or "offset" by the amount of their contributions, plus 3% a year in interest. The proposal did not include a "minimum benefit" guarantee to ensure that participants would receive a total benefit at least equal to the poverty threshold.

Analyzing the President's 2005 IA proposal using assumptions on investment returns and administrative costs provided by the Social Security Administration, CRS found that the total of the reduced Social Security benefit *plus* the annuity that would have been available using the actual IA balance would have exceeded Social Security current-law promised benefits if the account earned the 4.6% annual real rate of return projected by

---

* Excerpted from CRS Report RL32879, dated March 9, 2006.

the Social Security actuaries. However, if the account earned the 2.7% risk-adjusted annual real rate of return projected by the actuaries, workers would have faced a slight reduction in overall Social Security income relative to current law. Younger workers and those with higher lifetime earnings would have benefitted the most from IAs. Younger workers would have been able to contribute to their IA throughout their careers and would have had higher contributions as a result of continued wage growth. Higher earners would have benefitted from being able to accrue larger account balances as the dollar cap on contributions increased.

This chapter is based on the President's 2005 IA proposal. The version portrayed in his FY2007 budget submission is not significantly different from his 2005 proposal. The main substantive difference is that the average interest that a worker would need to earn to break even would be reduced to 2.7% from 3%. Thus, if the account earned the 2.7% risk-adjusted annual rate of return, the worker would experience no reduction in overall Social Security income relative to current law.

INTRODUCTION[1]

The Old-Age, Survivors, and Disability Insurance (OASDI) program, commonly referred to as Social Security, is facing a long-term financial deficit. In 2041, the Social Security Trust Funds will be depleted and tax revenues will be sufficient to cover approximately 74% of benefits promised at that time.

Given this challenge, President Bush made Social Security reform the key focus of his 2005 domestic social policy agenda. On February 2, 2005, the President issued a document, "Strengthening Social Security for the 21st Century," which laid out the specifications for a system of voluntary individual accounts funded out of the current payroll tax to be phased-in as part of a reformed Social Security system. Administration officials concede that the individual accounts themselves do not alleviate the solvency problem.[2] These accounts would likely worsen the solvency problem over the next 75 years. The intent of these accounts was (1) to offset at least a portion of the anticipated benefit reductions or tax increases that will be necessary to achieve solvency; (2) to make the Social Security system a better deal for younger workers, who are most likely to be affected by these changes; and (3) to provide a benefit that each worker would individually own that the government could not take away. The President stated that these accounts are just one piece of a comprehensive Social Security reform package and that additional measures will be needed to achieve long-term solvency.[3] The President later espoused the idea of "progressive price indexing" as one option for achieving solvency by indexing future benefits of high-wage workers to inflation while wage indexing future benefits of low-wage workers. However, no specific details of how this proposal would be implemented were released. Thus, this chapter focuses solely on the individual account component of the President's 2005 Social Security reform proposal.[4]

THE PRESIDENT'S 2005 SOCIAL SECURITY INDIVIDUAL ACCOUNT PROPOSAL

Individual Account Contributions

Under the President's proposal, individuals born prior to 1950 would have experienced no change in their Social Security benefits. Individuals born in 1950 and later would have had the option to participate in Social Security individual accounts (IAs). Workers born in years 1950 through 1965 could have first participated in 2009. Workers born in years 1966 through 1978 could have first participated in 2010. Workers born in years 1979 and later could have first participated in 2011. Those who chose to participate would have been able to divert up to 4% of their Social Security covered wages into an individual account.[5] The actual maximum dollar amount of contributions would have be gradually increased, such that low-earners would be able to immediately contribute a full 4% of earnings to their IA, while higher earners would initially have their contributions capped. In the first year of account availability, 2009, the cap on contributions would have been $1,000. According to the Social Security actuaries, this cap would increase by $100 each year and then be increased by the growth in the national average wage.[6] For example, in 2010, the contribution limit would be equal to $1,100 increased by the growth in average wages between 2007 and 2008, or $1,145. The actuarial memorandum only covers the years through 2015, and the contribution limit rises using this method each year until then. Although it is not specified in the actuarial memorandum, the February 2, document implies that this dollar contribution limit would continue to rise after 2015, but that contributions would never exceed 4% of covered wages.

Individuals who do not choose to participate in the IA system would continue to draw benefits from the traditional Social Security system; however, these benefits are likely to be reduced to achieve long-term solvency. Individuals who choose to participate in the IA system would not be permitted to discontinue their participation, would be subject to benefit reductions based on their participation in the IA, and would also be subject to benefit reductions to achieve long-term solvency.

ACCOUNT ADMINISTRATION AND INVESTMENT

Individual account contributions would be collected and records maintained by a central administrator. Private investment managers would be chosen through a competitive bidding process to manage pooled account contributions. The central administrator would be responsible for addressing participant questions and issuing periodic account statements. The Social Security Administration's actuaries estimate that the ongoing administrative costs for a centralized system with limited choice of fund investment would be roughly 0.3 percentage points (or 30 basis points).[7]

Individuals who opt-in to the IA system would choose from a few broad-based investment funds: a government bond fund; an investment-grade corporate bond index fund; a small-cap stock index fund; a large-cap stock index fund; and, an international stock index fund.[8] In addition, workers could choose a government bond fund with a guaranteed rate of return above inflation. Workers could also select a "life-cycle portfolio" that would automatically adjust the level of risk and return of the investments by gradually reducing the portion of the portfolio invested in stocks and increasing the proportion invested in bonds as the worker aged in an attempt to avoid sudden losses closer to retirement. This portfolio would be the default choice for workers reaching age 47, although the worker could opt-out if the worker and his or her spouse signed a waiver stating that they are aware of the risks. Workers would be able to adjust their allocations among these funds annually.

Life-cycle portfolios reduce the probability of a sudden loss of capital due to a decline in equity values, but they do not eliminate this risk. Furthermore, with the switch to heavier investment in bonds rather than stocks comes a reduced expected rate of return in the account balance. The rate of return one earns closer to retirement has a greater effect on the overall account balance than the rate of return earned at the start of a working career because that interest rate is applied to every dollar held in the account at that point in time, not just the account a few years into one's career. Shifting the asset allocation to favor bonds does reduce the down-side risk, but it also limits the up-side gains.[9]

In the scenario described in the President's proposal, the life-cycle portfolio would specify an asset allocation shift based on a worker's planned year of retirement. Thus, all workers retiring in a given year have the same portfolio of stocks and bonds. The primary appeal of these "targeted retirement date" life-cycle portfolios is the minimal involvement required by the investor. Once the individual joins the fund, the assets are on auto-pilot and the individual does not need to decide when or how to adjust the portfolio. However, this 'one size fits all' approach may not be ideal for those who have investments outside the Social Security IA system as it could undermine the intended overall asset allocation for that worker's age. For example, a worker who already has a great deal invested in bonds in a 401(k) plan may not want the automatic shift towards bonds specified by a life-cycle portfolio because it could place too great a portion of his or her assets in fixed income securities. This approach may also not be ideal for those with different tolerance for risk. For example, the asset allocation specified for someone at age 35 might be 80% in stock and 20% in bonds. However, some individuals may be risk averse and prefer a portfolio with 70% stock and 30% bonds.

Offset to Social Security Defined Benefit Based on Hypothetical Individual Account

If a worker chooses to participate in an IA, in exchange for the reduction in contributions to the defined benefit Social Security system, he or she would accept a future Social Security benefit reduction. The benefit reduction would apply to the Social Security retirement, spousal or aged widow(er) benefit that would otherwise be paid to him or her.[10] This future benefit reduction is equal to the contributions made to the worker's individual account plus 3% per year in interest. For each *actual* account that a worker contributes to and receives upon retirement, there is also a *hypothetical* "shadow" account that exists only as an accounting mechanism. The "shadow" account records all of the contributions made to the actual account and grows them at a fixed annual real rate of return (the rate one would earn after adjusting for inflation) of 3%, essentially equal to what the Social Security Administration actuaries project these contributions would have earned had they continued to be paid into the Social Security system and invested in Treasury bonds in the Trust

Funds.[11] Thus, the 3.0% offset is intended to reflect the portion of the Social Security benefit the worker chooses to forgo and replace with individual account proceeds by diverting a portion of his or her payroll tax away from the Social Security system.

Table 1 provides an example of how this would work. In this example, Mary works and contributes to her individual account for 10 years, between 2021 and 2031. Each year, Mary contributes an amount equal to 4% of her Social Security covered wages to her individual account. For example, she earns $15,000 in 2021 and therefore contributes $600 to her IA, where it is assumed to grow at a 4.6% annual real rate of return and results in an end of year account balance of $622. When she makes her $600 contribution to her actual IA, the "shadow" IA reflects this same contribution amount, but grows it at a fixed 3.0% annual real rate of return so that at the end of the first year her "shadow" IA records a balance of $617. This same process continues every year until she retires in 2031. At that point, her actual IA balance is $15,648 and her "shadow" IA balance is $14,327. Upon retirement, the account balance of this hypothetical "shadow account" is converted into a hypothetical CPI-indexed monthly annuity.[12] This hypothetical annuity would be used to reduce, or offset, the Social Security defined benefit.

Table 1. Mary's Actual and "Shadow" Individual Accounts

Year	Annual Wage (nominal)	Actual Account Contributions (nominal)	Shadow Account Contributions (nominal)	Actual Account Balance (assuming 4.6% real rate of return)	Shadow Account Balance (fixed 3.0% real rate of return)
2021	$15,000	$600	$600	$622	$617
2022	$17,500	$700	$700	$1,395	$1,374
2023	$20,000	$800	$800	$2,329	$2,278
2024	$22,500	$900	$900	$3,438	$3,338
2025	$25,000	$1,000	$1,000	$4,734	$4,564
2026	$27,500	$1,100	$1,100	$6,231	$5,964
2027	$30,000	$1,200	$1,200	$7,944	$7,550
2028	$32,500	$1,300	$1,300	$9,891	$9,332
2029	$35,000	$1,400	$1,400	$12,087	$11,321
2030	$37,500	$1,500	$1,500	$14,552	$13,531
Account balance in 2031				$15,648	$14,327

Source: Created by CRS.

Continuing the example above in table 2, based on Mary's 10-year work history, Mary could expect to receive a Social Security defined benefit equal to about $654 per month in 2031. Mary's "shadow" account would produce a CPI-indexed annuity of $82 per month. This "shadow" annuity is used to reduce, or offset, Mary's

Social Security benefit, leaving her with a Social Security defined benefit of $572. Assuming that Mary chooses to annuitize her entire actual IA balance, Mary's actual IA would produce a CPI-indexed annuity of $89 per month. The annuity from the actual IA plus her reduced Social Security defined benefit would provide Mary a combined Social Security income of $661.

**Table 2. How Mary's "Shadow" Account Offsets Her Social Security Defined Benefit
and How Her Actual Account Contributes to Her Social Security Income in 2031**

Mary's current-law Social Security defined monthly benefit	$654
Minus "shadow" account monthly annuity (based on fixed 3.0% annual real rate of return)	- $82
Equals remaining Social Security defined monthly benefit	= $572
Plus actual account monthly annuity (assuming 4.6% annual real rate of return)	+ $89
Equals combined Social Security monthly income	= $661

Source: Created by CRS.

Note: Example assumes current law provisions remain in place through 2031 and that Mary chooses to
annuitize her entire IA balance.

Individual Account Distributions

Workers would not be permitted to have access to their IA balances prior to retirement.
Upon retirement, the receipt of aged widow(er) benefits, or conversion from disabled worker
to retirement benefits, the IA accumulation would be available to the beneficiary. Individuals
may be required to purchase an annuity or take in phased withdrawals a portion of the IA
balance. The portion required to be annuitized or taken in phased withdrawals would be equal
to the dollar amount needed to provide the worker with a total monthly benefit equal to at
least 100% of the federal poverty threshold when combined with the reduced Social Security
defined benefit. For example, looking back at table 2, Mary's reduced Social Security defined
benefit would be equal to $572 (in 2005 dollars). In 2031, the year of Mary's retirement, the
monthly poverty level is projected to be equal to $766 (in 2005 dollars). Thus, Mary would be
required to annuitize or take in phased withdrawals whatever portion of her IA is needed to
provide a monthly stream of income equal to $194 ($766 - $572).

The annuity purchased or phased withdrawals taken would be required to be CPI-indexed
so that the annual amounts increase with inflation and, thus, retain purchasing power. If after
the purchase of this annuity or estimation of phased withdrawals the worker still has a balance
in his or her IA, the remainder may be withdrawn as a lump-sum or left as an inheritance.
There would be no "minimum benefit" guarantee to ensure that participants would receive a
total benefit at least equal to the poverty threshold.[13]

Under the system of phased withdrawals, also referred to as programmed withdrawals or
"self-annuitization," the worker's account balance is divided in such a way as to allow the
worker to withdraw an equal amount each month (indexed to inflation) until the retiree dies or
until the IA funds are depleted. This amount is calculated taking into account projected future
inflation, interest rates and life expectancy. It has not yet been specified who will take the role
of calculating the size of these withdrawals. The advantage of phased withdrawals as opposed
to an annuity is that a worker who does not expect to live to projected life expectancy could
withdraw whatever portion of their IA assets are needed to stay above poverty and, upon
death, the remaining balance would be available to pass along as an inheritance.[14]

When a worker purchases a CPI-indexed annuity, risks of higher than expected inflation,
lower than expected interest rates, and of living longer than an individual's projected life
expectancy are borne by the insurance company. When a worker opts to take phased
withdrawals, these risks are borne by the worker. Thus, if inflation grows faster than
originally expected, the amount of money that the worker must withdraw to remain above

poverty would increase, leading the worker to deplete his or her IA assets faster than planned. Under phased withdrawals, the worker retains the responsibility for investing the individual account assets in such a way as to ensure a rate of return that would maintain an account balance sufficient to provide the appropriate level of withdrawals until the expected date of death. If the worker fails to invest in such a way as to ensure the rate of return needed to maintain an account balance until they die, then the withdrawal amounts would eventually exceed the balance remaining in the IA, leading the worker to have insufficient resources to remain above poverty. Under a phased withdrawal system, the worker also faces the risk that they will live beyond the date of life expectancy that was used to calculate the phased withdrawal amounts. The date of life expectancy is, by definition, the average remaining number of years prior to death. Thus, on average, about 50% of those opting for phased withdrawals will die prior to running out of IA funds and 50% will live longer than expected and run out of IA funds. In this case, the worker would have received larger withdrawal amounts than could be sustained with the IA balance at retirement and the worker would risk running out of funds prior to death. Phased withdrawals do not guarantee that those with IA balances projected to be sufficient at retirement (when the monthly phased withdrawal amount is calculated) will avoid falling into poverty.

If a worker decides not to use inflation-indexed phased withdrawals of a portion of his or her IA to maintain above poverty level retirement income, he or she would be required to purchase a CPI-indexed annuity to achieve this goal. Although the President's plan requires the purchase of CPI-indexed annuities, there is currently a very limited market for these annuities in the United States. Although the Treasury has issued Treasury Inflation Protection Securities (TIPS) since 1997, the demand for inflation-indexed annuities remains small, possibly because many workers feel that they already have some form of inflation protection from current-law Social Security benefits. If, however, these types of annuities were to be mandatory and accompanied by the required reduction in Social Security benefits for IA participants, the experience in the United Kingdom indicates that it is likely that such a market would develop.[15]

ANALYSIS OF THE PRESIDENT'S 2005 IA PROPOSAL

Although the President's IA proposal would worsen Social Security solvency within the next 75 years, in the long-run, the shadow accounts and the resulting offsets in Social Security defined benefits would reduce benefit costs to the current-law program. Because of the short-run costs, and barring other benefit reductions or tax increases, the IA proposal is likely to increase publicly held debt and increase the unified budget deficit. Under the President's IA proposal, younger workers and higher earners who can contribute to the IA for longer periods of time or contribute larger amounts to the IA would have larger IA balances and annuities than those who contribute over fewer years or contribute fewer dollars. As a result of the larger IA balances, younger workers and higher earners would have a lower Social Security defined benefit. Whether a worker does better under the individual account proposal depends on whether he or she is able to obtain a higher annual rate of return (net of administrative expenses) than the 3.0% real rate of return used to calculate the shadow account.

Although these individual accounts are likely to make the solvency problem worse, the President has not yet specified how this additional shortfall will be financed. It could be financed through (1) increased government borrowing (to be paid off eventually through general revenues); (2) increased payroll taxes or other tax increases; or (3) additional benefit reductions. CRS has provided estimates of combined Social Security income under two scenarios: one where it is assumed that trust fund revenues are found and the trust fund can provide "scheduled" current law Social Security benefits, and one where it is assumed that trust fund revenues are not found and the current-law benefit is reduced to a "payable" level based on estimated current-law revenues. However, because the Social Security Administration actuaries were not provided with the plan specifications needed to produce a 75-year analysis of how the President's IA proposal would affect solvency, the size of the annual benefit reductions that would be required to maintain trust fund solvency under a payable baseline is not known. Therefore, the results below do not take into account the benefit reductions *on top of* those required under current-law and under the "shadow" account offset that would be necessary under the President's IA proposal to achieve solvency. Thus, this analysis tends to overstate the combined Social Security income that would be available under the IA proposal compared to a current-law payable baseline. However, the total Social Security income possible for a scaled average-wage worker using the 'expected' 4.6% annual real rate of return would be 31% higher than current-law payable benefits for younger cohorts.[16] Thus, if the additional benefit reductions required to achieve solvency under the IA plan reduce benefits by less than 31%, scaled average-wage workers under the IA plan would still come out ahead. One important limitation of using these assumed constant annual interest rates is that historical rates of return have not followed such a pattern. Interest rate fluctuations over time and where these fluctuations occur in a worker's career can have a large effect on the estimated account balances of workers under an IA system.

Effect on Social Security Solvency

Administration officials acknowledge that the proposed individual accounts alone do not improve the Social Security solvency problem. In the short-run, these individual accounts are likely to make the solvency problem worse. The President's plan permits individuals to contribute up to 4 percentage points (up to a dollar contribution limit) of the current 12.4% payroll tax into individual accounts, thus diverting current revenues away form the traditional Social Security system. By itself, this step would worsen the Social Security solvency problem because these dollars are taken from the Social Security surpluses and therefore the Trust Funds don't accrue the same balances that they otherwise would have and they also earn less interest on these reduced balances. Not including the lost interest earnings, the cost to the Trust Funds between 2005 and 2015 would be approximately $541 billion in constant 2004 dollars.[17] By the end of 2015, the IA proposal would increase publicly-held debt by $587 billion in 2004 dollars. The second piece of the President's IA proposal, the reduction in Social Security benefits based on the "shadow" account, has the effect of offsetting the cost of the IA proposal and potentially improving the solvency problem in the long run. However, because this reduction only takes place upon a worker's retirement, but the contributions to the IA begin almost immediately and continue up to the worker's year of retirement, the savings from the benefit offset takes many years to counter the loss of revenue to the Trust

Funds from the IA itself. Between 2005 and 2015, these offsets reduce Social Security benefits by only $3 billion constant 2004 dollars. The Social Security actuaries estimate that the year in which Social Security costs exceed Social Security tax revenue would be 2012 under the President's proposal instead of 2017 under current law.

If, as indicated in the actuarial memorandum, disability recipients are not subject to the "shadow" account offset (presumably because disabled workers would not have access to their accounts until their disability benefits convert to aged retirement benefits at the full retirement age), then the Trust Funds would be made worse off because they would still have the burden of paying full Social Security benefit amounts to disability recipients (who are by definition under the retirement age) even though these individuals may have participated in the IA system, thereby reducing the revenues available to pay these benefits. The actuarial memorandum implies that disabled individuals would be subject to the offset upon conversion from disability benefits to retirement benefits at the full retirement age, reducing the cost of their benefit payments from that point on.

The actual effect of the President's proposal on solvency is dependent upon the number of individuals who participate in the system of individual accounts and upon their level of earnings. The Social Security actuaries assume that approximately two-thirds of all eligible workers will opt-in to the account system. The actuaries do not attempt to predict what types of workers (e.g., high wage, low wage, etc.,) would participate in the IA system, but instead rely on estimates of the aggregate dollar amounts that would likely be diverted from current payroll taxes. The larger the number of individuals who participate in the accounts, the greater the dollar amount diverted away from the current Social Security system, and the greater the up-front negative impact on Social Security solvency. Of course, the greater the number of individuals who choose to participate in the IA system, the greater the eventual reduction in benefits promised to these individuals under the current Social Security system and the greater the potential long-term enhancement to Social Security solvency.

The Social Security actuaries, who estimate the effect of Social Security reform proposals on solvency, were unable to produce the standard 75-year estimate of the effect of the President's proposal because they were only given specifications through 2015. However, based on a similar individual account structure introduced by Senator Lindsey Graham as part of a larger reform proposal in the 108th Congress (S. 1878) and analyzed by the Social Security actuaries, it seems likely that over a 75-year period the President's individual account proposal would not pay for itself through benefit offsets, nor reduce the existing solvency problem.[18] In present value terms, Senator Graham's individual account proposal alone would have added $2.7 trillion in constant 2004 dollars to the $4.0 trillion current-law Social Security shortfall[19]

Some individual account proposals, such as that introduced by Representative Shaw (H.R.750 in the 109th Congress), use the actual individual account to provide revenue to the Social Security Trust Fund to pay Social Security benefits. The individual is still responsible for investing the IA assets, but instead of reducing the Social Security benefit based on contributions to the IA, the actual IA is handed over to the government for use in paying for the individual's Social Security benefits. The Social Security benefit payments are fixed, but the rate of return earned by each individual worker on his or her account, and thus the account balance, is *subject to fluctuation*. Thus, the Trust Fund is subject to the risk that the individual accounts will not be invested in a way that produces sufficient revenue to pay for an individual's lifetime benefits. Alternatively, the President's proposal provides the Trust Funds with a *guaranteed* source of revenue in the form of reduced benefit costs, which is equal to the individual's IA contributions grown at a real annual 3% interest rate. Therefore, the Trust Funds are not subject to any investment risk. With the lower "traditional" Social Security benefits, the President's proposal also lowers the impact on the Trust Funds from the costs of unexpected increases in inflation or longevity. Individuals are responsible for purchasing an annuity (in which case these risks are shifted to the insurance company that sold the annuity) or making phased withdrawals (in which case these risks are borne by the individual).

Effect on the Unified Budget

The unified budget (the combined on- and off-budget) could be affected by this proposal in two ways. First, if the government relies on general revenues to reimburse Social Security for the loss of revenue due to the diversion of funds for the IA, the Treasury would need to either increase tax revenues, reduce other government spending, or increase government debt. According to the Office of Management and Budget, the President's IA proposal will require transition financing of $664 billion over the next 10 years, or $754 billion including interest if additional debt is issued to cover these costs.[20] Second, as figure 1 below illustrates, diverting Social Security revenues into individual accounts reduces the Social Security surplus, thereby reducing the off-budget surplus. Social Security surplus dollars are not held by the Social Security Trust Funds. Rather, according to law, surplus receipts are credited to the Social Security Trust Funds in the form of special-issue nonmarketable Treasury bonds. The actual surplus dollars are held by the U.S. Treasury where they become part of the general revenue pool and can be used to increase spending, reduce taxes, or reduce the government debt.[21] In recent years, Social Security surpluses have been used to offset increased spending or reduced taxes since the rest of the government's budget (on-budget) has been in deficit. Thus, any reduction in the Social Security surplus (off-budget) would, barring other changes, lead to an increased unified budget deficit.

Effect on Combined Social Security Income

Based on the assumptions and methodology described below, CRS finds that the total of the reduced Social Security defined benefit *plus* the annuity that would be available using the actual IA balance would exceed Social Security current-law promised benefits if the account earns the 4.6% annual real rate of return projected by the Social Security actuaries. However, if the account earns the 2.7% risk-adjusted annual real rate of return projected by the actuaries, workers would face a slight reduction in overall Social Security income relative to current law.[22] Younger workers and those with higher lifetime earnings would benefit the most from IAs. Younger workers would be able to contribute to their IA throughout their careers and would have higher contributions as a result of continued wage growth. Higher earners would benefit from being able to accrue larger account balances as the dollar limit on contributions increases over time until it reaches the full 4% of covered wages.

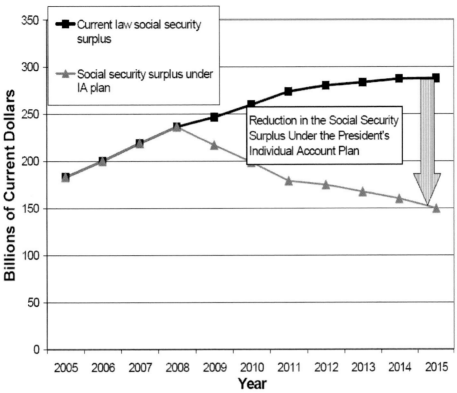

Source: Congressional Research Service (CRS) Calculations based on the 2004 Social Security Trustees Report, table VI.F.9 and the Feb. 3, 2005 Social Security Actuarial Memorandum to Charles Blahous, table 1.b.2.

Note: The 2004 Social Security Trustees Report is used because this was the basis for the estimates provided in the Social Security memorandum to Charles Blahous.

Figure 1. Effect of the President's Individual Account Proposal on Projected Social Security Surpluses (Billions of current dollars).

How an individual worker would fare under the IA proposal would depend entirely upon how the actual rate of return earned by the worker's IA compared to the fixed "benefit offset" rate of 3%. The worker would bear all of the investment risk. If a worker's actual account attained an annual real rate of return greater than 3%, the balance of the actual account would be higher than that of the "shadow" account. Thus, while the Social Security benefit would be reduced by the annuity based on the "shadow" account, an annuity from the actual account would be larger and would more than offset the reduction to the defined benefit. Therefore, the combined actual individual account annuity plus the Social Security benefit reduced by the "shadow" account would be larger than what the worker is scheduled to receive under current law. On the other hand, if a worker's actual account attained an annual real rate of interest lower than 3%, the balance of the actual account would be lower than that of the shadow account. Thus, while the Social Security benefit would be reduced by the annuity based on the "shadow" account, an annuity from the actual account would be smaller and would not offset the reduction to the worker's Social Security benefit. Therefore, the combined actual IA annuity plus the Social Security benefit reduced by the "shadow" account would be smaller than what the worker is promised to receive under current law. Because the hypothetical account rate of return (3.0%) is not reduced by administrative fees while the actual risk-adjusted rate of return is reduced by administrative fees (to 2.7%), the hypothetical account balance will exceed that of the risk-adjusted actual account in every case where the worker invests exclusively in government bonds as a way to "opt-out" of the IA system.

According to the actuarial memorandum, disability beneficiaries would not be subject to the offset and would not have access to their IA until conversion from disability benefits to aged retirement benefits at the full retirement age. The memorandum also indicates that the offset applies to all aged retirement benefits. If disability recipients were subject to the offset upon conversion, then these workers would experience a sudden change in the composition of their benefit from one of a guaranteed benefit to one that is partially guaranteed and partially dependent on the proceeds from the IA.

Limitations of this Analysis

According to the 2004 Trustees Report (the source of the assumptions used for this analysis), under current law, Social Security will be unable to fully pay promised benefits after 2042.[23] Estimates of combined Social Security income are provided under two scenarios: one where it is assumed that trust fund revenues are found and the trust fund can provide "scheduled" current law Social Security benefits, and one where it is assumed that trust fund revenues are not found and the current-law benefit is reduced to a "payable" level based on estimated current-law revenues. In the "scheduled" benefits scenario, the benefit estimates for both the current-law benefit and the Social Security benefit under the President's IA assume the use of yet unidentified sources of revenue. A comparison of the 'payable' baseline to the scheduled baseline shows to what degree the current-law scheduled benefits are overstated compared to current-law revenue sources. Because the individual accounts would actually make the Social Security solvency problem worse in the short run, to achieve solvency without revenue increases the President's proposal would require *larger* benefit reductions than those that would be required to achieve solvency under current law *unless* the entire transition cost were financed through increased debt or higher taxes. However, because the Social Security Administration actuaries were not provided with the plan specifications needed to produce a 75-year analysis of how the President's IA proposal would affect solvency, the size of the annual benefit reductions that would be required to maintain trust fund solvency is not known. Thus, a serious limitation of the "payable" analysis is that it *overstates* the value of the total Social Security income available under the IA plan because it fails to take into account the *additional* solvency-driven reductions (on top of the "shadow account" offset) to the Social Security defined benefit that forms the base of Social Security combined income.

Figure 2 shows that the total Social Security income possible for a scaled average-wage worker using the assumed 4.6% annual real rate of return would be 31% higher than current-law payable benefits for younger cohorts. Thus, if the additional benefit reductions required to achieve solvency under the IA plan reduce benefits by less than 31%, scaled average-wage workers who achieve the "expected" 4.6% annual rate of return under the IA plan would still come out ahead. However, if the ultimate benefit reductions are greater than 31%, workers would have higher benefits under current-law. Figure 2 also shows that the total Social Security income possible for a scaled average-wage worker using the risk-adjusted 2.7% annual real rate of return would be about 4% lower than current-law payable benefits for younger cohorts. Thus, any additional benefit reductions required to achieve solvency under the IA plan would make these scaled average-wage workers worse off than under current-law.

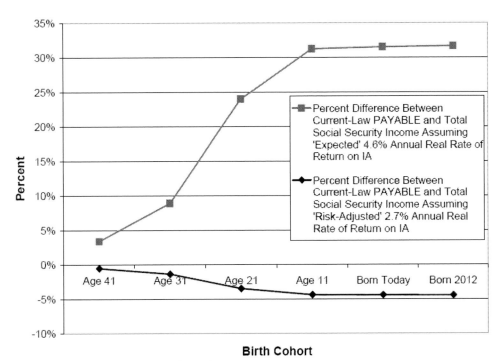

Source: Congressional Research Service estimates.

Figure 2. Percent Difference Between Current-Law Payable Social Security Benefits and Total Social Security Income (Reduced Current-Law Payable Social Security Benefits Plus the Individual Account Annuity).

Although it is not yet known how the additional shortfall due to the IAs will be financed, it would require at least the same solvency-driven reductions that would be required under a "do-nothing" scenario where only those benefits that can be paid with incoming tax revenues would be paid. In this analysis, these estimates are presented as "payable" benefits. According to the 2004 Trustees Report (the source of the assumptions used for this analysis), under current law, Social Security will be unable to fully pay promised benefits after 2042.[24] At that time, payroll tax revenues and revenues from the income taxation of Social Security benefits are projected to be sufficient to pay approximately 74% of scheduled benefits and a gradually declining percentage thereafter. Thus, under current law a benefit reduction of approximately 26% would be required in 2042, with gradually increasing reductions thereafter. In the examples presented below, only the worker age 21 today would have any change in Social Security benefits under the payable baseline as this worker's year of retirement (2051) occurs after the Trust Funds have been depleted and annual Social Security revenues are sufficient to pay only 74% of promised benefits. Thus, under the payable baseline, the 21-year-old's Social Security promised benefits are reduced by 26%.

For a series of hypothetical workers that vary by age and earnings history, the following section provides estimates of

- the worker's actual and "shadow" individual account balances; current-law promised Social Security benefits;
- benefit offsets based on the "shadow account" annuities; reduced promised Social Security benefits;
- the total reduced Social Security/IA benefit relative to the Social Security benefit promised under current law;
- the total reduced Social Security/IA benefit relative to the Social Security benefit payable under current law;
- required annuitization or phased withdrawal levels with reduced Social Security promised benefits;
- maximum amounts available at retirement as lump-sum or inheritance amounts with reduced Social Security promised benefits once the required annuitization or phased withdrawals have been deducted;
- required annuitization or phased withdrawal levels with reduced Social Security payable benefits;
- and, maximum amounts available at retirement as lump-sum or inheritance amounts with reduced Social Security payable benefits once the required annuitization or phased withdrawals have been deducted.

Because account balances and benefit reductions will differ by age and lifetime earnings, estimates for hypothetical low, average and high-wage earners born in various years (i.e., of various birth cohorts) are provided.

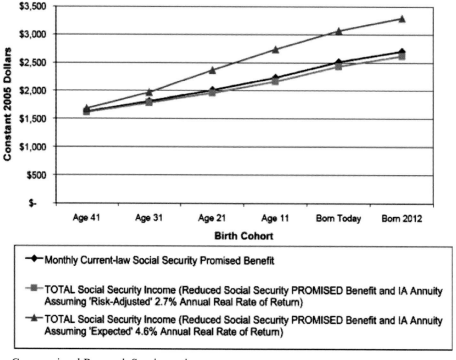

Source: Congressional Research Service estimates.
Figure 3. Total Social Security Income for Scaled Average-Wage Worker, by Birth Cohort.

Analysis by Birth Cohort

Assuming a 4.6% annual real rate of return, younger birth cohorts participating in the IA system would receive a larger total Social Security income (composed of the reduced Social Security benefit *plus* the IA annuity) compared with older cohorts of similar earnings levels (e.g., scaled low-wage worker). Figure 3 shows combined Social Security income for scaled average-wage workers of different birth cohorts.

Younger workers will have higher individual account balances than will older workers of similar earnings levels. As is evident from table 3, those workers who, as a result of their age, are able to contribute to their IA throughout their careers have much larger account balances upon retirement than do those who contribute at the same earnings level, but over fewer years. For example, upon retirement, the "expected" individual account balance of the average worker age 41 today is only 27% of that of the average worker age 21 today. Based on the assumptions used in this analysis, the increased account balance for younger generations is due to three variables: (1) the rise in real wages for individuals of similar earnings levels, and thus real contributions to the accounts; (2) the higher value of interest accumulated due to these higher wages; and, (3) the increasing number of years of contributions to the accounts and the effect of more years of interest (up to the point where each future cohort would have contributed to the IA for each of their 44 work years, the 1990 birth cohort). First, under the assumptions used by the Social Security actuaries, each future generation will earn real wages (i.e., an increase in earnings that is greater than the increase in inflation) larger than those of the generation before it.[25] Thus, the real contributions to the IA of each future generation will also be larger than those of the current generation. Second, these larger real contributions create a larger real account base for investment. Even with the same annual real rate of return applied (e.g., 4.6%) to the IA between different generations, the dollar value of the interest is higher with the higher real account base. Third, the 41-year-old worker participates in the account for only 22 years (2009-2030) whereas the 21-year-old participates for 40 years (2011-2050). The younger worker's greater of number of years participating in the IA leads both to greater aggregate contributions and greater interest earnings as a result of the increased years of investment of those contributions.

Because younger workers will have both larger actual accounts as well as larger "shadow" accounts, younger workers face a larger offset to their Social Security promised benefits relative to older workers. Table 4 illustrates that depending on age, the "shadow" account annuity reduces Social Security promised benefits by between 17% and 41% for the scaled average-wage worker.

The effect of the benefit offset in reducing the Social Security benefit is larger for younger cohorts whose Social Security benefits could be reduced to achieve long-term solvency. Table 5 provides the same information as for table 4, but for a baseline of current-law Social Security *payable* benefits instead of *promised* benefits. Only the worker age 21 today would have any change in Social Security benefits under the payable baseline as this worker's year of retirement (2051) occurs after the Trust Funds have been depleted and annual Social Security revenues are sufficient to pay only 74% of promised benefits. Thus, under the payable baseline, Social Security promised benefits are reduced by 26%. Because the Social Security benefit is lower under the payable baseline, but the "shadow" account offset remains the same, the percent reduction in Social Security benefits is larger than under the promised baseline. Thus, in the long-run, workers would receive an increasingly smaller portion of their Social Security defined benefit.

Younger workers would experience the largest percent increase in total Social Security income if a 4.6% annual real rate of return is achieved. Table 6 demonstrates that the total of the reduced Social Security benefit *plus* the annuity that would be available using the actual IA balance would exceed Social Security current-law promised benefits if the account earns the "expected" 4.6% annual real rate of return. Depending on age, the percent increase in combined Social Security income is estimated to be between 3% and 18% for the scaled average-wage worker. The percent increase in the total benefit amount is larger for younger workers who contribute to the IA for their entire careers and thus have more years for the difference in interest rates between the hypothetical account and the actual account to work in their favor. If, on the other hand, the account is only able to achieve a 2.7% annual real rate of return (the annual real annual rate of 3.0% minus 0.3% administrative costs), then the total of the reduced Social Security benefit plus the annuity would be less than that promised under current-law. The advantages for younger workers would be removed under this "risk-adjusted" interest rate as there is no percentage point difference to be utilized to enhance the longer IA participant's account balance.

Younger workers would experience an even larger percent increase in combined Social Security income when compared to what would be possible under a current-law payable scenario. Table 7 provides the same information as table 6, but for a benefits payable baseline. Again, the only worker that would be affected by the payable baseline is the worker age 21 today. Because the current-law payable benefit would be lower than the current-law promised benefit, the same dollar amount from the IA annuity (assuming a 4.6% annual real rate of return), would lead to a larger percent increase in combined Social Security income for this worker.

Analysis by Earnings Level

Assuming a 4.6% annual real rate of return, higher-wage workers would experience a greater percent increase in combined Social Security income than lower-wage workers. Figure 4 below demonstrates the levels of current-law promised benefits, the combined Social Security income assuming an annual real rate of return of 4.6%, and the combined Social Security income assuming an annual real rate of return of 2.7% for a worker age 21 today with three different lifetime earnings levels.

IA participants with higher earnings over their lifetime will have larger account balances when they retire than those of lower earners. Those with higher wages are able to contribute larger dollar amounts to their IAs leading to larger account balances. For example, in table 3 the scaled low-wage earner age 41 today has only 44% of the account balance of the scaled high-wage earner age 41 today. Even though these workers contribute to the IA over the same number of years, and even though the high-wage earner is subject to the contribution cap for 15 years out of the 22 spent participating in the IA, 4% of the high-wage worker's salary is larger than 4% of the low-wage worker's salary. The disparity in account balances between individuals with different earnings levels increases over time as the cap on IA contributions rises to the point where the hypothetical high-wage worker could contribute a full 4% of wages to the IA. By the time a worker age 21 today retires, the account balance of a low-wage worker equals only 34% of that of a high-wage worker of the same age.

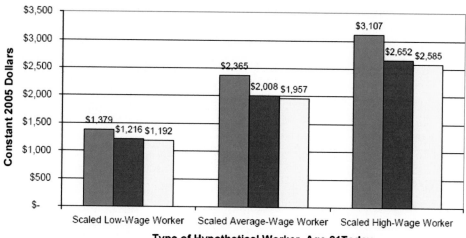

Note: Compares benefit amounts assuming funding is located to pay Social Security promised benefits.
Figure 4. Effect of the President's IA Proposal on Combined Social Security Income, by Earnings Level for Worker Age 21 Today.

Because of their larger account accumulations, higher earners would face a larger percent reduction in their Social Security scheduled benefits as a result of the benefit offset. Table 4 illustrates that depending on earnings level, the "shadow" account annuity reduces Social Security promised benefits by between 31% and 43% for a worker age 21 today. Low earners face smaller percent reductions to their Social Security promised benefits than do higher earners because the underlying Social Security benefit structure is progressive (i.e., it replaces a larger percentage of wages of low-wage workers compared to high-wage workers). Thus, a flat percentage of each workers wages (4%), grown at a flat percentage rate each year (3%) to arrive at the "shadow" offset, still maintains the progressive benefit structure by allowing low-wage workers to keep a larger percentage of their Social Security benefit (e.g., 69% for the age 21-year-old) than high-wage workers (e.g., 57% for the age 21-year-old).

Higher earners (scaled high and scaled average wage workers) would experience the largest percent increase in total Social Security income if a 4.6% annual real rate of return is achieved. Table 6 demonstrates that the total of the reduced Social Security benefit *plus* the annuity that would be available using the actual IA balance would exceed Social Security current-law promised benefits if the account earns the "expected" 4.6% annual real rate of return. Depending on earnings level, the percent increase in combined Social Security income is estimated to be between 13% and 18% for a worker age 21 today. Under the 4.6% rate of return scenario, the percent benefit increase would be larger for scaled high-wage workers than for scaled low-wage workers. This difference would occur because the 4% of earnings that high earners would be able to contribute to their IAs has a larger dollar value and would be able to take advantage of the 1.6 percentage point difference between the 4.6% rate of return on the IA and the 3.0% rate of return used to calculate the IA benefit offset. If, on the other hand, the account is only able to achieve a 2.7% annual real rate of return (the annual real annual rate of 3.0% minus 0.3% administrative costs), then the total of the reduced Social Security benefit plus the annuity would be less than that promised under current-law. The advantages for higher earners would be removed under this "risk-adjusted" interest rate as there is no percentage point difference to be utilized to enhance the higher earner's account balance.

As table 8 illustrates, the reduced Social Security promised benefit is still large enough compared to the monthly aged poverty thresholds to allow each hypothetical worker the option of withdrawing the entire IA balance as a lump-sum at retirement, rather than being required to purchase an annuity or take programmed withdrawals, or passing it on as an inheritance. If, however, additional benefit reductions are eventually introduced as part of a comprehensive Social Security proposal, some portion of the IA balance would probably need to be annuitized or taken as a phased withdrawal in order to achieve a combined monthly stream of income equal to the federal poverty threshold. This outcome is best demonstrated in table 9, which takes into account the effect of a reduction in promised benefits for the 21 year old to provide only those benefits payable at retirement. In this case, the low-wage and average-wage worker's payable benefits fall below the poverty threshold after being reduced by the "shadow" account annuity. As a result, this worker would be required to annuitize or take in programmed withdrawals enough of the individual account to guarantee a combined Social Security income equal to 100% of the federal poverty threshold. Once this portion of the individual account has been annuitized or set aside for programmed withdrawals, the worker would have the option to take the remainder of the account balance as a lump sum or pass it along as inheritance. The high-wage 21-year-old worker would not be required to annuitize or set aside for programmed withdrawals any portion of his or her account balance because even the 26% reduction in Social Security benefits under the payable baseline leaves this worker with a large enough Social Security benefit to remain above the federal poverty threshold. Thus, if benefit reductions are the primary method of achieving long-term solvency, lower- and average-wage workers would be less able to increase family wealth under the President's IA plan than would high-wage workers.

METHODOLOGY

All individual account estimates are based on the proposal specifications outlined above. To estimate the account balances of the actual and hypothetical "shadow" accounts for those retiring many years in the future, CRS assumes that the IA contribution limit continues to increase over the full work history of each worker according to the method outlined in the actuarial memorandum. If further details emerge that alter this contribution rate, these estimates would need to be recalculated accordingly. CRS estimates the account balances for the actual IA, which the worker will receive in full, using both the "expected" annual real rate of return specified by the Social Security actuaries (4.9%) as well as the "low-yield" or "risk-adjusted" annual real rate of return specified by the actuaries (3.0%), both reduced by the estimated administrative fee of 30 basis points per year. Thus the annual real rate of return net of administrative costs is 4.6% and 2.7%, respectively. The hypothetical account balance is estimated using the 3.0% rate of return specified in the proposal. This account balance is used to calculate the offset to the Social Security defined benefit. Because the hypothetical account rate of return is not reduced by administrative fees whereas the actual risk-adjusted rate of return is reduced by administrative fees, the hypothetical account balance will exceed that of the risk-adjusted actual account in every case. To calculate the CPI-indexed annuity for both the actual and hypothetical "shadow" accounts, annuity factors provided by the Social Security Administration were used.

One important limitation of using these assumed constant annual interest rates is that historical rates of return have not followed such a pattern. Interest rate fluctuations over time and where these fluctuations occur in a worker's career can have a large effect on the estimated account balances of workers under an IA system. For example, a negative rate of return in the years prior to an individual's retirement can significantly reduce the value of the assets in the IA. Similarly, the rate of return prevalent at the time of retirement can alter the monthly annuity payment that a worker would receive based on the same dollar amount in the individual account. The higher the interest rate assumed when calculating the annuity amount, the greater the assumed earnings on the assets used to fund the annuity, and the larger the annuity payment to the worker. For example, based on CRS analysis, at an interest rate of 6.0%, a 68-year-old person who purchased a level, single-life annuity for $200,000 would receive income from the annuity of $1,852 per month. At an interest rate of 4.0%, the same sum of money would buy a level, single-life annuity worth $1,584 per month, a difference of $268 in monthly income.

Some have argued that the establishment of individual accounts, as well as the tax increases, benefit reductions or government borrowing needed to achieve solvency, may affect the macroeconomy and, thus, affect the interest rates that individuals could expect to obtain on their IAs. These estimates do not incorporate any such potential macroeconomic feedbacks.

The effect of the proposal is estimated both on workers who would contribute to the IA for their entire career as well as those whose careers would be split between the current-law system and the IA system. To estimate the effect of the IA proposal on a worker age 21 today, CRS assumes that the worker is born in 1984, begins work at age 21 in 2005, and retires at the full retirement age of 67 in 2051. As a result, this worker spends 40 years of his or her 46 year work history contributing to the IAs and reflects what the system could provide to a worker once the plan is fully phased-in. To estimate the effect of the IA proposal on a worker age 31 today, CRS assumes that the worker is born in 1974, begins work at age 21 in 1995, and retires at the full retirement age of 67 in 2041. As a result, although this worker also has a career of 46 years, only 30 of them are spent contributing to the IA. Finally, to estimate the effect of the IA proposal on a worker age 41 today, CRS assumes that the worker is born in 1964, begins work at age 21 in 1985, and retires at the full retirement age of 67 in 2031. Thus, this worker also has a career of 46 years, but only 22 of them are spent contributing to the IA.

Account balance estimates for scaled low-wage workers, scaled-average wage workers, and scaled high-wage workers, as defined by the Social Security Office of the Chief Actuary are provided.[26] It is assumed that these workers follow typical lifetime earnings patterns that would produce a Social Security benefit equivalent to that of workers with career earnings of either: (1) a "low"wage (45% of a wage equal to Social Security's "average wage series"); (2) an "average wage"(a wage equal to Social Security's "average wage series"); or,

Table 3. Estimated Account Balances in Year of Retirement for Actual and "Shadow" Account Under the President's 2005 Social Security Personal Account Proposal, by Type of Hypothetical Worker (Constant 2005 dollars)

Individual Account	Scaled Low Earner			Scaled Average Earner			Scaled High Earner		
	Age 41 Today	Age 31 Today	Age 21 Today	Age 41 Today	Age 31 Today	Age 21 Today	Age 41 Today	Age 31 Today	Age 21 today
Actual Account Balance (Using "Expected" 4.6% Annual Real Rate of Return)	$28,149	$54,441	$90,173	$52,798	$111,257	$198,541	$64,148	$139,246	$268,788
Actual Account Balance (Using "Low-Yield"/"Risk Adjusted" 2.7% Annual Real Rate of Return)	$22,184	$38,885	$58,710	$42,427	$80,617	$129,568	$52,624	$103,782	$180,723
"Shadow" Account Balance (Accrues at Specified 3.0% Annual Real Rate of Return)	$23,022	$40,960	$62,700	$43,895	$84,732	$138,328	$54,266	$108,590	$192,046

Source: Estimates by the Congressional Research Service.

Note: For the worker age 21 today, the year of retirement at age 67 is 2051. For the worker age 31, the year of retirement at age 67 is 2041. For the worker age 41, the year of retirement at age 67 is 2031.

Table 4. Current-Law *Promised* Social Security Benefit, Estimated "Shadow" Annuity Amount in Year of Retirement, and Reduced *Promised* Social Security Benefit, by Type of Hypothetical Worker
(Constant 2005 dollars)

Individual Account	Scaled Low Earner			Scaled Average Earner			Scaled High Earner		
	Age 41 today	Age 31 today	Age 21 today	Age 41 today	Age 31 today	Age 21 today	Age 41 today	Age 31 today	Age 21 today
Monthly Current-Law Promised Social Security Benefit	$983	$1,093	$1,216	$1,623	$1,805	$2,008	$2,144	$2,384	$2,652
"Shadow" Monthly Annuity at Retirement (First year, increasing with CPI each year of life expectancy)	$142	$248	$371	$271	$512	$820	$336	$657	$1,138
Remaining Monthly Social Security Promised Benefit After Reduction by "Shadow" Annuity	$840	$846	$844	$1,352	$1,293	$1,189	$1,808	$1,728	$1,515
Percent Change in Current-Law Social Security Promised Benefit Due to "Shadow" Account Offset	- 14%	- 23%	- 31%	- 17%	- 23%	- 41%	- 16%	- 28%	- 43%

Source: Estimates by the Congressional Research Service.

Note: For the worker age 21 today, the year of retirement at age 67 is 2051. For the worker age 31 today, the year of retirement at age 67 is 2041. For the worker age 41, the year of retirement at age 67 is 2031.

Table 5. Current-Law *Payable* Social Security Benefit, Estimated "Shadow" Annuity Amount in Year of Retirement, and Reduced *Payable* Social Security Benefit, by Type of Hypothetical Worker
(Constant 2005 dollars)

Individual Account	Scaled Low Earner			Scaled Average Earner			Scaled High Earner		
	Age 41 today	Age 31 today	Age 21 today	Age 41 today	Age 31 today	Age 21 today	Age 41 today	Age 31 today	Age 21 today
Monthly Current-Law Payable Social Security Benefit	$983	$1,093	$900	$1,623	$1,805	$1,486	$2,144	$2,384	$1,963
"Shadow" Monthly Annuity at Retirement (First year, increasing with CPI each year of life expectancy)	$142	$248	$371	$271	$512	$820	$336	$657	$1,138
Remaining Monthly Social Security Payable Benefit After Reduction by "Shadow" Annuity	$840	$846	$528	$1,352	$1,293	$667	$1,808	$1,728	$825
Percent Change in Current-Law Social Security Payable Benefit Due to "Shadow" Account Offset	- 14%	- 23%	- 41%	- 17%	- 23%	- 55%	- 16%	- 28%	- 58%

Source: Estimates by the Congressional Research Service.

Notes: For the worker age 21 today, the year of retirement at age 67 is 2051. For the worker age 31, the year of retirement at age 67 is 2041. For the worker age 41, the year of retirement at age 67 is 2031. Only the worker age 21 today would have any change in current-law Social Security benefits under a payable baseline (shown in bold) as this worker's year of retirement occurs at a point where annual Social Security revenues are sufficient to pay only 74% of promised benefits. These results do not take into account the *additional* benefit reductions (on top of those due to the benefit offset and reductions to achieve solvency under current law) that would be necessary under the individual account plan in order to achieve solvency under a payable baseline. Thus, these results tend to overstate the benefit levels that would be payable under the President's IA proposal. Please refer to accompanying memorandum for detailed description of methodology used.

Table 6. Combined Social Security Benefit For Expected and Risk-Adjusted Account Balances Under President's Individual Account Proposal Compared to Current-Law *Promised* Benefit, by Type of Hypothetical Worker (Constant 2005 Dollars)

Individual Account	Scaled Low Earner			Scaled Average Earner			Scaled High Earner		
	Age 41 today	Age 31 today	Age 21 today	Age 41 today	Age 31 today	Age 21 today	Age 41 today	Age 31 today	Age 21 today
Current-Law Monthly Social Security PROMISED Benefit	$983	$1,093	$1,216	$1,623	$1,805	$2,008	$2,144	$2,384	$2,652
Remaining Monthly Social Security PROMISED Benefit After Reduction by "Shadow" Annuity	$840	$846	$844	$1,352	$1,293	$1,189	$1,808	$1,728	$1,515
Annuity Available Using "Expected" Actual IA Balance (Using 4.6% annual rate of return)	$174	$329	$534	$326	$673	$1,176	$397	$842	$1,593
TOTAL (Reduced Social Security PROMISED Benefit and IA Annuity)	$1,014	$1,175	$1,379	$1,678	$1,966	$2,365	$2,205	$2,570	$3,107
Percent Increase or Decrease in Total Social Security Income (Total reduced PROMISED benefit plus IA annuity relative to current law PROMISED benefit)	3%	7%	13%	3%	9%	18%	3%	8%	17%
Annuity Available Using Risk-Adjusted Actual IA Balance (Using 2.7% Annual Real Rate of Return)	$137	$235	$348	$262	$488	$768	$325	$628	$1,071
TOTAL Reduced Social Security PROMISED Benefit and Risk-Adjusted IA Annuity	$977	$1,081	$1,192	$1,614	$1,781	$1,957	$2,134	$2,355	$2,585
Percent Increase or Decrease in Total Social Security Income (Total reduced PROMISED benefit plus Risk-Adjusted IA annuity relative to current law PROMISED benefit)	- 1%	- 1%	- 2%	- 1%	- 1%	- 3%	0%	- 1%	- 3%

Source: Estimates by the Congressional Research Service.

Notes: For the worker age 21 today, the year of retirement is 2051. For the worker age 31 today, the year of retirement is 2041. For the worker age 41, the year of retirement is 2031. Thus, only the 21-year old would be subject to benefit reductions under a 'payable' baseline as this worker retires after the 2042 date when Social Security can only pay the portion of promised benefits equal to what can be paid annually out of revenues generated by payroll taxes and the income taxation of Social Security benefits. Please refer to accompanying memorandum for detailed description of methodology used.

Table 7. Combined Social Security Benefit For Expected and Risk-Adjusted Account Balances Under President's Individual Account Proposal Compared to Current-Law *Payable* Benefit, by Type of Hypothetical Worker (Constant 2005 dollars)

	Scaled Low Earner			Scaled Average Earner			Scaled High Earner		
	Age 41 today	Age 31 Today	Age 21 today	Age 41 today	Age 31 today	Age 21 today	Age 41 today	Age 31 today	Age 21 today
Current-Law Monthly Social Security PAYABLE Benefit	$983	$1,093	$900	$1,623	$1,805	$1,486	$2,144	$2,384	$1,963
Remaining Monthly Social Security PAYABLE Benefit After Reduction by "Shadow" Annuity	$840	$846	$528	$1,352	$1,293	$667	$1,808	$1,728	$825
Annuity Available Using "Expected" Actual IA Balance (Using 4.6% annual rate of return)	$174	$329	$534	$326	$673	$1,176	$397	$842	$1,593
TOTAL (Reduced Social Security PAYABLE Benefit and IA Annuity)	$1,014	$1,175	$1,063	$1,678	$1,966	$1,843	$2,205	$2,570	$2,417
Percent Increase or Decrease in Total Social Security Income (Total reduced PAYABLE benxefit plus IA annuity relative to current law PAYABLE benefit)	3%	7%	18%	3%	9%	24%	3%	8%	23%
Annuity Available Using Risk-Adjusted Actual IA Balance (Using 2.7% Annual Real Rate of Return)	$137	$235	$348	$262	$488	$768	$325	$628	$1,071
TOTAL Reduced Social Security PAYABLE Benefit and Risk-Adjusted IA Annuity	$977	$1,081	$876	$1,614	$1,781	$1,434	$2,13	$2,355	$1,896
Percent Increase or Decrease in Total Social Security Income (Total reduced PAYABLE benefit plus IA annuity relative to current law PAYABLE benefit)	-1%	-1%	-3%	-1%	-1%	-3%	0%	-1%	-3%

Source: Estimates by the Congressional Research Service.

Notes: For the worker age 21 today, the year of retirement is 2051. For the worker age 31 today, the year of retirement is 2041. For the worker age 41, the year of retirement is 2031. Thus, only the 21-year-old would be subject to benefit reductions under a 'payable' baseline as this worker retires after the 2042 date when Social Security can only pay the portion of promised benefits equal to what can be paid annually oxut of revenues generated by payroll taxes and the income taxation of Social Security benefits. These results do not take into account the *additional* benefit reductions (on top of those due to the benefit offset and reductions to achieve solvency under current law) that would be necessary under the individual account plan in order to achieve solvency under a payable baseline. Thus, these results tend to overstate the benefit levels that would be payable under the President's IA proposal. Please refer to accompanying memorandum for detailed description of methodology used.

Table 8. Poverty Thresholds in Year of Retirement, Reduced Social Security *Promised* Benefit, Required Annuitization Levels, and Remaining Individual Account Balance, by Type of Hypothetical Worker (Constant 2005 dollars)

	Scaled Low Earner			Scaled Average Earner			Scaled High Earner		
	Age 41 today	Age 31 today	Age 21 today	Age 41 today	Age 31 today	Age 21 today	Age 41 today	Age 31 today	Age 21 today
Monthly Aged Poverty Threshold in Year of Retirement	$766	$766	$766	$766	$766	$766	$766	$766	$766
Remaining Monthly Social Security PROMISED Benefit After Reduction by "Shadow" Annuity	$840	$846	$844	$1,352	$1,293	$1,189	$1,808	$1,728	$1,515
Monthly Annuity Amount Needed to Achieve 100% Poverty Level When Combined With Reduced Social Security PROMISED Benefit	$0	$0	$0	$0	$0	$0	$0	$0	$0
Portion of Actual IA Required to be Annuitized to Achieve 100% of Poverty	$0	$0	$0	$0	$0	$0	$0	$0	$0
Remaining Actual IA Balance (Using "Expected" 4.6% Annual Real Rate of Return)	$28,149	$54,441	$90,173	$52,798	$111,257	$198,541	$64,148	$139,246	$268,788
Remaining Actual IA Balance (Using "Low-Yield"/"Risk Adjusted" 2.7% Annual Real Rate of Return)	$22,184	$38,885	$58,710	$42,427	$80,617	$129,568	$52,624	$103,782	$180,723

Source: Estimates by the Congressional Research Service.

Notes: For the worker age 21 today, the year of retirement at age 67 is 2051. For the worker age 31, the year of retirement at age 67 is 2041. For the worker age 41, the year of retirement at age 67 is 2031. Please refer to accompanying memorandum for detailed description of methodology used.

Table 9. Poverty Thresholds in Year of Retirement, Reduced Social Security *Payable* Benefit, Required Annuitization Levels and Remaining Individual Account Balance, by Type of Hypothetical Worker
(Constant 2005 dollars)

	Scaled Low Earner			Scaled Average Earner			Scaled High Earner		
	Age 41 today	Age 31 today	Age 21 today	Age 41 today	Age 31 today	Age 21 today	Age 41 today	Age 31 today	Age 21 today
Monthly Aged Poverty Threshold in Year of Retirement	$766	$766	$766	$766	$766	$766	$766	$766	$766
Remaining Monthly Social Security PAYABLE Benefit After Reduction by "Shadow" Annuity	$840	$846	$528	$1,352	$1,293	$667	$1,808	$1,728	$825
Monthly Annuity Amount Needed to Achieve 100% Poverty Level When Combined With Reduced Social Security PAYABLE Benefit	$0	$0	$238	$0	$0	$100	$0	$0	$0
Portion of Actual IA Required to be Annuitized to Achieve 100% of Poverty	$0	$0	$40,185	$0	$0	$16,822	$0	$0	$0
Remaining Actual IA Balance (Using "Expected" 4.6% Annual Real Rate of Return)	$28,149	$54,441	$49,989	$52,798	$111,257	$181,719	$64,148	$139,246	$268,788
Remaining Actual IA Balance (Using Risk-Adjusted 2.7% Annual Real Rate of Return)	$22,184	$38,885	$18,525	$42,427	$80,617	$112,747	$52,624	$103,782	$180,723

Source: Estimates by the Congressional Research Service.

Notes: For the worker age 21 today, the year of retirement is 2051. For the worker age 31, the year of retirement is 2041. For the worker age 41, the year of retirement is 2031. Thus, only the 21-year-old would be subject to benefit reductions under a 'payable' baseline as this worker retires after the 2042 date when Social Security can only pay the portion of promised benefits equal to what can be paid annually out of revenues generated by payroll taxes and the income taxation of Social Security benefits. As a result of the lower Social Security benefit, the effect of the reduction from the "shadow" annuity is to reduce the Social Security benefit to the level where it falls below the poverty threshold for the scaled low-earner, forcing this worker to annuitize a portion of his or her actual individual account balance to reach poverty threshold. These results do not take into account the *additional* benefit reductions (on top of those due to the benefit offset and reductions to achieve solvency under current law) that would be necessary under the individual account plan in order to achieve solvency under a payable baseline. If additional benefit reductions were required under the individual account scenario, workers would be required to annuitize a larger portion of their individual accounts to reach the poverty threshold. Thus, these results tend to overstate the benefit levels that would be payable under the President's IA proposal. Please refer to accompanying memorandum for detailed description of methodology used.

(3) a "high" wage (160% of a wage equal to Social Security's "average wage series"). For example, based on projections in the 2004 Social Security Trustees Report, a worker retiring in 2005 would have had *career average earnings* of $15,776 for a scaled "low" earner, career average earnings of $35,057 for a scaled "average" earner, and career average earnings of $56,091 for a scaled "high" earner.[27] These scenarios are for illustration only and are not meant to fully represent every possible scenario that actual workers may experience. For example, by relying on stylized workers, no gaps in employment are assumed. If present, these gaps would reduce both the Social Security benefit and the IA balance of these workers. However, because under a system of individual accounts the earlier contributions are made the more interest they accrue, the timing of gaps in employment has a greater effect on individual account balances than they would on the traditional Social Security benefit level. Although the plan does not require annuitization, but allows individuals to take programmed withdrawals from their IAs, CRS has followed the Social Security Administration's practice of assuming universal annuitization as it is not clear which type of worker might opt for programmed withdrawals. Because hypothetical workers with no spouses or other dependents are used, the annuity levels calculated for both the actual and hypothetical accounts are based on the purchase of a unisex CPI-indexed single-life annuity assuming an inflation rate of 2.8% per year and a nominal interest rate of 5.884% per year. Furthermore, the poverty level estimates for the year of retirement are also based on a single-person household. The aged poverty level in 2004 was $9,060. This level was indexed to the year of retirement using the CPI. Unless otherwise specified, all assumptions are based on the 2004 Social Security Trustees Report. Unless otherwise specified, all dollar amounts are presented in real 2005 dollars.

REFERENCES

[1] The President's FY2007 budget submission included an updated version of his individual account proposal. This version, outlined in a Social Security Administration actuarial memorandum dated Feb. 6, 2006, included three specific changes: (1) the proposal would become effective in 2010 instead of 2009; (2) the initial contribution cap would be $1,100 instead of $1,000; and (3) the offset to the worker's traditional benefit would be based on the amount of their contributions, plus 2.7% in interest instead of 3%. Of these three changes, only the reduction of the offset rate alters the conclusions presented in this report based on analysis of the 2005 proposal. Under the 2005 proposal, if the account earned the 2.7% risk-adjusted annual real rate of return projected by the actuaries, workers would have faced a slight reduction in overall Social Security income relative to current law. In the January 2006 version of the IA proposal, if the account earned the 2.7% risk-adjusted annual rate of return, the worker would experience no reduction in overall Social Security income relative to current law. Please note that the numbers presented in the remainder of this report have not been updated to reflect this change.

[2] White House Background Press Briefing on Social Security, Feb. 2, 2005.

[3] President George W. Bush, State of the Union Address, Feb. 2, 2005.

[4]   For additional information on price indexing, please see CRS Report RL32900, "Indexing Social Security Benefits: The Effects of Price and Wage Indexes."

[5]   In 2005, Social Security covered wages are capped at $90,000. This cap is indexed annually to increases in the national average wage.

[6]   Social Security Administration Memorandum to Charles P. Blahous, Special Assistant to the President for Economic Policy, National Economic Council from Stephen C. Goss, Chief Actuary, "Preliminary Estimated Financial Effects of a Proposal to Phase In Personal Accounts — INFORMATION," Feb. 3, 2005.

[7]   Some have argued that this assumption may understate the true administrative costs of such a system. The actuaries did not provide an estimate of the costs associated with annuitization.

[8]   An index fund is a fund composed of securities intended to replicate the movement of a specific securities index (e.g., the Dow Jones, Standard and Poors 500, etc.). Index funds are considered to be passive investments since the portfolio manager does not have to decide among various securities for investment. Rather, the manager knows the securities that make up the index and their relative importance to the overall index and seeks to match it. Because the management of the investment is less active, the expenses and transaction costs are low. The advantage of index funds is that, since most funds do not beat the index anyway, the investor has a greater chance of at least matching industry averages. The limitation of the index fund is that it must purchase all of the securities in the index even if the market indicates that a particular security in the index is going to lose value. (Taken from p. 501, "How the U.S. Securities Industry Works," by Hal McIntyre).

[9]   Robert J. Shiller of Yale University recently conducted a computer simulation using financial data going back to 1871. He found that people enrolled in life-cycle accounts would have lost money 32% of the time under the President's IA proposal because the rate of return earned is less than the 3% real rate of return required to break even in the proposal. For additional information please see Robert J. Shiller's study, "The Life-Cycle Personal Accounts Proposal for Social Security: An Evaluation," Yale ICF Working Paper No. 05-06, Apr. 2005, available at [http://papers.ssrn.com/sol3/papers.cfm?abstract_id=703221].

[10] According to the Social Security actuarial memorandum, disability benefits would not be reduced.

[11] Unlike the actual individual account, which is reduced on an annual basis by 0.3% of assets and results in an "expected" net 4.6% annual rate of return or a "risk-adjusted" 2.7% rate of return, the "shadow" account is not reduced for any administrative fees. See the Methodology section for additional detail.

[12] An annuity is an insurance instrument that provides a stream of periodic payments in return for an up front payment called the "premium." In this case, the premium would be the individual's account balance at retirement.

[13] The plan does not specify whether the poverty threshold to be used is for the single worker, for all individuals who are expected to receive benefits off of the worker's record, or all household members.

[14] Not all individual accounts are likely to have large enough balances to provide a monthly withdrawal amount that, when combined with the reduced Social Security defined benefit, is able to provide a combined Social Security income equal to 100% of

the federal poverty threshold, whether provided in the form of an annuity or as a phased withdrawal. The current-law Social Security program also does not guarantee a benefit amount equal to 100% of the federal poverty threshold.

[15] Brown, Jeffrey, Olivia Mitchell and James Poterba, *The Role of Real Annuities and Indexed Bonds in an Individual Accounts Retirement Program*, National Bureau of Economic Research, Working Paper no. 7005, Mar. 1999.

[16] For details on "scaled" wage workers, please refer to the Methodology section.

[17] Social Security Administration Memorandum to Charles P. Blahous, Special Assistant to the President for Economic Policy, National Economic Council from Stephen C. Goss, Chief Actuary, "Preliminary Estimated Financial Effects of a Proposal to Phase In Personal Accounts — INFORMATION," Feb. 3, 2005.

[18] The default option under Sen. Graham's plan was an individual account funded by a carve-out equal to 4% of the current payroll tax, with contributions capped at $1,300 in 2006 and increased with the percent increase in the national average wage thereafter. The benefit offset was calculated using account contributions grown at a real annual interest rate of 2.7%.

[19] The Congressional Research Service (CRS) calculation based on Social Security Administration Memorandum from Chris Chaplain and Alice H. Wade to Stephen C. Goss on the "Estimated OASDI Financial Effects of 'Social Security Solvency and Modernization Act of 2003' introduced by Senator Lindsey Graham — INFORMATION," Nov. 18, 2003. For details on how CRS calculated this estimate, please refer to CRS Report RS22010, *Social Security: 'Transition Costs'*, by Laura Haltzel.

[20] "Strengthening Social Security for the 21st Century," White House, Feb. 2005, available at [http://www.whitehouse.gov/infocus/social-security/200501/strengthening-socialsecurity.html]. For additional information on transition costs, see CRS Report RS22010, *Social Security: Transition 'Costs'*, by Laura Haltzel.

[21] For additional information on how Social Security financing works, please refer to CRS Report 94-593, *Social Security: Where Do Surplus Taxes Go and How Are They Used?*, by Geoffrey Kollmann.

[22] The higher rate of return one expects to earn from investing in stocks is due to the higher risk such an investment carries. The difference between the rate of return on stocks and the rate of return on government bonds is known as the "risk premium," the amount of compensation the market demands for taking on the additional risk of investing in stocks relative to the lower risk of investing in government bonds. In this case, because stocks are assumed to earn a real rate of return of 6.5% while government bonds are assumed to earn a real rate of return of 3% the risk premium is 3.5 percentage points. Thus, the "risk-adjusted" rate of return used in this analysis represents the stock rate of return adjusted downward by this risk premium. This rate of return omits any expected return over that of government bonds.

[23] The 2005 Social Security Trustees Report indicates that the year of exhaustion of the OASDI Trust Funds in 2041. To maintain consistency with the underlying assumptions used in this analysis, CRS has continued using 2042 as the date of exhaustion for the "payable" baseline estimates.

[24] The 2005 Social Security Trustees Report indicates that the year of exhaustion of the OASDI Trust Funds in 2041. To maintain consistency with the underlying assumptions

used in the Social Security actuarial analysis of the President's IA proposal, CRS has continued using 2042 as the date of exhaustion for the "payable" baseline estimates.

[25] The Social Security actuaries assume long-term average real wage growth of 3.9% per year.

[26] Social Security Administration, Office of the Actuary, *Internal Rates of Return Under the OASDI Program for Hypothetical Workers*, Actuarial Note No. 144, June 2001. The pattern in these "scaled" earnings histories shows relatively low earnings at the beginning of the career, fairly rapid growth through the middle of the career, and a gradual tapering off of earnings at the end of the career.

[27] Career average earnings levels are defined for retired workers as the highest 35 years of earnings, indexed for growth in average wages to the year prior to benefit entitlement. This concept is similar to that of the AIME, except that career average earnings for these scaled workers are indexed to the year prior to entitlement instead of two years prior to eligibility and earnings are averaged on an annual rather than a monthly basis. Thus, the indexing year for the 2005 retiree is 2004, and the 2004 average wage index is the basis for the career average earnings levels for each hypothetical worker.

In: Social Security: New Issues and Developments   ISBN: 978-1-60456-243-9
Editors: P. O. Deaven, W. H. Andrews, pp. 73-100   © 2008 Nova Science Publishers, Inc.

Chapter 3

SOCIAL SECURITY: THE CHILEAN APPROACH TO RETIREMENT[*]

Christopher Tamborini

ABSTRACT

Over the past few years, there has been intense debate about Social Security reform in the United States. A number of options, ranging from changing the benefit formula to adding individual accounts, has been discussed. The policy debate takes place against the backdrop of an aging population, rising longevity, and relatively low fertility rates, which pose long-range financial challenges to the Social Security system. According to the 2007 Social Security Trustees Report's intermediate assumptions, the Social Security trust funds are projected to experience cash-flow deficits in 2017 and to become exhausted in 2041.

As policymakers consider how to address Social Security's financing challenges, efforts of Social Security reform across the world have gained attention. One of the most oft-cited international cases of reform is Chile. Chile initiated sweeping retirement reforms in 1981 that replaced a state-run, pay-as-you-go defined benefit retirement system with a private, mandatory system of individual retirement accounts where benefits are dependent on the account balance. As a pioneer of individual retirement accounts, Chile has become a case study of pension reform around the world. Although Chile's experience is not directly comparable to the situation in the United States because of large differences between the countries, knowledge of the case may be useful for American policymakers.

This CRS report focuses on the Chilean individual retirement accounts system. It begins with a description of the U.S. Social Security policy debate, along with a brief comparison of Chile and the United States. Next, the report explains what Chile's individual retirement accounts system is and how it works. The pension reform bill sent to the Chilean Congress for debate in 2007 is also discussed. The report does not address other components of Chile's social security system, such as maternity, work injury, and unemployment.

The final section provides an assessment of Chile's now 26-year-old individual retirement accounts system. Pension reforms have contributed to the rapid growth in the

---

[*] Excerpted from CRS Report RL34006, dated May 17, 2007.

Chilean economy over the past two decades and returns on pension fund investments have been greater than expected. Administrative costs, however, have been high and participation rates have been modest at best. There is concern that the system does not cover the entire labor force and provides inadequate benefits to low income workers.

INTRODUCTION

As policymakers contemplate ways to address Social Security's long-term financial challenges, pension reforms across the world have gained new attention.[1] This chapter focuses on Chile, one of the most oft-cited cases of pension reform internationally. In 1981, Chile initiated sweeping reforms that replaced a state-run, pay-as-you-go defined benefit retirement system with a private, defined contribution individual retirement accounts system.[2] As a pioneer of individual accounts, Chile has become a case study for many countries seeking to reform their retirement systems. Although the Chilean experience is not directly comparable to the United States situation because of large differences between the countries, the case may offer some valuable insights for policymakers who are interested in individual retirement accounts.

The report[3] begins with a description of the U.S. Social Security policy debate and a brief comparison of Chile and the United States. It discusses the backdrop against which the Chilean pension reforms were implemented. Next, the report explains what Chile's individual retirement accounts system is and how it works. A pension reform bill, which is scheduled for consideration by the Chilean Congress in 2007 and expected to be passed before May 2008, is detailed. The final section provides an assessment of the individual retirement accounts system's performance relative to some of its initial goals.

BACKGROUND

The U.S. Social Security System

The U.S. Old-Age, Survivors, and Disability Insurance (OASDI) programs collectively make up the system referred to as Social Security. The program is a social insurance system, whereby premiums are paid by workers to obtain coverage and benefits are intended to replace part of the earnings lost to the worker and the family when the worker retires, becomes disabled, or dies. Virtually all working men and women in the United States are covered by Social Security — about 96% of the labor force pay payroll taxes.[4]

Social Security is financed primarily on a pay-as-you-go (PAYGO hereafter) basis, in which today's workers pay for the benefits of today's retirees. The primary revenue source is a payroll tax paid by current workers and their employers.[5] When revenues exceed outgo, as they do now, surpluses are invested in bonds and credited to the Social Security trust funds managed by the Treasury Department.

Financial Challenges

The Social Security system faces a long-term financing problem. Under the intermediate assumptions of the Social Security trustees, the system is projected to begin running cash flow deficits in the year 2017, at which point the system must begin redeeming any bonds (including interest) accumulated in previous years. Financial projections of the trustees also show that the trust funds will be exhausted in 2041, at which point 75% of scheduled annual benefits would be payable with income revenue.[6]

A primary factor underlying Social Security's long-term financial problem is the program's PAYGO financing structure in combination with the demographics of an aging society, specifically the looming retirement of the large baby boom cohort (persons born between 1946 and 1964), along with rising longevity and a low birth rate.[7] Demographics are important because PAYGO systems, such as Social Security, are sensitive to the ratio of workers to beneficiaries, which is declining in the United States.[8] Presently, there are about three covered workers for every beneficiary, and according to the Social Security trustees, this ratio will eventually fall to less than two to one. Between 2010 and 2030, the number of individuals age 65 or older is projected to grow by 76%, while the number of workers supporting the system is projected to grow by 6%.[9]

The Social Security Debate

The longer it takes to address Social Security's financing challenge, the greater the changes will need to be. There are, however, fundamentally diverging views on reform. One approach would maintain the current program structure and make relatively modest changes to restore the system's long-term solvency, such as increasing the retirement age, reducing the cost-of-living adjustments, or raising the amount of earnings subject to the payroll tax.[10] A second approach would change the program's underlying structure and create a partially or fully funded system based on personal savings and investments in individual retirement accounts.[11]

Over the past several years, there has been an intense national discussion on whether to create some form of individual accounts (IAs) within the Social Security system.[12] During the 109th Congress, 10 Social Security reform bills were introduced; all but two of these would have allowed workers to invest some part of their earnings in individual retirement accounts, either to supplement the Social Security system (often referred to as add-on accounts) or to replace part of the system (often referred to as carve-out accounts).[13] No legislation received congressional action. During the same period, President Bush had made efforts to advance his initiative to restructure Social Security through the creation of individual accounts, such as voluntary carve-out accounts.[14] During the 110th Congress, two comprehensive Social Security measures had been introduced at the time this chapter was written: H.R. 1090 (Social Security Guarantee Plus Act of 2007) and H.R. 2002 (Individual Social Security Investment Program Act of 2007). H.R. 1090, introduced by Representative Ron Lewis, would establish voluntary individual accounts funded with general revenues, among other program changes, and H.R. 2002, introduced by Representative Sam Johnson, would establish individual accounts funded with a redirection of current payroll taxes, among other program changes.[15]

The Debate and the Chilean Case

As policymakers consider how to address Social Security's challenges in the United States, other countries' experiences with retirement reforms have gained attention.[16] Much of this attention has been directed toward countries that have adopted some sort of individual accounts program as part of their retirement system.[17] The case of Chile, the first country to introduce a fully funded individual retirement accounts system in 1981, is often cited by both proponents and opponents of individual accounts.

Policymakers who advocate introducing individual accounts in the United States have tended to point to Chile as a successful case. Adopting a Chilean-type system, some argue, would put the Social Security system on a path of sustainable solvency beyond the traditional 75-year projection period, since a fully funded system is not sensitive to changes in the number of workers per beneficiary. These proponents believe government-run, PAYGO systems are unsustainable in aging societies. They argue that a fully funded system, such as Chile's, would reduce future demands on the government for financing the growing costs associated with an increasingly elderly population.

In addition, advocates of individual accounts maintain that a Chilean-style model would change the way Americans save for retirement, providing workers with a sense of ownership over their retirement savings. Individual retirement accounts, proponents maintain, would strengthen the link between contributions and benefits and thus would provide more incentives for workers to save for retirement. Moreover, American workers may earn significant returns on their contributions under an individual retirement accounts system, because their capital would be invested in stocks and bonds.

By contrast, policymakers who advocate a more traditional approach to reform have tended to highlight the risks of a Chilean-type system. They argue that individual accounts would expose workers to the risk of investment market volatility. Implementing individual retirement accounts, others maintain, would also erode the social insurance nature of the U.S. system, which is designed to pool risk and protect workers and their families against loss of earnings due to retirement, disability, or death. A Chilean-type model, it is pointed out, would eliminate the system's progressive benefit formula, which replaces a higher share of earnings for lower earners than for higher earners. Under an individual accounts system, benefits would become strictly a function of workers' earnings and the returns achieved by their plan's investments. As a result, some workers could be worse off for reasons including poor investment decisions or downturns in financial markets. Some also argue that individual accounts do not necessarily provide the annuity features of the current U.S. system. Furthermore, critics may cite problems facing Chile's individual retirement accounts system, such as coverage gaps and high administrative costs, as evidence that implementing individual accounts in the United States would be problematic.

Another concern raised by opponents relates to the transition costs from switching from a PAYGO to a fully funded system — that is, the cost of paying accrued obligations while funding individual accounts.[18] Adopting a Chilean-type funded system would require today's younger workers to save for their own retirements while continuing to pay taxes to cover current retirees' benefits. Others contend that, depending on the funding mechanism, an individual retirement accounts system could worsen the U.S. program's financial outlook and exacerbate current budget deficits. For example, diverting revenues from payroll taxes into individual accounts, such as carve-out accounts, would only reduce the system's long-term financing problem to the extent that the benefit offset (from lower benefits) is greater than the diverted revenues.[19]

Chile and the United States in Comparative Perspective

Before examining how Chile's individual retirement accounts system works, it is important to note some of the major demographic, political, and economic differences between Chile and the United States.

Basic Demographics

Chile has a relatively small population compared to the United States (roughly 16 million compared to 300 million respectively), and a smaller share of persons 65 or older (see table 1). Both Chile and the United States are projected to face population aging, although Chile is expected to remain younger than the United States. In 2025, 18% of Americans and 14% of Chileans are projected to be age 65 years or older. Also note that the share of workers (aged 20-64) is declining among the U.S. population, but rising in Chile.

Table 1. Basic Demographics, the United States and Chile

Country	Population (in thousands)		Life Dxpectancy (at birth)		MedianAage (both sexes)		Percent Age 65 or older		Percent WorkingAage (20-64)	
	2005	2025	2005	2025	2005	2025	2005	2025	2005	2025
United States	295,734	349,666	77.7	80.5	36.3	38.5	12.4	18.2	60.0	55.4
Chile	15,981	18,521	76.6	79.9	30.1	36.8	8.0	14.2	58.0	60.2

Source: U.S. Census Bureau, International Data Base, August 2006 version.

Political and Economic Differences

The political situation in Chile when the individual retirement accounts system was first adopted is very different than the United States today. Individual accounts were implemented in Chile under the military dictatorship of Augusto Pinochet (1973-1990). According to many analysts, this allowed the Chilean government to implement far-reaching pension reforms quickly and without a great amount of political consensus building.[20] A democratic government was reinstated in Chile in 1990 and has continued the individual retirement accounts system.

The fiscal conditions of Chile prior to the 1981 privatization reforms and the United States today are very different. A large budget *surplus* (e.g., 5% of Gross Domestic Product (GDP) in 1980) helped the Chilean government cover the transition costs to the new system. By contrast, in 2006 the U.S. federal budget recorded a *deficit* of $248 billion (representing 1.9% of GDP).[21] Moreover, Chile used individual accounts to help develop its financial markets. Such markets are already well established in the U.S.

Another difference between the countries is the condition of the PAYGO retirement system. Chile's PAYGO system was insolvent at the time that their retirement system was overhauled. In 1980, the program had a deficit equivalent to 2.7% of gross domestic product, and general revenues financed roughly 28% of outgoing payments.[22] The U.S. Social Security system, by contrast, currently has a surplus (1.4% of GDP in 2006)[23] and is projected to remain solvent until 2041. Moreover, in Chile, factors such as government mismanagement, high rates of contribution evasion, and public distrust, among other reasons, helped set the stage for replacing their PAYGO system.[24] By contrast, the U.S. Social

Security program is well-managed, covers almost the entire labor force, and enjoys broad public support.[25]

The two countries differ in the size and scope of their economies. Chile is a relatively small developing county recognized for its robust economic performance in the Latin American region since the 1980s. With a per capita GDP of $5,747 in 2005, Chile is classified by the World Bank as an upper middle income country, whereas the United States, with a per capita GDP of $37,574, is classified by the World Bank as an OECD developed high income country.[26] Chile has a large number of self-employed workers (around 27% of the labor force), many of whom are part of the informal sector — a segment that did not participate widely in the PAYGO system or in the current individual retirement accounts system. In contrast, the United States has a very small informal sector and the self-employed must contribute to Social Security.

Finally, the definition of social security in Chile, as in many countries, includes sickness and maternity insurance, work injury insurance, unemployment and family allowances in addition to old-age, survivors and disability insurance. This CRS report focuses on the retirement component of Chile's social security system.

OVERVIEW OF CHILEAN INDIVIDUAL RETIREMENT ACCOUNTS

Background

In 1924, Chile became the first Latin American country to establish a national social insurance system, with the goal of insuring against elderly poverty, disability and death. It was a state-run, pay-as-you-go system with defined benefits, primarily financed by payroll contributions from employees and employers. While the program grew in size and complexity between 1924 and 1980, its basic structure remained relatively unchanged.

Several major problems associated with Chile's PAYGO retirement system set the stage for pension reforms in 1981. It was highly fragmented, with more than three dozen different retirement schemes, each with different eligibility requirements and contribution rates.[27] In 1973, for example, the combined employer/employee payroll contributions ranged from 19.5% to 26.0% of wages, depending on occupational type.[28] The system was also vulnerable to political manipulation and was widely seen as inequitable. White-collar workers tended to fare better than those on the lower end of the economic spectrum. The multitude of plans and contribution rates resulted in another difficulty — high administrative inefficiencies and expenses.

In May 1981, Chile replaced its state-run, PAYGO system with a private, fully funded individual retirement accounts system.[29] The switch had a number of goals, including to restore the long-term financial balance of the system; to provide efficiency gains in the system; to reduce inequities of the old system and cover more workers; to give workers "ownership" over their retirement resources; to increase national savings; and to stimulate the national economy.

Mandatory individual retirement accounts comprise the centerpiece of the new Chilean retirement system. Individual accounts are supplemented by a minimum guaranteed pension program, a social assistance pension program, and voluntary private savings accounts system. The main features of the system are summarized in table 2 and in the sections that follow.[30]

Table 2. Features of the Chilean Individual Retirement Accounts System

Element	Individual Retirement Accounts System
Year Started	• 1981
Participation	• Mandatory for new workers • Voluntary for self-employed • Optional for workers under the old system
Compensation from prior contributions	• Yes, recognition bonds
Mandatory contribution rate (% of taxable wages)	• Employee (10%) — capped at 60 UFs • Employer (none) • Additional contribution for administrative fees and survivors/disability insurance (See text box)
Additional savings (voluntary) mechanisms	• Additional contribution on top of the mandatory 10% of earnings • Separate savings account
Management of individual accounts	• Private pension fund management companies (*Administradoras de Fondos de Pensiones*, or AFPs)
Fees	• Charged to participant by AFP
Pension fund investments	• Five funds varying by risk (beginning in 2002)
Default fund on investments	• Depends on age, with older workers defaulted in fixed-income securities (since 2002).
Legal retirement age	• 65 (men), 60 (women)
Payout options	• Annuity (joint if married) • Programmed withdrawals • Programmed withdrawals with immediate annuity/deferred annuity
Government benefit guarantee	• Minimum pension guarantee (with 20 years of contributions to individual account)[31]

Source: Congressional Research Service.

Participation

Workers who entered the Chilean labor force after January 1, 1983 were no longer covered by the old system. Instead, they were required to pay a proportion of their earnings into a private pension fund; that is, the individual retirement accounts system. Participation of self-employed workers in the individual retirement accounts system was made voluntary. The police and members of the armed forces remain in their own separate system to date. Those already in the workforce when the reforms were implemented were permitted to join the new system or remain in the old one, and persons already receiving a pension continued under the old law.

Compensation for Previous Contributions to the Old System

Workers who switched to the new system received government-financed "recognition bonds" (*bonos de reconocimiento*) to compensate them for accrued benefits under the previous system. The recognition bond is paid out of general revenues into a worker's individual account at retirement. Its value takes into account, among other things, the life expectancy of workers and the number of years they contributed to the old system.[32]

Contribution Rate

Workers must contribute 10% of their monthly earnings to an individual retirement account, plus an additional amount (variable percentage) for administrative fees and survivors and disability insurance. There is a monthly maximum earnings limit on contributions of 60 UFs (*unidad de fomento*) —US$2,043 as of January 2007.[33] Contributions and interest are tax-deferred until retirement. Employers are responsible for sending the monthly contribution to workers' pension fund management companies (*Administradoras de Fondos de Pensiones*, AFPs). Employers are not required to contribute but may do so. There is and additional contribution for fees and survivors and disability insurance. (See text box below.)

What about Survivor and Disability Benefits?

Under the current Chilean system, survivors and disability pensions are provided through the private market and not the central government. The insurance is financed as a fraction of workers' additional required monthly contribution which varies by AFP —averaging around 0.75%-0.76% of the worker's gross earnings per month. These resources are used by the pension fund management companies (AFPs) to take out disability and group life (survivor) insurance from private insurance companies.

Workers who lose earnings capacity due to an injury or illness may receive a disability benefit. A total disability benefit is provided to members who have lost at least 66% of earning capacity (a smaller benefit is provided for partial disability). A survivor benefit is provided to the surviving widow, disabled widower, the mother of children of the insured born out of wedlock, children younger than age 18 (age 24 if a student, no age limit if disabled), and in some cases, to the parents of the deceased worker.

Qualifying widows and disabled widowers are required to have married the insured person at least six months before his or her death or three years before if the marriage took place when the member was already receiving an old-age or disability pension. As of the time of writing, men can qualify for a survivors pension only if they are totally or partially disabled. A reform bill under consideration in Chile would extend survivors benefits to widowers.[34]

Source: This information has been adapted from the Superintendent of Pension Fund Management Companies (SAFP), *The Chilean Pension System*, 4th edition (Santiago de Chile, 2003).[35]

Voluntary Savings Mechanisms

Chilean workers can supplement their individual retirement accounts in several ways. They can contribute on top of their required 10% contribution on earnings, up to a monthly ceiling (60 UF) to an individual account. Since August 1987, workers may also put money aside, regularly or sporadically, in a separate voluntary savings account.[36] The tax code provides a variety of incentives for voluntary contributions and accounts, which were extended to the self-employed not participating in the new system and to members of the old system beginning in 2002. As of December of 2005, there were roughly 1.5 million voluntary savings accounts, compared to 7.4 million mandatory individual retirement accounts.[37]

Management of Individual Accounts

In Chile, mandatory individual retirement accounts are administered by private pension fund management companies known as *Administradoras de Fondos de Pensiones* (AFPs).[38] The design emphasizes competition between AFPs in an attempt to lower administrative costs, promote higher returns on investments, and encourage better customer service.

Workers may select one AFP to manage their mandatory retirement accounts, which are invested in a mix of stocks, bonds, and other financial instruments. Workers may switch from one AFP to another at any time. When the system began, there were 12 AFPs operating. The number of AFPs peaked to 21 in 1994, and since then, a number have merged and some have been liquidated. As of January 2007, six pension fund management companies were in operation.[39]

AFP Fees

AFPs may levy an array of different fees for managing workers' mandatory individual retirement accounts.[40] These typically include a fixed flat fee when contributions are made (varies by AFP),[41] a proportional fee on contributions, and a fee to open a new account. All fees are levied when contributions are made. Since 1987, a management fee on a worker's account has not been permitted. At retirement, there are up-front fees for the purchase of an annuity or programmed withdrawals, but no exit fee or fee to transfer pension fund companies may be levied (since 1987).

In addition to administrative fees, workers pay AFPs for survivors and disability insurance, and each AFP takes out group life and disability insurance from separate private insurance companies. While typically included in the calculation of total administrative costs, survivors and disability insurance premiums are distinct from fees related to administering the individual accounts and provide protection against disability and death for the worker and his family.

Although total administrative costs in the Chilean system have declined from their peak in 1984, when they represented 3.6% of taxable earnings, they remain too high, according to observers.[42] Table 3 breaks down administrative costs (fees plus survivors and disability insurance) for the system in 2003. In that year, total administrative charges averaged 2.26% of taxable earnings, representing 22.6% of workers' 10% deposit or around 18% of the total deduction on workers' wages (12.26%). Note that, premiums paid for survivors and disability insurance typically make up around 0.75%-0.76% of the worker's taxable earnings per month.[43]

Table 3. Administrative Costs, Chilean Individual Retirement Accounts, 2003

Country	(a) Deposit in individual account as % of wages	(b) Administrative costs (fees + premium) as % of wages	(c) Total deduction as % of wages	Administrative Costs as % of	
				(d) Total deduction (b÷c)	(e) Deposit in individual account (b÷a)
Chile	10.00%	2.26%	12.26%	18.43%	22.60%

Source: Carmelo Mesa-Lago, "Evaluation of a Quarter Century of Structural Pension Reforms in Latin America," in Carolin A. Crabbe, ed., *A Quarter Century of Pension Reform in Latin America and the Caribbean: Lessons Learned and the Next Steps*, Inter-American Development Bank, 2005, table 2.6, pp. 43-82. (Hereafter cited as Mesa-Lago, 2005.)

Notes: Administrative costs are deducted on top of the 10% deposit in the individual account. Unlike the 10% mandatory contribution, however, administrative costs represent a variable percentage (over time and across AFPs). The 2.26% figure referenced in the table (b) includes roughly 0.75% for survivors and disability insurance premiums.

Pension Fund Investments

Pension fund investments are subject to a number of rules set by the Chilean government. To reduce risk, investments were initially limited to bonds of financial institutions, bank deposits, mortgage bonds, government securities, and a limited amount of corporate bonds. Investments in domestic or foreign equities were not permitted. As the system has matured, investment rules and restrictions have been relaxed. Investment in domestic equities has been allowed since the mid-1980s, and investment in foreign assets (both fixed and variable return investments) has been allowed since the mid-1990s. The limit on asset allocation in foreign instruments was raised from 20% to 30% in 2004; recent proposals seek to raise the limit to 80%.

The asset mix of Chilean pension funds has shifted dramatically since the system's inception, moving toward greater diversification (see figure 1). Investment in domestic equities began in the mid-1980s, peaked in the early 1990s at 32% of total assets, then declined to 15% of total assets in 2003 as the portfolio moved toward international diversification. In recent years, investments in foreign instruments have grown dramatically, rising from 0.6% of total portfolio assets in 1993 to 24% in 2003 (in 2005, this figure was at 30%).[44] A detailed summary of the asset allocation from 1981 to 2003 is provided in Appendix table 1.

The growth of the funds' size between 1981 and 2005 in relation to the Chilean economy has been considerable (figure 2). By 2005, pension funds represented almost 60% of Chile's GDP. The returns on investments have also been sizeable (figure 3). From the system's inception in 1981 to 2003, the pension funds have returned an average annual real rate of 10.4%; the average real return between 1991 and 2003 was 8.7% (before administrative costs). Negative returns were recorded in two years — 1995 (-2.5%) and 1998 (-1.1%)[45] — highlighting how capital markets vary during boom or bust times.

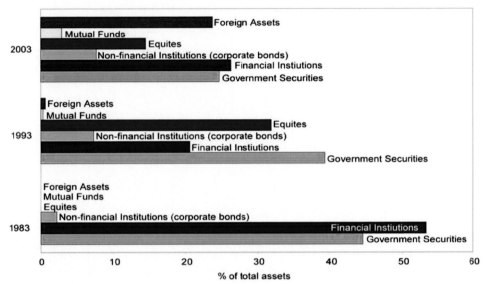

Source: Based on Arenas de Mesa, 2005, table 3.5, p. 92.

Notes: Totals may not equal the sums of rounded components. Categories less than 1% were dropped (i.e., disposable assets). *Foreign assets* include foreign mutual funds, foreign issued bonds, and equity of foreign corporations publicly traded on the New York Stock Exchange, NASDAQ, the London Stock Exchange, etc. *Mutual Funds* include investment funds of business firms plus others from the external sector (domestic issuer). *Equities* include stocks of financial institutions (domestic issuer). *Non-financial institutions* include the corporate bonds of business firms. *Financial institutions* include banking deposits and mortgage securities.

Figure 1. Aggregate Allocation of Chilean Pension Funds, 1983-2003.

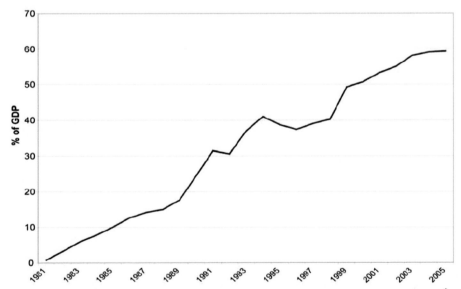

Source: Data for 1981-2005 are as of December, SAFP, *El Sistema Chileno de Pensiones*, 6th edition (Santiago de Chile, 2007), p. 258.

Figure 2. Value of Chilean Pension Funds as % of GDP, 1981-2005.

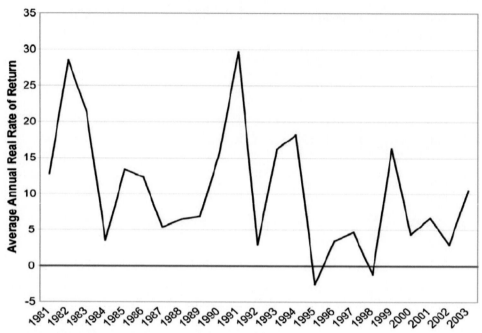

Source: Data reported in Arenas de Mesa, 2005, table 3.4, p. 91.

Figure 3. Annual Real Rates of Return in Chilean Pension Funds, 1981-2003 (before administrative costs).

AFPs must follow a number of other regulations. They have a minimum capital start up requirement. They have a minimum and maximum rate of return tied to the average real rate of return of all AFPs over a three-year period. Under the new multi-funds system established in 2002 (described in more detail below), the minimum and maximum rates of return are calculated separately for each fund type.[46] When an AFP has "excess returns" based on a defined percentage, they must put the funds into a reserve fund. Regulations also require that AFPs hold a margin account equal to 1% of the fund's value. If an AFP does not achieve a minimum return, it makes up the difference from the aforementioned 1% and excess returns funds. It should also be mentioned that from the beginning of the program to March 2000, each AFP was permitted to offer only one fund. Although the intent was to limit investor risk, the one fund per AFP rule, along with the maximum and minimum rates of return, resulted in almost identically held portfolios among AFPs.

To provide workers with a greater array of investment choices, legislation passed in January 2002 established multiple funds, which permitted each AFP to offer up to five Funds (A, B, C, D, and E), each with differing degrees of risk (see table 4).[47] Fund A has the highest proportion of its portfolio invested in equities, therefore the highest risk and potentially the greatest return. Under the multi-funds system, plan members are also permitted to allocate their contributions between two funds within the same AFP. Contributors who do not elect a specific fund are assigned one according to their age, with older workers automatically shifted into lower risk funds. As of September 2006, the majority of active contributors who have chosen a fund have selected A- and B-type funds. However, the majority of pension fund assets are in the C-type fund, which is the default fund for workers aged 36 to 55.[48]

Table 4. Features of Multi-funds, Equity Allowance and Default Age

Fund	Percent of Equities by Fund		Default Age Assignment	
	Minimum	Maximum	Men	Women
A	40%	80%	n/a	n/a
B	25%	60%	Up to 35	Up to 35
C	15%	40%	36 to 55	36 to 50
D	5%	20%	56 or older	51 or older
E	None (fixed-income securities)		n/a	

Source: SAFP, 2003.

Notes: In March 2000, regulations began permitting AFPs to offer a fixed-income fund (Fund 2) to workers already receiving a pension or to those within 10 years or less of retirement age. Participants previously in Fund 2, when there were two funds, who did not subsequently elect a fund after the multi-funds system was implemented, were assigned to the E-type Fund.

Payout Options

The legal retirement age under Chile's individual retirement accounts system is 65 years for men and 60 years for women. An individual need not stop working to receive his or her pension at legal retirement age. Early retirement is permitted but only if capital in the individual account would fund an "adequate" annuity, in terms of a monetary amount and a replacement rate of former earnings.[49] The amount of the pension benefit depends on the amount accumulated in the mandatory individual account and the type of payout option a worker chooses.

Chilean workers have three options to withdraw income from their retirement accounts: (1) purchase an annuity, (2) withdraw a predetermined amount each month, or (3) a combination of the two. A retiree can use the accumulated capital in the individual account to purchase an annuity from a private life insurance company. The annuity must be inflation-protected and provide survivors benefits.[50] The second option is a programmed withdrawal, which is actuarially determined using official life tables, the account balance, and a variable interest rate. If individuals who choose the monthly programmed withdrawal outlive their resources, they could qualify for a minimum pension. If the retiree dies before all withdrawals are made, the remaining balance forms part of his or her estate. A third option available since 2004 is to combine an annuity and programmed withdrawal, with the advantage that the retiree is guaranteed an income stream for life, and if the individual dies early, the remaining account balance can be passed on to dependents.[51] A lump-sum withdrawal is allowed, but only under designated conditions that few workers meet.[52]

Government Role

The Chilean government maintains a number of important roles in the individual retirement accounts system. Regulatory oversight is provided by the governmental agency known as the Superintendent of Pension Fund Management Companies (SAFP), which licenses and oversees the pension fund management companies.

The government acts as the guarantor of the AFP system. If an AFP goes bankrupt, the account holder (who is not retired or a retiree taking programmed withdrawals) does not lose any money in his or her individual account. The guarantee is effective only after the AFP uses its reserve funds. Also, the government insures 75% of a worker's annuity over the minimum pension level if an insurance company goes bankrupt. To date the government has yet to need to do so.[53] The government also continues to administer the old PAYGO pension system (current pensioners under the old system and those who switched from the old system to the new system) through the National Pension Fund, INP.[54]

Two government programs form the safety-net under the system of individual retirement accounts. A *minimum pension guarantee* (MPG) is available to all workers who have at least 20 years of contributions but who have not accumulated enough in their individual account to finance a minimum lifetime pension. The MPG is a *top-up* benefit — if the individual account is not sufficient to fund a minimum pension, the government makes up the difference. If a person who has programmed withdrawals runs out of money in their individual account, or the amount they receive is below the minimum benefit, the government also tops this up. The minimum benefit level is set by the government and equals roughly 75% of Chile's minimum wage or 25% of the average wage.[55]

A second non-contributory program targets the very poor aged. The means-tested *social assistance pension* (known as PASIS) is available to the indigent elderly with fewer than 20 years of contributions. The benefit equals approximately half the value of the minimum pension. Not all who would qualify for a PASIS pension, however, receive one. To control costs, the government has set a limit on the number of persons who can receive the social assistance pension. A large share of qualified candidates has been placed on a waiting list. A reform bill currently under consideration by the Chilean Congress aims to extend PASIS-type benefits to all of the aged population who qualify, as discussed below.[56]

Recent Developments

In recent years, there have been growing calls to modify Chile's individual retirement accounts system. Pension reform was a major theme during Chile's presidential campaign of 2005 and early 2006. The two main candidates, Sebastian Piñera of the center right National Renewal Party and Michelle Bachelet of the center left Socialist Party, agreed on the need to improve the existing individual retirement accounts system.[57]

In January 2006, Michelle Bachelet won the presidency in a runoff election, and soon after taking office in March, she created an Advisory Commission on Pension Reform. In July, the Commission presented the government with 70 proposals for improving the individual retirement accounts system.[58] By December of the same year, President Bachelet sent a pension reform bill based on the Commission's recommendations to the Chilean Congress for debate and approval.

The pension reform bill would strengthen the role of the state in the existing system and has several areas of focus. A main part of the reform is the addition of a new pillar (*Sistema de Pensiones Solidarias,* SPS) to the individual retirement accounts system. The SPS, which would take effect July 1, 2008, would increase retirement benefits to low-income persons aged 65 or older who have lived in Chile for at least 20 years. It would replace the means-tested PASIS pension and the guaranteed minimum pension such that (a) individuals not eligible for any other pension would receive a *basic solidarity pension* of 60,000 pesos a month ($111); and (b) individuals whose pension from the individual accounts equals less than 200,000 pesos ($369) a month would receive a monthly top up benefit of up to 60,000 pesos ($ 111), known as a *solidarity-based pension contribution*.[59]

Another goal of the proposed reforms is to increase the participation of self-employed and informal sector workers and younger low-income workers in individual retirement accounts. To this end, one provision calls for a government cash subsidy to low-income workers (defined as earnings of less than 1.5 times the minimum wage) between the ages 18 and 35 for the first 24 months they are formally employed.[60] Another measure would require self-employed workers, roughly 27% of the Chilean labor force, to enroll with an AFP seven years after the bill's implementation. Their participation is currently voluntary.

Gender equity is also addressed in the pension reform bill. The legal retirement age would remain 60 for women and 65 for men, but starting July 1, 2009, women retiring at age 65 would receive a bonus credit for each child's birth —equivalent to 12 monthly contributions at minimum wage (at the time the child was born), plus 4% annual interest from the child's birth date until the woman reaches age 65. Survivor pensions would be extended to widowers (currently, men qualify only if they are disabled). In the case of divorce or annulement, capital in an individual account would be divided evenly between spouses. Social security law in Chile does not yet address the new marital status of divorced as provided by the civil marriage law of 2004 (legalizing divorce).[61]

The proposed legislation also aims to increase competition among AFPs and to reduce administrative costs. Among other modifications, the bill would

- allow banks to set up an AFP and offer pension funds;
- permit the Superintendent of Pension Fund Managers (SAFPs) to direct new entrants in the workforce to the management company with the lowest commissions;
- eliminate the flat fee charged to plan members by most AFPs, which is regressive; and
- raise the limit on foreign investment from 30% to 80%, three years after the reform bill's enactment.

Other measures seek to improve financial education and boost retirement savings. The reform bill calls for the creation of a Pension Education Fund as a way to help improve workers' knowledge of the individual retirement accounts system. This measure comes on the heels of a growing body of research showing a lack of knowledge of the retirement system, especially among workers with low incomes, with less education, and among women.[62] The bill would also create an employer-sponsored voluntary retirement savings plan, known as *Ahorro Previsional Voluntario Colectivo* (APVC), in which employers, as well as other persons, could contribute to an individual's voluntary savings account.

ASSESSING THE CHILEAN APPROACH TO RETIREMENT

This section provides a brief assessment of some of the major impacts of Chile's individual retirement accounts system. The section does not analyze potential effects of the reform bill under debate in the Chilean Congress as of May 2007. Note that a complete analysis of the Chilean individual retirement accounts system cannot be made until the first cohort of workers entirely under the new system reaches retirement age — around 2020.

Macroeconomic Effects

Many economists argue that individual accounts have significantly contributed to Chile's rapid economic growth since the mid-1980s. One study estimates that Chilean pension reforms contributed roughly 0.5 percentage points per year (in a range from 0.2 to 0.9 percentage points) to economic growth from 1981 to 2001, a period when Chile's economy grew at an average annual rate of 4.6%.[63] Individual accounts are also viewed as having helped the Chilean labor market; for example, by lowering the cost of labor (i.e., reducing total rate of payroll taxes), which encouraged employment creation.[64]

The implementation of individual accounts has helped develop Chile's domestic capital markets. Chilean capital markets were very underdeveloped at the time individual accounts were adopted. AFPs are now the largest institutional investors in Chile's capital markets, and pension fund assets have grown to represent a huge portion of the Chilean economy, from around 1% of GDP in 1981 to 63% of GDP as of June 2006.[65]

Among the oft-cited benefits of moving from a PAYGO to a fully funded system is the increase in national savings.[66] Empirical studies, however, have not reached a consensus on whether pension reforms have directly boosted Chile's national savings rate.[67] Measuring changes in the savings rate is difficult as estimates depend on assumptions of the savings levels that would have existed if no reform had taken place.

System Financing

A primary rationale for moving to a fully funded system in Chile was that it would help the retirement system achieve solvency. The transition to an individual retirement accounts system from a PAYGO system, however, has proved fiscally expensive for Chile in the short term. During the first five years of the reforms in Chile, total transition costs — expenditures for current pensioners and for those who remained in the old system, plus the costs of redeeming recognition bonds — ranged from 4.2% to 4.7% of GDP per year, according to the Congressional Budget Office (CBO).[68] Transition costs peaked in the late 1980s, and during the 1990s averaged roughly 4.1% of GDP annually.[69] The entire transition period in Chile is not expected to end until about 2050 — the year that benefits to those who stayed in the old system are projected to cease completely.[70]

Another area of concern relates to new fiscal burdens on the government resulting from the growth of minimum pension guarantees (not including the proposed expansion of the program). As Chile's individual retirement accounts system matures, forecasts project that an increasing number of future retirees will qualify for a minimum pension guarantee as many current workers are not accumulating enough in their mandatory individual accounts to fund at least a minimum pension at retirement. The share of individual account holders requiring a "top up" benefit to provide a minimum pension level is projected to increase to more than 30 percent as the system matures, costing the government up to 1% of GDP.[71]

It is worthwhile to point out several strategies that helped the Chilean government finance the transition costs, especially during the early and most expensive years of implementation. These included increasing taxes on consumption,[72] selling a large array of state-owned enterprises, borrowing from the public, and tightening spending. These methods helped Chile build a substantial budget surplus prior to the reform (5.5% of GDP in 1980). According to the CBO, "in general, the Chilean privatization has been quite successful in managing the transition from a pay-as-you-go to a fully funded privatized retirement system."[73]

Efficiency and Costs to Participants

Chile's switch to individual retirement accounts was also intended to improve the efficiencies of the old system. However, among the current system's greatest problems are high administrative costs. The extent of administrative costs has become a focal point of controversy in Chile because management fees reduce a workers' net investment over their working lives and hence their final pension from the individual account. If administrative costs are reduced, more of workers' contributions can be invested (in their IAs) and therefore raise the accumulated capital in their individual accounts.

Studies have shown that the cumulative impact of administrative charges on a workers' final capital accumulation and pension in Chile may be substantial.[74] Over time it has been estimated that administrative fees have consumed a quarter (25%) of the accumulations of an average Chilean worker who began contributing in 1982 and retired in 2002.[75] Administrative charges also reduce workers' rate of return. Estimates from the Superintendent of Pension Fund Management Companies (SAFP) have indicated that when commission fees are considered, average annual returns on Chilean pension funds between July 1981 and August 2001 decline from 10.83% to 7.33% for low earners and 7.59% for high earners.[76] The disparity between high and low earners stems from a flat-fee on monthly contributions that exists in most AFPs. Unlike proportional fees, fixed charges tend to be regressive.

There are a number of reasons for high administrative costs in the Chilean system. Given pension fund managers' incentive to entice plan members to their AFP, the system, especially in the 1990s, experienced high marketing costs and a dramatic growth in sales personnel. Increased advertising and sales representatives also led individual participants to change AFPs excessively, thereby increasing total operating costs.[77] A lack of competition and market transparency may also contribute to high administrative costs. From the inception of the program until present, there has been a concentration of assets in a few AFPs. In July 2006, two out of the six total AFPs controlled roughly 66% of all fund assets. High administrative costs and industry concentration may have resulted from government regulation in the AFP system (e.g., regulation of fee structure, legal barriers to entry such as start-up requirements or minimum reserve fund).[78]

Furthermore, many Chilean workers do not to appear to be well-informed about the fees associated with their individual retirement accounts. A high level of knowledge about administrative charges, some argue, may boost competition in the AFP system by encouraging more plan members to shop around for the AFP with the lowest fee structure. A recent analysis conducted by two Chilean pension experts shows that only 3.7% of plan members were aware of variable commissions charged by AFPs (and hence unable to compare fees and performance), and 52% did not know what percentage of their income went toward contributions into an individual retirement account.[79]

The administrative costs reported in Chile would not necessarily be replicated in other countries given the diverse factors that drive such costs.[80] For example, whether administrative functions are managed by the government or private entities and whether administration tasks are covered by a single entity (centralized) or diverse entities (decentralized) may play a role in administrative costs. A centralized management system of investment funds could build on the existing tax collection and record-keeping systems of the government, generate economies of scale, and spread administrative costs over more workers, thereby lowering total costs.[81] The relatively low administrative costs in the U.S. government employees' Thrift Savings Plan (TSP) is often cited as evidence of the cost advantages of a centralized single, private entity.[82] By contrast, Chile has a decentralized structure of private pension fund management companies.

Coverage

The individual retirement accounts system was expected to improve participation rates in Chile, in part by linking benefits more tightly to contributions. However, active participation in the new system remains lower than expected.[83] Whereas almost the entire Chilean workforce is enrolled in the AFP system,[84] the share of persons actively contributing to their accounts is much smaller (see table 5).[85] In 2003 approximately 62% of the Chilean labor force, or 68% of those employed, are estimated to have contributed to their individual retirement accounts.[86] This figure is roughly similar to the level of coverage provided under Chile's old PAYGO retirement system in the mid-1970s.[87]

**Table 5. Active Members and Total Contributors,
Chilean Individual Retirement Accounts, 1981-2005**

Years	Number of Members [a]	Number of Contributors [b]
1981	1,400,000	n/a
1983	1,620,000	1,229,877
1985	2,283,830	1,558,194
1987	2,890,680	2,023,739
1989	3,470,845	2,267,622
1991	4,109,184	2,486,813
1993	4,708,840	2,792,118
1995	5,320,913	2,961,928
1997	5,780,400	3,296,361
1999	6,105,731	3,262,269
2001	6,427,656	3,450,080
2003	6,979,351	3,618,995
2005	7,394,506	3,784,141

Source: SAFP, *El Sistema Chileno de Pensiones*, 6th edition (Santiago de Chile, 2007), p. 247.
Notes: (a) Members are those who are still alive and who are not receiving a pension and enrolled in an AFP, December; (b) The number of members who contributed in December in each year.

Furthermore, not all of those that actively contribute to their accounts at one point in time will contribute to them regularly over their working life.[88] One study estimates that an average Chilean worker entering the labor force at 20 years old and retiring at 60 years old will have 21 years of contributions.[89] Another study estimates that an average plan member makes contributions for about 54% of his/her potential working life.[90] While around one fifth of plan members make contributions nearly 100% of the time over their careers, a substantial portion of the population does not make regular contributions. Individuals may not contribute regularly for various reasons, such as interruptions in employment or job seasonality, non-employment, and low wages in relation to daily expenses over a lifetime.

These trends reflect a growing concern in Chile that the current system does not cover the entire labor force and provides inadequate benefits to an important segment of workers. According to a Chilean government's study baseline projection, nearly 40% of workers affiliated with an AFP will accumulate enough capital to fund a benefit above the minimum level, 10% will qualify for a minimum benefit "top up," and nearly half will reach retirement with less than the minimum pension and fewer than 20 years of contributions.[91]

Several factors help explain why participation in the Chilean individual retirement accounts system has not been greater. The labor market in Chile has a high share of self-employed workers, roughly 27% of the labor force, and a large informal sector. The participation rate for self-employed workers (which is voluntary) dropped from 12% to 7% between 1986 and 2003, while salaried workers rose from 63% to 76%.[92] Chilean men contribute to their accounts almost 40% more months than women, who work fewer years, experience interrupted periods of employment due to child rearing and have lower lifetime earnings.[93] Another factor may be the minimum pension guarantee, which may create incentives for lower income workers to contribute just long enough to qualify for the minimum pension (20 years), and soon thereafter stop making contributions.[94]

CONCLUSION

Obtaining knowledge of other countries' experience with reforms in their social insurance programs has gained importance in recent years as policymakers contemplate how to address Social Security's long-term financial challenges. It is difficult, however, to draw general lessons from one country's experience, as there is no universal solution to reform. Social security systems operate differently in different countries; each faces its own unique set of political and socioeconomic conditions and has a different set of income support programs for the elderly. Moreover, what is viewed as successful or desirable in one country may not be in another. Nevertheless, information of reformed retirement systems around the globe can provide valuable insight to policymakers.

The performance of Chile's individual retirement accounts system is mixed.[95] Individual retirement accounts have contributed to the Chilean economy in a number of ways and the returns on pension fund investments have been greater than expected. The system seems to work well for workers with stable jobs who contribute regularly to their accounts over their working lives. However, the transition to an individual retirement accounts system has proved fiscally expensive for Chile. Concerns remain about low participation rates, especially among women and low-income workers, including members of the informal sector. Analysts also agree that administrative costs have been too high.

In an attempt to address these problems and improve the system, a pension reform bill was sent to the Chilean Congress for consideration in 2007. The bill aims to reduce administrative costs, increase benefits, and expand coverage to supplement the shortfalls in the existing system's safety net. This development suggests that the Chilean individual retirement accounts model continues to evolve after 26 years of existence.

APPENDIX. CHILEAN PENSION FUNDS

Table A1. Allocation of Chilean Pension Funds, 1981-2003
(as a percent of total investments)

Year	Government Securities	Financial Institutions	Non-Financial Institutions (corporate bonds)	Equities	Mutual Funds and Others	Foreign Assets
1981	28.1	71.3	0.6	0.0	0.0	0.0
1982	26.0	73.4	0.6	0.0	0.0	0.0
1983	44.5	53.4	2.2	0.0	0.0	0.0
1984	42.1	55.6	1.8	0.0	0.0	0.0
1985	42.4	56.0	1.1	0.0	0.0	0.0
1986	46.6	48.7	0.8	3.8	0.0	0.0
1987	41.4	49.4	2.6	6.2	0.0	0.0
1988	35.4	50.1	6.4	8.1	0.0	0.0
1989	41.6	39.2	9.1	10.1	0.0	0.0
1990	44.1	33.4	11.1	11.3	0.0	0.0
1991	38.3	26.7	11.1	23.8	0.0	0.0
1992	40.9	25.2	9.6	24.0	0.2	0.0
1993	39.3	20.6	7.3	31.9	0.3	0.6
1994	39.7	20.0	6.3	32.2	0.9	0.9
1995	39.4	22.4	5.2	30.1	2.6	0.2
1996	42.1	23.6	4.7	26.0	3.0	0.5
1997	39.6	29.3	3.3	23.4	3.2	1.1
1998	41.0	31.7	3.8	14.9	3.0	5.6
1999	34.6	33.2	3.8	12.4	2.7	13.3
2000	35.7	35.1	4.0	11.6	2.5	10.8
2001	35.0	32.4	6.2	10.6	2.5	13.2
2002	30.0	34.2	7.2	9.9	2.5	16.1
2003	24.7	26.3	7.7	14.5	2.9	23.8

Source: Based on Arenas de Mesa, A. "Fiscal and Institutional Considerations and the Chilean Prescription," table 3.5, p. 92 (using data from the Superintendent of Pension Fund Companies).

Notes: Totals may not equal the sums of rounded components. Categories less than 1% were dropped (i.e., disposable assets). *Financial institutions* include banking deposits and mortgage securities, but not equities of financial institutions. *Non-financial institutions* include corporate bonds of business firms. *Equities* are stocks of financial institutions plus those of the business sector (domestic issuer). *Mutual Funds and others* include investment funds of the business firms plus others from the external sector (domestic issuer). *Foreign assets* includes foreign issuers less others from the external sector (includes foreign mutual funds, foreign issue bonds, and equity of foreign corporations publicly traded on the New York Stock Exchange, NASDAQ, the London Stock Exchange, etc.

REFERENCES

[1] U.S. Government Accountability Office, *Social Security Reform: Other Countries' Experiences Provide Lessons for the United States*, United States Government Accountability Office Report to Congressional Requesters, 2005, GAO-06-126, at [http://www.gao.gov/new.items/d06126.pdf]; (Hereafter cited as GAO, 2005). U.S. Congressional Budget Office, *Social Security Privatization: Experiences Abroad*, January 1999, at [http://www.cbo.gov/ftpdocs/10xx/doc1065/ssabroad.pdf]; (Hereafter cited as CBO, 1999). U.S. Social Security Administration, *Social Security Programs Throughout the World: The Americas, 2005* (Washington: GPO, 2006), [http://www.socialsecurity.gov/ policy/ docs/progdesc/ ssptw/2004-2005/americas/ ssptw05americas.pdf]; (Hereafter cited as SSA, 2006).

[2] Retirement programs are legally classified as either *defined benefit* plans or *defined contribution* plans. In *defined benefit* or "DB" plans, the retirement benefit is normally tied to an employee's earnings history, years of service, and age of retirement, among other factors. A *defined contribution* or "DC" plan operates much like a savings account in which the retirement benefit is tied to an employee's history of contributions, as well as administrative costs, investment returns and payout options, among other factors. See CRS Report RL30122, *Pension Sponsorship and Participation: Summary of Recent Trends*, by Patrick Purcell.

[3] This report was written by Christopher R. Tamborini while on detail to CRS. Questions should be addressed to Kathleen Romig at (7-3742).

[4] Being covered by Social Security means that a worker is employed in a job or is self-employed and contributes a portion of his or her earnings to Social Security. Workers not covered by Social Security are either covered by a similar eligible contributory system offered by their employers outside of Social Security (such as some local and state employees), do not have high enough earnings for mandatory participation, or have another special exemption. See CRS Report 94-27, *Social Security Brief Facts and Statistics*, by Gary Sidor.

[5] Covered workers and their employers each pay 6.2% of wages to Social Security up to a taxable maximum ($97,500 in 2007). Self-employed workers pay 12.4% of wages to Social Security up to the taxable maximum.

[6] U.S. Social Security Administration, 2007 Annual Report of the Board of Trustees of the Federal Old-Age and Survivors Insurance and Disability Insurance Trust Funds, April 23, 2007, figure II.D2, p. 8, at [http://www.ssa.gov/OACT/TR/TR07/tr07.pdf].

[7] A PAYGO system of financing would be sustainable if payroll taxes collected on behalf of current workers exceed benefits paid to current beneficiaries.

[8] This can be referred to as the age dependency ratio or support ratio. See CRS Report RL32981, *Age Dependency Ratios and Social Security Solvency*, and CRS Report RL32701, *The Changing Demographic Profile of the United States*, by Laura B. Shrestha.

[9] Another factor influencing the long-term financial health of Social Security is the projected increase in the real value of Social Security benefits due in large part to wage-indexing rules put into effect in 1979. Wages are projected to exceed price growth in the future. This results in greater Social Security benefits for future retirees since initial

benefits are indexed to wages. See Congressional Budget Office, *The Future Growth of Social Security: It's Not Just Society's Aging, An Issue Summary from* CBO, no. 9, July 2003, at [http://www.cbo.gov].

[10] See CRS Report RL33840, *Options to Address Social Security Solvency and Their Impact on Beneficiaries: Results from the Dynasim Microsimulation Model,* by Laura Haltzel, Dawn Nuschler, Kathleen Romig, Gary Sidor, Scott Szymendera, Mikki Waid, and Debra Whitman.

[11] See CRS Report RL33544, Social Security Reform: Current Issues and Legislation, by Dawn Nuschler.

[12] CRS Report RL33398, The Structure of Social Security Individual Account Contributions and Investments: Choices and Implications, by Debra B. Whitman.

[13] CRS Report RL33544.

[14] See CRS Report RL32879, Social Security Reform: President Bush's 2005 Individual Account Proposal, by Laura Haltzel; and the final report of President's Commission to Strengthen Social Security, Strengthening Social Security and Creating Personal Wealth for all Americans, 2001, at [http://www.csss.gov/reports/Final_report.pdf].

[15] For more information, see CRS Report RL33544.

[16] See CBO, 1999; GAO, 2005; SSA, 2006.

[17] For a useful review of pension reforms in Latin America and Eastern Europe see Barbara Kritzer, "Individual Accounts in Other Countries," *Social Security Bulletin,* vol. 66, no. 1 (2005), pp. 31-37; and Stephen Kay and Barbara Kritzer, "Social Security Reform in Latin America: Policy Challenges,"*Journal of Aging and Social Policy,* vol. 14, no. 1 (2002), pp. 9-21.

[18] CRS Report RS22010, *Social Security: "Transition Costs,"* by Laura Haltzel.

[19] CRS Report RL31498, *Social Security Reform: Economic Issues,* by Jane Gravelle and Marc Labonte; CRS Report RL33544, *Social Security Reform: Current Issues and Legislation,* by Dawn Nuschler.

[20] Studies show that democratic and authoritarian regimes have been equally as likely to implement private pension schemes, albeit in varying scopes. See Carmelo Mesa-Lago and Katharina Mueller, "The Politics of Pension Reform in Latin America," *Journal of Latin American Studies,* vol. 34, no. 3 (August 2002), pp. 687-715; and Raúl L. Madrid, *Retiring the State: The Politics of Pension Privatization in Latin America and Beyond* (Stanford: Stanford University Press, 2003).

[21] CRS Report RS22550, The Federal Budget: Sources of the Movement from Surplus to Deficit, by Marc Labonte; and CRS Report RL31235, The Economics of the Federal Budget Deficit, by Brian W. Cashell, p. 2.

[22] CBO, 1999, pp. 11-12.

[23] CRS Report RL31498.

[24] Rodrigo Acuña and Augusto Iglesias, "Chile's Pension Reform after 20 Years," Social Protection Discussion Paper No. 0129 (2001), The World Bank.

[25] CRS Report RL33544.

[26] Per capita GDP is GDP divided by midyear population. It is the sum of gross value added by all resident producers in the economy plus any product taxes and minus any subsidies not included in the value of the products. For more information see World Bank, *World Development Indicators,* 2006, at [http://devdata.worldbank.org/data-query/].

[27] For example, government employees qualified for a full pension after 30 years of service, bank employees 24 years, and legislators 15 years. For more information see R. Myers, "Chile's Social Security Reform, After Ten Years," *Benefits Quarterly*, vol. 8, Third Quarter (1992), pp. 41-55.

[28] Wage workers contributed 6.5% of wages (7% in arduous occupations); self-employed contributed 10% of earnings; and salaried employees, 8% of salary. Employers contributed 13% of wages for wage earners (15% to 17% in arduous occupations), and 17.8% of salary for salaried employees. See U.S. Department of Health, Education, and Welfare (Social Security Administration), *Social Security Programs Throughout the World, 1973*, 1973, p. 36.

[29] The implementation of individual retirement accounts (Decree Law 3500) was part of a broader set of free-market reforms.

[30] For a detailed overview of the system, see the Superintendent of Pension Fund Managers (SAFP), *The Chilean Pension System*, 4th edition (Santiago de Chile, 2003), at [http://www.safp.cl/sischilpen/english.html]. (SAFP, 2003 hereafter.) See also Robert Holzmann and Richard Hinz, *Old Age Income Support in the 21st Century* (Washington, DC: The World Bank, 2005).

[31] An "assistance pension" (PASIS) may be available to indigent elderly with less than 20 years of contributions. Not all who qualify, however, receive an assistance pension. To control costs, the government sets a limit on the number of persons who can receive social assistance benefits. A recent reform bill under consideration in the Chilean Congress attempts to extend a PASIS-type benefit to all who qualify.

[32] CBO, 1999, pg. 12.

[33] Chilean pensions are expressed in a currency called *Unidad de Fomento* (UF), which is adjusted monthly to prices. As of January 2007, one UF is equal to 18,327.50 Chilean pesos or about $34.

[34] For information on Chile's new civil marriage law as it relates to survivor benefits, see the Chilean Pension Fund Administrators' Association, *Research Series AFP Association*, Number 55, March 2006, at [http://www.afp-ag.cl/ingles/estudios/Estudio55.pdf].

[35] For more information on disability benefits in individual accounts systems, see Patrick Wiese, "Financing Disability Benefits in a System of Individual Accounts: Lessons from International Experience," WP2006-4, Center for Retirement Research at Boston College, 2006.

[36] These separate savings accounts are limited to four withdrawals per year. Voluntary contributions and accounts may be transferred to workers' mandatory individual accounts at retirement. For more details see Chilean Pension Fund Administrators' Association, "Characteristics of APV (Voluntary Social Security Saving Scheme)" at [http://www.afp-ag.cl/ingles/pdf/apv_web.pdf]. See also B. Kritzer, "Recent Changes to the Chilean System of Individual Accounts," *Social Security Bulletin*, vol. 64, no. 4 (2001/2002), pp. 66-71.

[37] Superintendent of Pension Fund Management Companies (SAFP), *El Sistema Chileno de Pensiones*, 6th edition (Santiago de Chile, 2007), p. 256.

[38] A government agency known as the Superintendent of Pension Fund Managers issues extensive guidelines for private pension fund companies, among other responsibilities. Their website is available at [http://www.safp.cl/].

[39] Superintendent of Pension Fund Companies (SAFP), *Preguntas Frecuentes ¿Que AFP's Operan en el Mercado Chileno?*, January 2007, at [http://www.safp.cl/].

[40] The Chilean government places limits on the structure of fees.

[41] The amount and the application of a fixed fee varies by AFPs. Fixed fee means an amount that does not vary by the level of contribution or quantity of capital in the account.

[42] For general information on administrative costs see, Whitehouse, E., "Administrative Charges for Fund Pensions: Comparison and Assessment of 13Countries" in *Private Pensions Systems: Administrative Costs and Reforms*, Private Pensions Series No. 2, (Paris: Organization of Economic Co-operation and Development [OECD], 2001).

[43] Recent figures from the Superintendent of Pension Fund Management Companies (SAFP) indicate that administrative charges have remained steady since 2003. In January 2007, administrative fees and premiums for survivors and disability insurance ranged from 2.23%-2.55% of taxable earnings, depending on the AFP.

[44] SAFP, "Evolucion de la Inversion de los Fondos de Pensiones Por Sector Institucional e Instrumentos Financieros," 2006, at [http://www.safp.cl/inf_afiliados/index.html].

[45] Arenas de Mesa, 2005, table 3.4, p. 91.

[46] To avoid excessive divergence from the average yield, the defined minimum rate of return has been widened for the two funds with the highest share invested in equities within the multi-funds system. For more information see, SAFP, 2003, pp. 173-211.

[47] For more information on multi-funds see Guillermo Larraín Ríos, "Enhancing the Success of the Chilean Pension System: The Addition of Multiple Funds and Annuities," in Carolin A. Crabbe, ed., *A Quarter Century of Pension Reform in Latin America and the Caribbean: Lessons Learned and the Next Steps,* Inter-American Development Bank, 2005), pp. 219-239; and B. Kritzer, "Recent Changes to the Chilean System of Individual Accounts," *Social Security Bulletin*, vol. 64, no. 4 (2001/2002), pp. 66-71.

[48] The Chilean Pension Fund Administrators' Association, "Multi-Funds Results and Trends," *Bulletin No. 14*, 2006, at [http://www.afp-ag.cl/ingles/estudios/multifondos14.pdf].

[49] Until 2004, an "adequate" annuity was defined as providing at least 50% of the insured's average wage during the past 10 years and at least 110% of the guaranteed minimum pension. In 2004, this threshold was raised to 55% of the insured's average wage and at least 130% of the minimum pension. The percentages will increase gradually until 2010.

[50] For analysis on Chile's annuity market see Roberto Rocha, Marco Morales, and Craig Thorburn, "An Empirical Analysis of the Annuity Rate in Chile," World Bank Policy Research Working Paper 3929, 2006.

[51] See U.S. Social Security Administration, "International Update," March 2004, at [http://www.ssa.gov/policy/docs/progdesc/intl_update].

[52] As of 2006, an account surplus can be withdrawn if the account balance exceeds a specified threshold — at least 70% of the worker's average wage over the past ten years and at least 150% of the minimum pension.

[53] Estelle James, Guillermo Martínez, and Augusto Iglesias, "The Payout Stage in Chile: Who Annuitizes and Why?," Working Paper no. 14, SAFPs, December 2005, at [http://www.safp.cl/files/doctrab/DT00014.pdf].

[54] Created in 1980, the INP (*Instituto de Normalización Previsional*) unified the diverse "Cajas de Previsión" (Social Security institutions) under the old system. The INP also issues the recognition bonds — the credit given for the accrued contributions to the old pension system from those who switched to the new system.

[55] As of 2006, the set minimum monthly level corresponds to about 88,000 Chilean pesos ($166) for 69 and under; 96,000 pesos ($181) for 70 to 74; and 102,000 pesos ($194) for 75 or older, source: SAFP.

[56] Both the minimum and assistance pensions are financed through general revenues and are indexed to prices, as well as ad hoc increases by the government. In April 2006, the Chilean Congress increased the minimum guaranteed pension and means-tested assistance pension by 10% (U.S. Social Security Administration, "International Update," May 2006 at [http://www.socialsecurity.gov/policy/docs/progdesc/ intl_update/].

[57] Larry Rohter, "Chile's Candidates Agree to Agree on Pension Woes," *New York Times*, January 10, 2006.

[58] Consejo Asesor Presidencial para la Reforma Previsional. *Informe Final*, July 2006, at [http://www.consejoreformaprevisional.cl/view/informe.asp]. See also Reuters News, "Chile Commission Recommends Pension Overhaul," July 6, 2006 and "Chile Preparing Pension reform Bill for December," November 14, 2006.

[59] This section draws heavily from the U.S. Social Security Administration, "International Update," July 200 and January 2007, at [http://www.socialsecurity.gov/policy/ docs/progdesc/ intl_update/]. See also Larry Rohter, "Chile Proposes to Reform Pension System," *New York Times*, December 26, 2006.

[60] The subsidy consists of a direct payment to the worker of up to 5% of minimum wage and a deposit of 5% of minimum wage into the worker's individual retirement account.

[61] In 2005, the SAFP ruled that ex-wives (through divorce or annulment) have no right to a widow's pension. The main issue lies in the interpretation of the original pension law, which do not envision divorce as a marital status. Divorce was legalized in Chile in 2004. For more information see the Chilean Pension Fund Administrators' Association, "Women who are Divorced or whose Marriages have been Annulled are not Entitled to a Widow's Pension," *Research Series AFP Association*, Number 55, March 2006, at [http://www.afp-ag.cl/ingles/estudios/Estudio55.pdf].

[62] Alberto Arenas de Mesa et al., "The Chilean Pension Reform Turns 25: Lessons from the Social Protection Survey," National Bureau of Economic Research Working Paper 12401, 2006, at [http://www.nber.org/papers/w12401]; see also Jeremy Skog, "Who Knows What About Their Pensions? Financial Literacy in the Chilean Individual Account System," University of Pennsylvania Working Paper, September 2006, at [http://bpp.wharton.upenn.edu/waldfogj/900/papers0607/Skog-Knowledge-9-11-06.pdf].

[63] See Vittorio Corbo and Klaus Schmidt-Hebbel, "Macroeconomic Effects of Pension Reform in Chile," in International Federation of Pension Funds Administrators, ed., *Pension Reform: Results and Challenges*, 2003.

[64] Sebastían Edwards, "The Chilean Pension Reform: A Pioneering Program," in Martin Feldstein, ed., *Privatizing Social Security* , 1998, pp. 33-62. (Hereafter cited as Sebastían Edwards, 1998).

[65] La Asociación Internacional de Organismos de Supervisión de Fondos de Pensiones (AIOS), "Los Regímenes de Capitalización Individual en América Latina," *Boletín Estadístico AIOS*, no. 15, June 2006, p. 13.

[66] CRS Report RL30708, *Social Security, Saving, and the Economy*, by Brian W. Cashell.

[67] See Mauricio Soto, "Chilean Pension Reform: the Good, the Bad, and the In Between," Issues in Brief Number 31, Center for Retirement Research, 2005, at [http://www.bc.edu/centers/crr/issues/ib31.pdf], (Hereafter cited as Soto, 2005);and Peter R. Orszag and Joseph E. Stiglitz, "Rethinking Pension Reform: Ten Myths About Social Security Systems," in Robert Holzmann and Joseph Stiglitz, eds., *New Ideas About Old Age Security* (Washington, DC: The World Bank, 2001), pp. 17 - 56.

[68] The *transition cost* range from 1982 to 1986 was from 4.2% to 4.7% of GDP (CBO, 1999, table 3, p. 18). As a point of comparison, the *total cost* of the U.S. Social Security system in 2007 will account for 4.3% of GDP. Social Security's cost as a percentage of GDP is projected to rise to 6.2% of GDP in 2030 (2007 Social Security Trustees' Report, pp. 11-12).

[69] Milko Matijascic and Stephen J. Kay, "Social security at the crossroads: Toward effective pension reform in Latin America," *International Social Security Review*, vol. 59, no. 1, 2006, pp. 3-26. (Hereafter cited as Matijascic and Kay, 2006.)

[70] Arenas de Mesa, 2005, p. 89.

[71] Soto, 2005.

[72] A value-added tax (VAT) was established in 1975.

[73] CBO, 1999, p. 24.

[74] Measuring the precise impacts of administrative costs on workers' accumulated capital in their individual accounts is difficult. Some fees are proportional to contributions and some are fixed. Fees also may vary by year, AFP, and investment returns. See, Whitehouse, E., "Administrative Charges for Funded Pensions: Comparison and Assessment of 13 Countries" in *Private Pensions Systems: Administrative Costs and Reforms*, Private Pensions Series No. 2, (Paris: Organization for Economic Co-operation and Development [OECD], 2001).

[75] Soto, 2005, figure 4, pp. 4-5.

[76] SAFP, Boletín Estadístico, 2001.

[77] In October 1997, the government tightened the rules for transferring pension companies. See Solange Berstein and Alejandro Micco, "Turnover and Regulation in the Chilean Pension Fund Industry," Central Bank of Chile Working Paper No. 180, September 2002, at [http://www.bcentral.cl/esp/estpub/estudios/dtbc/pdf/dtbc180.pdf].

[78] Some estimates, however, point out that administrative costs under Chile's individual retirement accounts system are on average 42% lower than the old PAYGO system, (Sebastián Edwards, 1998, p. 45).

[79] Solange Berstein and Rubén Castro, "Costos y Rentabilidad de los Fondos de Pensions: ¿Qué Informar a Los Afiliados?," Working Paper no. 1, Superintendent of Pension Fund Management Companies, April 2005, at [http://www.safp.cl/files/doctrab/DT00001.pdf].

[80] For a general discussion of administrative costs see Olivia S. Mitchell, "Administrative Costs in Public and Private Pension Systems." National Bureau of Economic Research Working Paper No. 5734, 1996, at [http://www.nber.org/papers/w12401].

[81] CRS Report RL32756, Social Security Individual Accounts and Employer-Sponsored Pensions, by Patrick Purcell, p. 6.

[82] However, the TSP may enjoy economies of scale that would be unavailable to private sector firms if individual accounts were administered competitively (see CRS Report RL31498).

[83] Dow Jones Industrial News. "Chilean Pensions' Poor Coverage Sparks Reform Debate," April 19, 2004.

[84] A person is "affiliated" with the system as long as he or she has contributed one month over a period of 20 years. In 2005, around 7.3 million Chileans were affiliated. See Superintendent of AFP,"Afliados activos por AFP," Información Estadística y Financiera, March 17, 2006, at [http://www.safp.cl/inf_estadistica/series_excel/anuales.html].

[85] Contributions are mandatory for wage and salary workers, but remain voluntary for self-employed workers (about 27% of the Chilean labor force). In Chile, the self-employed are generally located on the lower end of the income distribution, and many are part of the country's large informal or "underground" economy. The vast majority of self-employed do not contribute to the individual retirement accounts system (around 93%). There is also a segment of wage workers who should be making individual accounts contributions, but in practice do not comply with the law. Such workers are also likely to be part of the informal economy.

[86] Soto, 2005, pp. 4-5.

[87] See SAFP, El Sistema Chileno de Pensiones, 6th edition (Santiago de Chile, 2007), figure VI.3, p. 149. See also, Rodrigo Acuña and Augusto Iglesias, "Chile's Pension Reform after 20 Years," Social Protection Discussion Paper No. 0129 (2001), The World Bank.

[88] Pension analysts call this contribution density — the frequency with which workers contribute to their individual account over their working lives.

[89] Alberto Arenas de Mesa, 2005 (estimates were calculated by taking the number of months of reported contributions divided by the number of months between the worker's entry into the data set — typically age 15 — and their age in 2002). Other Chilean pension observers, such as Alejandra Cox Edwards, have estimated higher contributions densities, partly due to using an older set age in which a worker enters the labor force.

[90] Estelle James, Guillermo Martínez, and Augusto Iglesias, "The Payout Stage in Chile: Who Annuitizes and Why?," Working Paper no. 14, Superintendent of Pension Fund Companies, 2005, at [http://www.safp.cl/files/doctrab/DT00014.pdf]; see also, Alberto Arenas de Mesa, Jere Behrman, and David Bravo, "Characteristics of and Determinants of the Density of Contributions in a Private Social Security System," WP 2004-077, University of Michigan Retirement Research Center, 2004, at [http://www.mrrc.isr.umich.edu/publications/papers/pdf/wp077.pdf].

[91] Cited in Matijascic and Kay, 2006, p. 6.

[92] Arenas de Mesa, 2005.

[93] Arenas de Mesa, Behrman, and Bravo, 2004.

[94] Salvador Valdés-Prieto, "Social Security Coverage in Chile, 1990-2001," (Office of the Chief Economist, Latin America and Caribbean Region, The World Bank Background Paper for Regional Study on Social Security Reform, 2004).

[95] A number of comprehensive studies have gauged the system's performance to date. See, for example, Alberto Arenas de Mesa, et al., "The Chilean Pension Reform Turns 25: Lessons from the Social Protection Survey," National Bureau of Economic Research Working Paper 12401, 2006, at [http://www.nber.org/papers/w12401]; see also Mesa-Lago, 2005.

In: Social Security: New Issues and Developments
Editors: P. O. Deaven, W. H. Andrews, pp. 101-113

ISBN: 978-1-60456-243-9
© 2008 Nova Science Publishers, Inc.

Chapter 4

SOCIAL SECURITY, SAVING, AND THE ECONOMY*

Brian W. Cashell

ABSTRACT

One issue that never seems far from the minds of policymakers is Social Security. At the heart of the issue is the large shortfall of projected revenues needed to meet the mounting costs of the system. For the moment, the amount of Social Security tax receipts exceeds the amount of benefits being paid out. The Social Security trustees estimate that, beginning in 2017, the amount of benefits being paid out will exceed tax collections. According to the trustees' best estimate, the trust fund will be exhausted in the year 2040.

Some have argued that because the Social Security trust fund is intended to meet rising future costs of the program, its surplus should not be counted as contributing to official measures of the budget surplus. With regard to current saving, however, it makes no difference whether the surplus is credited to the trust fund or simply seen as financing current federal government outlays (including Social Security benefits). Off-budget surpluses contribute to national saving in exactly the same way as on-budget surpluses do. The additional saving they represent adds to the national saving rate and allows current investment spending to be higher than it would otherwise be.

With respect to household saving for retirement, how much is "enough" may be a subjective matter. But, one standard might be whether accumulated wealth is sufficient to avoid a decline in living standards upon retirement. A number of studies have found, however, that Americans may not tend to save enough to avoid such a decline in their living standard.

Social Security may affect saving in several ways. It may reduce household saving as participants pay some of their Social Security contributions by reducing what they otherwise would have set aside. It reduces the risk associated with retirement planning and so may free participants to cut precautionary saving. It may, however, encourage additional saving by making it possible to retire earlier, thus giving participants a longer period of retirement to plan for. To the extent that Social Security involves a transfer of income from workers to retirees, it tends to reduce household saving by shifting resources from potentially high savers to those who save less.

---

* Excerpted from CRS Report RL30708, dated June 13, 2007.

Proposed reforms have different effects on saving. Those that would move toward a more fully funded system would be likely to increase national saving, investment, and the size of the economy in the future. Reforms that would partially "privatize" using individual accounts, might tend to reduce national saving, unless contributions to those accounts were mandatory. Those that invested Social Security funds in private sector assets would be unlikely to have any effect on national saving.

INTRODUCTION

One issue of perennial concern to policymakers is Social Security. At the heart of the issue is the large shortfall of projected revenues needed to meet the mounting costs of the system, beginning in about 2017. Taxes on those currently in the workforce are credited to the trust fund and benefits to retirees are debited from the trust fund. The balance of the fund itself consists of Treasury securities.

At the moment, the amount of tax receipts exceeds the amount of benefits being paid out, and so the balance in the trust fund is growing. The current "best estimate" of the Social Security trustees is that beginning in 2017, the amount of benefits being paid out will exceed tax collections. At that time, the trust fund will have a balance of $4.7 trillion credited to it. According to the trustees' best estimate, the trust fund will be exhausted in the year 2040.[1]

Because benefits are projected to exceed receipts in 2017, there is concern among many policymakers that changes need to be made now. If steps are not taken now, it is argued, much more drastic changes will be needed down the road.

The major function of Social Security is to provide a base upon which to secure the income of the retired population. It does so by transferring income from the working population to those who are no longer in the labor force because of retirement or disability. This is also known as an intergenerational compact, by which those currently working support the retired population with the expectation that future workers will, in turn, provide for their retirement benefits. It also serves a social welfare function, by paying relatively more to retirees who were low-income earners, and survivors and dependents.

From a macroeconomic perspective, however, what matters is the effect on national saving. In a general sense, the economy is blind to the sources of saving. What matters is that saving, whether from the household, business, or public sector is channeled into investments which increase the capital stock, raise productivity and add to economic growth.

If individuals set aside substantial amounts during their working lives then the accumulated wealth and their expected Social Security benefits may be sufficient to provide for their retirement years. The more individuals save for their retirement, the higher their standard of living will be when they retire. If individuals are not saving enough to provide for some minimal standard of living in retirement, then increased saving in the public sector is one way of increasing national resources out of which to fund retirement benefits in the future. The larger the economy, the better able the nation will be to ensure a given minimum standard of living to all retirees.[2]

This paper examines the determinants of household saving and how household saving may be affected by Social Security. The potential effects of possible changes in Social Security on household and national saving are also discussed.[3]

SAVING AND THE ECONOMY

By definition, saving is that proportion of income that is not consumed. Rather, it is made available to sustain and increase the stock of productive capital. Combined with labor and technological advances, it is this capital that contributes to the production of all the goods and services that make up national output.

Reducing the share of income that is consumed and increasing the share that is saved, will tend to raise the amount of capital available to the labor force. The more capital available to the workforce, the greater the production of goods and services will be. In other words, by saving more now, people will be able to consume more in the future.

From a macroeconomic perspective, it makes little if any difference where the saving comes from. In terms of the collective resources of the nation, a dollar of saving means a dollar of investment whether it is household, business, or public sector saving.

The measure that matters with respect to the federal government's saving is the unified budget. For some purposes, the budget is divided into two accounts; one is referred to as "on-budget" and the other is "off-budget." The so-called off-budget surplus consists almost entirely of Social Security receipts and outlays.[4]

Some have argued that Social Security should not be counted as contributing to official measures of the budget surplus. Keeping Social Security off budget is a procedural device by which Congress signals that the Social Security program should be insulated from other operations of the budget. "Lockbox" proposals go further in an attempt to deter the current and future Congresses from using Social Security surpluses to justify spending increases for other federal programs or for tax cuts.[5]

With regard to current saving, however, it makes no difference whether those revenues are credited to the trust fund or simply seen as financing current federal government outlays (including Social Security benefits).[6] Without the excess revenues from Social Security taxes, the deficit would be larger, and the federal government's requirements for a share of the national savings pool would be larger as well. Off-budget surpluses contribute to national saving in exactly the same way as on-budget surpluses do. The additional saving they represent adds to the national saving rate and allows current investment spending to be higher than it would otherwise be.

EXPLAINING HOUSEHOLD SAVING

Any examination of Social Security and its effects on households must begin with an explanation of household saving behavior. What do households take into account when deciding whether, and how much, to save?

Life Cycle Saving

Most economists analyze household saving behavior using what is known as the life-cycle model of consumer behavior. The life-cycle model begins with the basic assumption that most individuals are not myopic but rather take their expected lifetimes into account when deciding how much out of current income to save and how much to spend.

The life-cycle model assumes that individuals seek to avoid large fluctuations in their standard of living over the course of their lifetimes. The model further takes as a given that individuals' incomes tend to follow a predictable pattern over the course of their lifetimes. Typically, that would mean relatively low levels of income during the initial years of work, increases in income up to retirement, and then a drop in income during retirement.

If consumption followed the same pattern as income, it would make for substantial changes in living standards over the course of a lifetime. Instead, consumers are presumed to vary the rate at which they save out of income in order to dampen the effect of changes in income on consumption. Thus, the typical pattern would be that individuals save relatively little in the early stages of their working lives. Then, during peak earning years, saving rates tend to be higher in order to accumulate wealth off of which to live during retirement, when saving tends to fall off considerably.[7]

Precautionary Saving

There is a second consideration that may motivate household saving in addition to retirement. While there may be a typical pattern to incomes, on average, over lifetimes, there is also a certain amount of uncertainty associated with an individual's income at a given time in the future. For example, some incomes vary over the course of the business cycle, and from time to time people may also experience episodes of either voluntary or involuntary unemployment. Thus, in addition to serving as a buffer against lifetime income fluctuations, some fraction of saving may also act to insure against the risks of shorter-term fluctuations in income. This kind of saving may also help to insure against whatever risk might be associated with an individual's pension plan. It is generally referred to as precautionary saving.

Although this may not account for all the possible incentives households have to save, it is enough of a framework to make some general observations about household saving behavior. For example, a temporary decline in incomes will not necessarily have an effect on consumer spending, or on an individual's long-term saving rate, since households have already set funds aside for just such a rainy day. But, any change in prospects that are likely to extend over an entire lifetime might well affect saving behavior.

Recent Trends in Household Saving

Social Security was created to help secure the economic condition of the retired population by forcing them to save more now in exchange for expected future benefits. Concern remains, however, that many are still not setting aside enough on their own in order to provide adequately for retirement.[8]

It has often been noted that Americans save less than they used to, and that they save less than most other industrialized nations. Those concerns were part of the motivation for the policies that contributed to the elimination of the federal budget deficit.[9] Personal saving, as measured in the standard economic accounts, has been falling steadily since 1990. Figure 1 shows personal saving as a percentage of aftertax personal income since 1970. The personal saving rate has fallen steadily from more than 10% in the early 1980s to less than zero in 2006.

Source: Department of Commerce, Bureau of Economic Analysis.
Figure 1. Personal Saving as a Percentage of Aftertax Personal Income.

However, this measure of saving may give an exaggerated picture of the drop in saving. One of the most marked characteristics of the economy during much of the 1990s was the dramatic rise in equity prices. But, capital gains are not included in the measure of saving shown in figure 1. A measure of saving based on changes in household net worth would tell a different story. In fact, much of the decline in measured savings, at least through 1999, may have been due to a large increase in equity prices. Between 1990 and 1999, total household net worth more than doubled, while the ratio of household net worth to aftertax income rose from 472% to 633%.[10] The increase in wealth resulting from the rise in equity prices may have led some to feel they did not need to save as much.[11]

Between 1999 and 2003, however, equity prices fell by about one-third, and during that period, the saving rate continued to decline. Stock prices have since recovered, but that household saving continued to be anemic even after the stock market cooled suggests that there are other factors that need to be considered. One candidate would seem to be the boom in the housing market. Since late 1997, the price of housing has risen rapidly relative to prior years. Between the third quarters of 1997 and 2006, the house price index published by the Office of Federal Housing Enterprise Oversight (OFHEO) almost doubled, increasing by 98.5%.[12]

A number of studies have suggested that housing price appreciation may have had a significant effect on household saving. Belsky and Prakken, for example, found that in the long run, the effects on household saving of house and equity price variations were similar.[13] They also found that house price appreciation had a more immediate effect and that the effect of equity price appreciation took longer to be fully reflected in the saving rate. The authors suggested that may be because historically equity prices have been more volatile than house prices, and so households may be more confident in the durability of house price gains. The authors also indicated that the strong effect of the post-2000 boom in house prices may have been partly due to the simultaneous decline in interest rates, which encouraged homeowners to refinance as well as borrow. They left open the question of whether, in other circumstances, house price appreciation would have the same effect on household saving.[14]

Although there are reasons to think that housing price appreciation might not be a substitute for saving, the empirical studies, not quite amounting to a consensus, found evidence to suggest that it might. If house prices come down in the future, however, households will end up with less wealth than they anticipate. That would make the current low saving rate seem more of a problem.

With respect to household saving, how much is "enough" may be a subjective matter. One standard might be whether accumulated wealth is sufficient to avoid a decline in living standards upon retirement. The life cycle model discussed above assumes that individuals seek to avoid substantial ups and downs in consumption over the course of a lifetime. It might be assumed, then, that the goal of retirement saving is to avoid a significant drop in living standards after retirement.

A number of studies have found, however, that Americans may not save enough to avoid such a decline in their living standard. One, by Hamermesh, of consumption patterns over time found that accumulated wealth, both private and through Social Security, was not sufficient to sustain consumption in early retirement. This study found that, typically, households gradually reduced their consumption spending within several years of having retired.[15]

A more recent study, by Bernheim and Scholz, also found that Americans were not saving enough to prepare for retirement.[16] In particular, they found a distinct difference in saving behavior between those with a college education and the rest of the population. In general, those households with a college education were found to have saved enough to avoid a substantial cutback in consumption on retiring, whereas those with less than a college education had not.[17]

In a separate study of household saving behavior, Bernheim concluded that the typical baby-boom household was saving at about one-third the rate at which they would need to save in order to continue to maintain their current standard of living into retirement.[18]

Engen, Gale, and Uccello make several interesting points regarding the adequacy of household saving for retirement. First, they point out that the ups and downs of the stock market may have little effect on many of those households that are not saving enough, since the ownership of financial assets is heavily concentrated among those households likely to already be saving enough. Second, with regard to what level of saving is considered adequate, it is important to consider the large increase in the consumption of leisure when comparing consumption before and after retirement. Those studies that do not account for the value of leisure time may overestimate the extent of any decline in post-retirement consumption.[19]

SOCIAL SECURITY AND HOUSEHOLD SAVING

Social Security was intended to provide a base upon which to secure the income of the retired population. As such, it might have been expected to increase the national rate of saving by adding to what households were already setting aside.

However, there is an important question as to whether or not Social Security is a close substitute for personal saving. If it is, Social Security may lead individuals to save less than they would have in its absence.

Consider the stereotypical saver described by the life cycle model discussed above. How would the introduction of a program which required workers to contribute to a retirement fund for their own eventual benefit affect their saving behavior? Whether and how much individual savings are affected by the introduction of such a program would likely depend on the specific features of the program. Suppose that the contributions yielded the same return as other forms of financial assets households might otherwise buy with their saving. In that case, it might be reasonable to expect that individuals would be indifferent between either saving directly or via the contributions to their retirement fund. The introduction of such a program might simply cause individuals to reduce other saving to offset the amount of their contribution.

Suppose, however, that when the program is introduced, retirement benefits are immediately available to everyone who is qualified. This would be closer to a pay-as-you-go system. In this case, those who were very near retirement would contribute relatively little to the program while still receiving the full stream of benefits in retirement. Because those who immediately receive benefits would have contributed little to the program there would be a significant transfer of income from those still working to those in retirement.

Of these two groups, workers tend to save more than do those who are retired. The transfer of income from relatively high savers to relatively low savers would tend to bring down the overall household saving rate. In a strictly pay-as-you-go pension system there would be no offsetting saving on the part of the public sector; all of the contributions would be distributed. Thus, the introduction of a pure pay-as-you-go Social Security system would tend to reduce the national saving rate.

Another way in which Social Security might influence saving was suggested by economist Martin Feldstein. Feldstein argued that Social Security, or any pension for that matter, might lead people to retire sooner than they otherwise would have. For one thing, once covered workers become eligible for an annuity, their pay effectively drops by the amount of the annuity, since they are only working for the difference between their earnings and what their annuity would be.

In an effort to measure the effect of Social Security on saving, Feldstein examined the effect of Social Security wealth on personal saving using data from 1930 to 1992. Social Security wealth was defined as the discounted present value of promised Social Security benefits. Feldstein found that, for each dollar increase in Social Security wealth, personal savings fell by two or three cents.[20] Other studies on the effect of changes in wealth on household saving have found that for each dollar increase in household wealth, saving out of current income falls by somewhere between 1 cent and 7 cents.[21]

If Social Security encourages workers to retire early, then there is a longer period of retirement to save for. But, workers anticipating an earlier retirement might tend to save more on their own. That aspect of Social Security might then tend to raise the personal saving rate. There are two potentially offsetting effects — Social Security substituting for personal saving, and encouraging longer retirement. The first effect tends to reduce personal saving, the second tends to raise it.

Social Security may also affect the precautionary motive for saving. Social Security, as it now stands, is a defined benefit program. In other words, retirement benefits, although they are based on career earnings, are fixed in real terms upon retirement. After that, they do not vary and continue as long as the beneficiary survives. In contrast, were individuals to provide entirely for their own retirement, there would be several sources of risk. For example, there would be uncertainty regarding how long a period of retirement would have to provided for, and there would be some risk associated with those investments which make up individuals' nest eggs.

Thus, Social Security may affect saving in several ways. It may reduce household saving as participants pay some of their Social Security contributions by reducing what they otherwise would have set aside in other investments. It reduces the risk associated with retirement planning and so may free participants to cut precautionary saving. It may also encourage additional saving by making it possible to retire earlier thus providing participants a longer period of retirement to plan for. To the extent that Social Security involves a transfer of income from workers to retirees, it tends to reduce total saving by shifting resources from high savers to relatively low savers.

SAVING AND SOCIAL SECURITY REFORM

As it now stands, Social Security is partially funded. In 2017, benefit payments are projected to exceed tax receipts and, if that happens, will have to be funded out of general revenues. Because of that, some policymakers urged that changes need to be made. The argument is that whatever costs there are to assuring future benefit payments and boosting the confidence of participants in the program will be more easily borne if they are spread out over a long period of time rather than put off until some inevitable day of reckoning.[22]

In the long run, from a national perspective, what matters is how much people save now. Whether it is household saving, business saving, or a federal budget surplus, increased saving means increased investment, a larger capital stock, and higher future living standards. The more that is saved now, the larger the economy will be in the future. If Social Security is changed, those changes could affect saving in one way or another. Using the basic model of life-cycle and precautionary saving explained above it is possible to make a few relevant observations about the potential effects of various kinds of Social Security reform proposals on saving.[23]

There are two broad kinds of reform possibilities that have been most discussed. One is a shift towards a fully-funded plan. The second is a switch from the *defined benefits* that currently characterize Social Security to one that is at least partly a *defined contribution* plan with variable benefits. This second kind of proposal includes some of the suggestions that would privatize some or all of the Social Security program. Another proposal that has been advanced would have some of the trust fund invested in private securities such as corporate stock.

Fully Funded vs. Pay as You Go

If Social Security were fully funded, that would mean that each generation contributed enough to fully provide for their benefits on retirement, and there would be no intergenerational transfers. A pure pay-as-you-go system, on the other hand, would have no trust fund at all, and all Social Security retirement benefits would be paid for by the current contributions of the working population. In this case there would be a continuing transfer of income between generations. Because Social Security is only partially funded, at some point in the future all benefits will be transfers from the working population to retirees if no changes are made.

Switching to a more fully funded program would necessarily involve some combination of increased contributions and reduced benefits. However, any increase in taxes, or cut in benefits, might be partially offset by a reduction in other forms of household saving. A reduction in benefits could also lead households to save less as they seek to maintain a constant level of consumption given a cut in income. For those still working, a cut in prospective benefits might encourage additional saving.

A shift towards a fully funded system would also tend to reduce the intergenerational redistribution of income. A pure pay-as-you-go system takes income from workers, who tend to be savers, and gives it to retirees who tend to save relatively little. In a fully funded system, workers would finance their own retirement benefits. Shifting from a pay-as-you-go system to a fully funded one might reduce the overall bias against saving which is due to the shift of income from savers to dis-savers.

Shifting Social Security closer to a fully funded program might also increase confidence on the part of participants that future benefits would be paid. This might serve to diminish the precautionary incentive to save and tend to reduce household saving.

A shift toward a more fully funded system might lead to a reduction in measured household saving, but it is unlikely that the reduction in household saving would offset the increase in public sector saving. The net result is that such a shift would be likely to raise the national saving rate.

Defined Benefit vs. Defined Contribution

Other proposals for Social Security reform involve at least a partial shift from a *defined benefit* plan to a *defined contribution* plan. A defined benefit plan is one where the benefits are set in advance, and while participants must contribute, their benefits do not depend on the performance of those assets in which they are invested. Participants in a defined contribution retirement plan contribute a set amount periodically into an account, and their ultimate retirement benefits depend on the return on the investments held in those accounts.

Depending on the existing level of confidence in future benefits, a shift toward a defined contribution plan might involve an increase in the perceived, or actual, risk faced by participants. To some extent, future benefits would depend on the performance of those assets in which contributions were invested. An increase in risk might lead households to save more for precautionary reasons. A switch toward a defined contribution plan might not, however, involve a great increase in perceived risk given the apparent skepticism among those working now as to whether or not they will get their full Social Security benefits on retiring. If the assets in which the defined contributions are invested yield a higher return, participants might have an incentive to reduce other forms of saving.

Switching to a defined contribution plan, or partially privatizing Social Security, would reduce the federal government surplus because money that had been collected as taxes would be invested directly by individuals. The measured household saving rate would go up as households themselves invested those funds which previously had been paid into the Social Security trust fund. If these new contributions were mandatory, there would be no net effect on national saving as the increase in household saving would offset the decrease in federal government saving.

If the defined contributions were not mandatory, however, it is possible that the household saving would not rise enough to offset the decline in the federal government saving rate. Many would be likely to spend at least a portion of the reduction in taxes and some, who might not ever plan to retire might spend all of it. Unless the contributions were made mandatory, the net effect of a switch in the direction of a defined contribution plan could reduce the national saving rate.

There could also be some indirect effects on saving. For example, there might be some increase in the risk associated with retirement savings with a switch to a defined contribution plan which could encourage additional precautionary saving.

Investing the Trust Fund in Private Securities

Another reform proposal that has been advanced is that some of the Social Security trust fund, which currently consists exclusively of Treasury securities, be invested in private securities. Such a change would have no effect on national saving.[24]

If the trust fund were to invest in private securities, corporate stock for example, it would have to either sell some of the Treasury securities it now holds or it would buy stocks out of current tax receipts, and the Treasury would have to find another market for any securities it would otherwise issue to the trust fund. In any case, the supply of Treasury securities would increase, their prices would tend to go down, and their yields would tend to go up. At the same time the demand for corporate stock would increase, and the yield on those stocks would tend to fall. Ultimately the public sector would own some private assets, and the private sector would hold a larger proportion of public sector debt. The only change would be in how the public and private sectors invested their money. There is no evidence indicating that households would increase, or reduce, their saving simply as a result of a shift in relative rates of return on selected financial assets.

If trust fund assets were invested in private sector securities, which yielded a higher rate of return, the trust fund might be made better off. But the improvement in the trust fund would come at the expense of the rest of the federal government budget and those private investors that would otherwise have purchased those assets. The borrowing costs of the federal government would rise because of the increased supply of government securities. The income from capital of other private investors would fall because the increase in demand for private sector securities would be likely to reduce their rate of return.[25]

If individual accounts were created out of trust fund assets and those accounts were invested in private securities the situation would be similar. If Social Security funds were held in personal accounts and invested in private securities, their yield would likely be higher than if they were invested in government securities. But, someone would have to buy the assets that would otherwise have been purchased by the trust fund. And those who did would experience a drop in income from capital.

None of this is to say that investing the trust fund in private securities is undesirable, or would have no effect. Rather, it is to say that such a change would be unlikely to affect the national saving rate.

Social Security will never function exactly like a collective retirement plan where each individual sets aside a given amount in order to provide for his own retirement. Even with a fully funded plan, there will be income transfers among participants. For example, those who live longer than average will gain at the expense of those who die prematurely. As long as the plan is less than fully funded, there will be an ongoing transfer from the working population to those who are already retired.

In the case of individuals, how much they set aside during their working years will determine how well they live in retirement. Similarly, for the nation as a whole, how much people save now will play a role in the size of the economy in the future. The collective saving of households, business, and the public sector will determine how much is invested. The more people invest, the larger a stock of capital people will have and the more productive the labor force will be. A more productive labor force means higher standards of living in the future.

By saving more now, the economy in the future will be larger than it otherwise would be. The larger the economy is and the higher incomes are will make it easier to afford paying retirement benefits no matter how they are financed.

REFERENCES

[1]   The trustees publish three estimates using different assumptions about costs. They call the intermediate projection their "best estimate." This refers to both Old-Age and Survivors Insurance (OASI) and Disability Insurance (DI), which collectively are referred to as OASDI. See the 2007 OASDI trustee's report, at [http://www.ssa.gov/OACT/TR/TR07/].

[2]   A larger economy will make it relatively easier to provide retirement benefits. In dealing with the long-range Social Security funding problem, for example, a larger economy would ease any actions needed to fully fund benefit obligations. Increasing federal government saving now reduces outstanding federal debt and reduces outlays now devoted to financing the existing public sector debt.

[3]   For a more comprehensive discussion of Social Security reform proposals, see CRS Report RL31498, *Social Security Reform: Economic Issues*, by Jane Gravelle and Marc Labonte.

[4]   The Postal Service is also included in the off-budget account.

[5]   Some proponents of accounting devices that isolate Social Security from the rest of the budget claim that this would result in greater government saving. This assumes that spending and tax policy decisions depend on what happens to the trust fund.

[6]   Neither would it matter with respect to Social Security deficits, currently projected to begin in 2017.

[7]   People with higher incomes tend to save more than those with lower incomes; not necessarily just because their incomes are higher, but also because they are more likely to be in their peak earning years.

[8]   Social Security is not the only source of retirement income. In fact, in the national income and product accounts published by the Department of Commerce, contributions to Social Security are not counted as part of household saving.

[9]   Such as the omnibus Budget Reconciliation Act of 1993, which included both tax increases and spending cuts. There has also been a reduction in defense spending relative to GDP. See Alberto Alesina, "The Political Economy of the Budget Surplus in the United States," *Journal of Economic Perspectives*, vol.14, no. 3, summer 2000, pp. 3-19.

[10] Figures are from the Board of Governors of the Federal Reserve System.

[11] See CRS Report RL33168, Why is the Household Saving Rate So Low? by Brian W. Cashell.

[12] See CRS Report RL31918, *U.S. Housing Prices: Is There a Bubble?*, by Marc Labonte.

[13] Eric Belsky and Joel Prakken, "Housing's Impact on Wealth Accumulation, Wealth Distribution and Consumer Spending," National Association of Realtors National Center for Real Estate Research, 2004, 26 pp.

[14] Whether or not house price appreciation might substitute for other forms of saving may depend on if there is a strong bequest motive for saving. Those who save in order to leave a bequest to their children may desire to leave a larger bequest if their children are expected to face higher house prices.

[15] Daniel S. Hamermesh, Consumption During Retirement: The Missing Link in the Life Cycle, *The Review of Economics and Statistics*, vol. LXVI, no. 1, February 1984, pp. 1-7.

[16] B. Douglas Bernheim and John Karl Scholz, "Do Americans Save Too Little?," Federal Reserve Bank of Philadelphia *Business Review*, September-October 1993, pp. 3-20.

[17] Income and education tend to be correlated, as are saving and income. Nonetheless, Bernheim and Scholz suggest that one reason some save less than others is that they may not be fully aware of the importance of saving, and that education might be effective in encouraging them to save more.

[18] American Council for Capital Formation, Center for Policy Research, *Special Report*, "Do Households Appreciate Their Financial Vulnerabilities? An Analysis of Actions, Perceptions, and Public Policy," August 1994.

[19] Eric M. Engen, William G. Gale, and Cori Uccello, *Are Households Saving Adequately for Retirement? A Progress Report on Three Projects*, paper presented at the third annual conference of the Retirement Research Consortium, May 2001, p. 19.

[20] Martin Feldstein, "Social Security and Saving: New Time Series Evidence," *National Tax Journal*, June 1996, vol. 49, no. 2, pp. 151-164.

[21] CRS Report RL30518, *The Stock Market and the Economic Outlook*, by Brian W. Cashell. (Out of print; for copies, contact author, 202-707-7816.)

[22] In principle, the Social Security trust fund represents the obligation of the federal government to pay future benefits. In practice, in an economic sense, it is current Social Security receipts and outlays that matter.

[23] See Eric M. Engen and William G. Gale, "Effects of Social Security Reform on Private and National Saving," in *Social Security Reform: Links to Saving, Investment, and*

Growth, Federal Reserve Bank of Boston, Conference Series No. 41. June, 1997, pp. 103-142.

[24]   Under current rules, if the trust fund purchased private sector securities, those expenditures would be counted as outlays in the unified budget. The increase in measured outlays would reduce the unified budget surplus. But, federal government saving would not change. The Congressional Budget Office is considering changing they way they count purchases of private securities in the budget to eliminate this inconsistency. Whether budget policy depends in any way on particular accounting practices is an issue beyond the scope of this paper. For a discussion, see Congressional Budget Office, Cost Estimate H.R. 4844, Railroad Retirement and Survivors' Improvement Act of 2000.

[25]   That is, unless the yields on government bonds had to rise so much, and the yields on the private securities purchased by the trust fund had to fall so much to allow the markets to clear that the shift resulted in no change in capital income to either the private sector or the trust fund.

In: Social Security: New Issues and Developments   ISBN: 978-1-60456-243-9
Editors: P. O. Deaven, W. H. Andrews, pp. 115-124   © 2008 Nova Science Publishers, Inc.

Chapter 5

PRIMER ON DISABILITY BENEFITS: SOCIAL SECURITY DISABILITY INSURANCE (SSDI) AND SUPPLEMENTAL SECURITY INCOME (SSI)*

Scott Szymendera

ABSTRACT

Generally, the goal of disability insurance is to replace a portion of a worker's income should illness or disability prevent him or her from working. Individuals may receive disability benefits from either federal or state governments, or from private insurers. This chapter presents information on two components of federal disability benefits, those provided through the Social Security Disability Insurance (SSDI) and the Supplemental Security Income (SSI) programs. The SSDI program is an insured program that provides benefits to individuals who have paid into the system and meet certain minimum work requirements. The SSI program, in contrast, is a means-tested program that does not have work or contribution requirements, but restricts benefits to those who meet asset and resource limitations.

The SSDI program was enacted in 1956 and provides benefits to insured disabled workers under the full retirement age (and to their spouses, surviving disabled spouses, and children) in amounts related to the disabled worker's former earnings in covered employment. The SSI program, which went into effect in 1974, is a needs-based program that provides a flat cash benefit assuring a minimum cash income to aged, blind and disabled individuals who have very limited income and assets.

To receive disability benefits under either program, individuals must meet strict medical requirements. For both SSDI and SSI disability benefits, "disability" is defined as the inability to engage in substantial gainful activity (SGA) by reason of a medically determinable physical or mental impairment expected to result in death or last at least 12 months. Generally, the worker must be unable to do any kind of work that exists in the national economy, taking into account age, education, and work experience.

Both programs are administered through the Social Security Administration (SSA) and therefore have similar application and disability determination processes. Although SSDI and SSI are federal programs, both federal and state offices are used to determine

---

* Excerpted from CRS Report RL32279, dated December 26, 2006.

eligibility for disability benefits. SSA determines whether someone is disabled according to a five-step process, called the sequential evaluation process, where SSA is required to look at all the pertinent facts of a particular case. Current work activity, severity of impairment, and vocational factors are assessed in that order. An applicant may be denied benefits at any step in the sequential process even if the applicant may meet a later criterion.

The SSDI program is funded through the Social Security payroll tax and revenues generated by the taxation of Social Security benefits, portions of which are credited to a separate Disability Insurance (DI) trust fund. In contrast, the SSI program is funded through appropriations from general revenues.

Generally, the goal of disability insurance is to replace a portion of a worker's income should illness or disability prevent him or her from working. Individuals may receive disability benefits from either federal or state governments, or from private insurers.

This chapter presents information on two components of federal disability benefits, those provided through the Social Security Disability Insurance (SSDI) and the Supplemental Security Income (SSI) programs.[1] The SSDI program is an insured program that provides benefits to individuals who have paid into the system and meet certain minimum work requirements. The SSI program, in contrast, is a means-tested program that does not have work or contribution requirements, but individuals must meet the asset and resource limitations. To receive disability benefits under either program, individuals must meet strict medical requirements.

SOCIAL SECURITY DISABILITY INSURANCE

The SSDI program is a part of the Old Age, Survivors, and Disability Insurance (OASDI) program administered by the Social Security Administration (SSA). The disability insurance portion of OASDI was enacted in 1956 and provides benefits to disabled workers under age 65 (and to their spouses, surviving disabled spouses, and children) in amounts related to the disabled worker's former earnings in covered employment. The SSDI benefits, like those of the Old Age and Survivors Insurance (OASI), are meant to replace income from work that is lost by incurring one of the risks the social program insures against. Funding for the SSDI and OASI programs is primarily through a payroll tax levied on workers in jobs covered by Social Security, and the benefits are based on an individual's career earnings. At the end of November 2006, nearly 8.6 million disabled workers and their dependents were receiving SSDI benefits.[2]

SUPPLEMENTAL SECURITY INCOME

The SSI program, which went into effect in 1974, is a means-tested program that provides cash payments assuring a minimum income for aged, blind or disabled individuals who have very limited income and assets.[3] This program is often referred to as a "program of last resort" since individuals who apply for benefits also are required to apply for all other benefits to which they may be entitled, such as Social Security retirement or disability benefits, pensions, or unemployment benefits. Although the SSI program is administered by SSA, it is funded through general revenues — not payroll taxes. The federal benefit provided through this program, unlike through the SSDI program, is a flat amount (adjusted for other income the individual may have), and is not related to prior earnings. In addition to the federal SSI payment, many states provide additional supplements to certain groups or categories of people. At the end of November 2006, over 7.2 million individuals received federally administered SSI payments.[4] Of these, over 6 million were entitled to benefits on the basis of disability or blindness.[5]

TYPE OF BENEFITS AND AVERAGE BENEFIT LEVELS

SSDI

SSDI benefits are based on the worker's past average monthly earnings, indexed to reflect changes in national wage levels (up to five years of the worker's low earnings are excluded).[6] The benefits are adjusted annually for inflation, as measured by the consumer price index for workers (CPI-W). Benefits are also provided to dependents (such as spouses or children), subject to certain maximum family benefit limits. Disability benefits may be offset if the disabled worker is simultaneously receiving workers' compensation or other public disability benefits. In addition, individuals who receive SSDI benefits also receive Medicare benefits after a 24-month waiting period.

At the end of November 2006, the average monthly SSDI benefit was $946.40 for disabled workers; $249.10 for spouses of disabled workers; and $280.80 for children of disabled workers.[7] The average age of a disabled worker beneficiary in 2005 was 51.8 years.[8]

SSI

The basic federal SSI benefit is the same for all beneficiaries. In 2007, the maximum SSI payment (also called the federal benefit rate), regardless of age, is $623 per month for an individual living independently or $934 per month for a couple living independently. Federal SSI benefits are increased each year to keep pace with inflation (as measured by the CPI-W). The monthly SSI benefit may be reduced if an individual has other income or receives in-kind (non-cash) support or maintenance. However, states may voluntarily supplement this payment to provide a higher benefit level than that specified in federal law.

SSI recipients living alone or in a household where all members receive SSI benefits are also automatically eligible for food stamps. States have three options for determining Medicaid eligibility for SSI recipients. In 32 states and the District of Columbia, individuals who are eligible for SSI are automatically eligible for Medicaid. SSI recipients in seven states and the Northern Mariana Islands are eligible but must complete a separate application for Medicaid. Eleven other states have the option to impose Medicaid eligibility requirements that are more restrictive than SSI criteria.

Individuals may receive SSDI, SSI based on disability (or blindness or age), or both (some may also receive other benefits). The amount of the SSI benefit may be adjusted based on receipt of other income, such as SSDI benefits (the SSDI benefit is not reduced if the recipient also receives SSI benefits, because SSDI is not means-tested). As figure 1 shows, over the past few years, the number of adults (age 18-64) receiving disability-related Social Security benefits has increased faster than those receiving disability-related SSI benefits or those receiving both types of benefits.[9]

At the end of November 2006, the average monthly federally administered SSI payment amount was $452.40 for all recipients; $536.50 for children under age 18; $468.70 for adults age 18-64; and $373.80 for adults age 65 and older.[10]

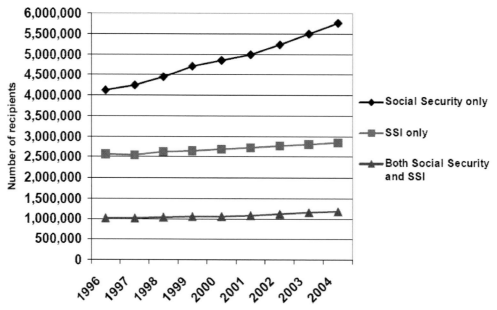

Source: Social Security Administration, *SSI Annual Statistical Report, 2004*, (Washington: GPO 2005), table 17.

Note: The number of individuals receiving Social Security benefits includes disabled workers, disabled widow(er)s, and disabled adult children. The SSI number includes those receiving federal SSI benefits, federally administered state supplements, or both.

Figure 1. Adults (Age 18-64) Receiving Social Security Benefits, SSI, or Both Based on Disability.

ELIGIBILITY REQUIREMENTS

Definition of Disability

For both SSDI and SSI disability benefits, "disability" is defined as the inability to engage in substantial gainful activity (SGA) by reason of a medically determinable physical or mental impairment expected to result in death or last at least 12 months. Generally, the worker must be unable to do any kind of work that exists in the national economy, taking into account age, education, and work experience.

The definition of disability for disabled children receiving SSI benefits is slightly different from adults. Instead of demonstrating work limitations, children are required to demonstrate that they have "marked or severe functional limitation," and in addition, they are subject to slightly different criteria for the medical listings.

SSDI

To be eligible for SSDI benefits, a worker must be (1) insured, and (2) disabled according to the definition of disability. To be insured, they must have worked a minimum amount of time in employment covered by Social Security (similar to eligibility for OASI benefits). However, for disability benefits, if an individual does not have 40 quarters of coverage (generally about 10 years), they must have one quarter of coverage (one quarter of coverage is equal to $1,000 in 2007 and indexed to the annual increase in wages) for each year after 1950 or from age 21 up to the onset of disability. In addition, there is a recency of work test that requires the worker to have 20 quarters of coverage in the 40 quarters preceding the onset of disability (generally five years of work in the last 10). Workers under age 31 need to have credit in one-half of the quarters during the period between when they attained age 21 and when they became disabled (a minimum of six quarters is required).

Once an individual's application for SSDI benefits has been approved, he or she will receive benefits after a five-month waiting period from the time the disability began, and will receive Medicare coverage 24 months after SSDI benefits begin. Disability benefits will continue as long as the individual remains disabled, or until he or she reaches the full retirement age (currently age 65 and six months for workers born in 1940) when the benefits automatically convert to retired worker benefits. According to law, SSA periodically conducts continuing disability reviews, or CDRs, to determine whether the individual is still disabled. How often the beneficiary's medical condition is reviewed depends on how severe it is and the likelihood it will improve. The SSDI award notice explains when the first review is expected.. If medical improvement is expected, the first review will be six to 18 months after first receiving disability benefits. If medical improvement possible the case will be reviewed about every three years. If medical improvement is unlikely, the case will be reviewed only about once every five to seven years. If the beneficiary has received SSDI benefits for at least 24 months, a medical review will not be initiated solely on account of work activity.

Of the individuals whose SSDI benefits are terminated, the majority are due to factors other than medical recovery. In 2005, of the nearly 500,000 disabled workers' benefits that were terminated, 42% were because of conversion to retirement benefits and 39% were due to the individual's death. Another 6% of those terminated had a medical improvement, while 7% had earnings from work above the substantial gainful activity earnings limit.

Table 1. Reasons for SSDI Worker Benefit Termination, 2005

	Number of Workers	Percent of Terminations
Total terminations/ suspensions	499,662	100.0%
Attainment of normal retirement age	210,952	42.2%
Death of beneficiary	196,729	39.4%
Medical improvement	32,203	6.4%
Work above SGA	36,263	7.3%
Other	23,515	4.7%

Source: Social Security Administration, Annual Statistical Report on the Social Security Disability Insurance Program, 2005, (Washington: GPO 2006), table 50.

SSI

To receive SSI aged benefits, an individual must be at least 65 years old. To receive SSI disability benefits, an individual must meet the same definition of disability that applies under the SSDI program (see the section below on the "Disability Determination Process"). To qualify for SSI benefits because of blindness, an individual must have visual acuity of 20/200 or less with the use of a correcting lens in the person's better eye, or tunnel vision of 20 degrees or less. In addition to age, disability, or blindness, an individual must meet income and resource tests to qualify for SSI benefits. They must also (1) be a citizen of the United States, or if not a citizen, (a) be a refugee or asylee who has been in the country for less than seven years, or (b) be a "qualified alien" who was receiving SSI as of August 22, 1996 or who was living in the United States on August 22, 1996 and subsequently became disabled; (2) be a resident of the United States or the Northern Mariana Islands, or a child of a person in the military stationed outside the United States;[11] (3) apply for all other benefits to which they are entitled; and (4) if they are disabled, accept the vocational rehabilitation services that they are offered. There is no recency of work test for SSI benefits as there is for SSDI benefits.

The countable resource limit for SSI eligibility is $2,000 for individuals and $3,000 for couples. These amounts are not indexed for inflation and have remained at their current levels since 1989. Some resources are not counted in determining eligibility for SSI. Among the excluded resources are: an individual's home; a car used for essential transportation (or, if not essential, up to $4,500 of its current value); property essential to income-producing activity; household goods and personal effects totaling $2,000 or less; burial funds of $1,500 or less; and life insurance policies with total face value of $1,500 or less.

Two types of income are considered for purposes of determining SSI eligibility and payment amounts: earned and unearned. Earned income includes wages, net earnings from self-employment, and earnings from services performed. Most other income not derived from current work (including Social Security benefits, other government and private pensions, veterans' benefits, workers' compensation, and in-kind support and maintenance) is considered "unearned." In-kind support and maintenance includes food, clothing, or shelter that is given to an individual. If an individual (or a couple) meets all other SSI eligibility requirements, their monthly SSI payment equals the maximum SSI benefit minus countable income.

Not all income is counted for SSI purposes, and different exclusions apply to earned and unearned income. Monthly unearned income exclusions include a general income exclusion of $20 per month that applies to non needs-based income. Food stamps, housing and energy assistance, state and local needs-based assistance, in-kind support and maintenance from non-profit organizations, student grants and scholarships used for educational expenses, and income used to fulfill a plan for achieving self-support (PASS) are also excluded from unearned income. Once the $20 exclusion (and any other applicable exclusion) is applied to unearned income, there is a each dollar for dollar reduction in SSI benefits (each dollar of countable unearned income reduces the SSI benefit by one dollar).

Monthly earned income exclusions include any unused portion of the $20 general income exclusion, the first $65 of earnings, one-half of earnings over $65, impairment-related expenses for blind and disabled workers, and income used to fulfill a PASS. As a result of the one-half exclusion for earnings, once the $65 exclusion (and any other applicable exclusion) is applied to earned income, SSI benefits are reduced by $1 for every $2 of earned income. In 2007, the monthly earned income amount at which an individual with no unearned income and no special earned income exclusions no longer qualifies for a federal SSI payment (not including any state supplement) is $1,331 (also called the earned income "breakeven" amount); the monthly earned income amount at which a couple no longer qualifies is $1,953. The earned income breakeven amount may be lower for SSI recipients with unearned income and those who do not live independently; it may be higher for those who receive special earned income exclusions related to a PASS or to work.

In some cases, the income and resources of non-recipients are counted in determining SSI eligibility and payment amounts. This process is called "deeming" and is applied in cases where an SSI-eligible child lives with an ineligible parent, an eligible individual lives with an ineligible spouse, or an eligible non-citizen has a sponsor.

In contrast to SSDI, the majority of adults who have their SSI disability benefits suspended for at least one year are suspended due to having too much income. Unlike SSDI benefits, SSI benefits may be suspended for one month, and paid in the next depending on an individual's income or resources. Table 2 shows SSI recipients who had their benefits suspended for at least 12 months. For both SSDI and SSI recipients age 18-64, less than 10% of suspensions are due to recovering from disability.

Table 2. SSI Recipients with Benefits Suspended for at Least 12 Months by Age and Reason, 2003

	Number of Recipients		Percent of Recipients	
	Under age 18	Age 18-64	Under age 18	Age 18-64
Total Suspensions	63,700	431,400	100%	100%
Excess Income	25,600	256,900	40.2%	59.6%
Excess Resources	5,000	10,400	7.9%	2.4%
Death of Recipient	3,700	83,700	5.8%	19.4%
No longer disabled	14,100	25,100	22.1%	5.8%
Other	15,300	55,300	24.0%	12.8%

Source: Social Security Administration, *SSI Annual Statistical Report, 2004,* (Washington: GPO 2005), table 61.

DISABILITY DETERMINATION PROCESS

The application process for SSDI and SSI disability benefits is very much the same.[12] Although SSDI and SSI are federal programs, both federal and state offices are used to determine eligibility for benefits. An individual applies for benefits at a local Social Security Administration office where they are interviewed to obtain relevant medical and work history and to see that required forms are completed. The case may be denied at that point because the applicant does not have SSDI insured status or is earning too much money from work (work above the SGA earnings limit) in the case of Social Security disability cases, or is above the income and resource limits in the case of SSI disability cases — otherwise it is forwarded to the state disability determination service (DDS) for a medical determination.

The medical determination for both types of disability benefits is made on the basis of evidence gathered in the individual's case file. Ordinarily there is no personal interview with the applicant on the part of the state personnel who decide the claim.

SSA determines whether someone is disabled according to a five-step process, called the sequential evaluation process, where SSA is required to look at all the pertinent facts of a particular case. Current work activity, severity of impairment, and vocational factors are assessed in that order. An applicant may be denied benefits at any step in the sequential process even if the applicant may meet a later criterion. For example, a worker that meets the medical listings for disability but earns an amount exceeding the SGA earnings limit would be denied benefits at Step 1. The five steps are as follows:

- Step 1. *Work test.* Is the individual working and earning over SGA ($900 per month for a non-blind individual or $1,500 per month for a blind individual in 2007)? If yes, the application is denied. If no, the application moves to Step 2.
- Step 2. *Severity test.* Is the applicant's condition severe enough to limit basic life activities for at least one year? If yes, the application moves to Step 3. If not, the application is denied.
- Step 3. *Medical listings test.* Does the condition meet SSA's medical listings, or is the condition equal in severity to one found on the medical listings?[13] If yes, the application is accepted and benefits are awarded. If no, the application moves to Step 4.
- Step 4. *Previous work test.* Can the applicant do the work he or she had done in the past? If yes, the application is denied. If not, the application moves to Step 5.[14]
- Step 5. *Any work test.* Does the applicant's condition prevent him or her from performing any other work that exists in the national economy? If yes, the application is accepted and benefits are awarded. If no, the application is denied.

PROGRAM FINANCING INFORMATION

The SSDI program is primarily funded through the Social Security payroll tax, a portion of which is credited to a separate Disability Insurance (DI) trust fund. By contrast, the SSI program is funded through appropriations from general revenues.

SSDI

The payroll tax is a 15.3% tax on earnings that is split equally between employees and employers. Payroll tax revenues are used to pay benefits under the Social Security OASDI program and the Medicare Hospital Insurance (HI) program. The Social Security portion of the payroll tax is 12.4% (6.2% each per employee and employer) on earnings up to the taxable maximum ($97,500 in 2007). Of the 12.4%, 10.6% is paid to the OASI trust fund and 1.8% is paid to the DI trust fund. In addition to these payroll tax contributions, the DI trust fund receives some revenue from the taxation of Social Security benefit payments. These combined revenues are invested in non-marketable government bonds, which earned an effective annual interest rate of 5.5% in 2005.[15]

The resources in the DI trust fund are used to pay SSDI benefits. Currently, the DI trust fund is running a surplus as revenues coming into the trust fund exceed benefits paid out. Under current projections, this trend will continue for the next nine years, but after that the program expenditures are projected to exceed its revenues, leading to the exhaustion of the DI trust fund in 2026. In contrast, the OASI trust fund will be depleted in 2043, and taken together the OASDI trust fund will be depleted in 2041.[16] Among other things, the rapid rise in expenditures will be a reflection of the aging of the baby boom, as more of them are projected to apply for SSDI benefits when they reach ages 50-65, at which higher rates of disability incidents occur.

SSI

The SSI program is financed through the general revenue of the United States. Each year, Congress appropriates money to pay both SSI benefits and administrative costs. The SSI Appropriation for FY2005 was $40.722 million, with $37.928 million going to pay SSI benefits and $2.844 million going to pay administrative costs.[17]

REFERENCES

[1]   This paper was originally written by Laura Haltzel and updated by April Grady and Julie M. Whittaker.

[2]   Social Security Administration, *OASDI Monthly Statistics, November 2006*, (Washington: GPO 2006), table 1, available on the website of the Social Security Administration at [http://www.ssa.gov/policy/docs/statcomps/oasdi_monthly/2006-11/index.html].

[3]   See CRS Report 94-486, *Supplemental Security Income (SSI): A Fact Sheet*, by Scott Szymendera, and CRS Report RS20294, *SSI Income and Resource Limits: A Fact Sheet*, by Scott Szymendera.

[4]   Includes federally administered state supplementation. As of 2005, ten states provide supplemental payments that are federally administered (other states that provide supplemental payments administer them at the state level).

[5]   Social Security Administration, *SSI Monthly Statistics, November 2006,* (Washington: GPO 2006), tables 1 and 2, available on the website of the Social Security Administration at [http://www.ssa.gov/policy/docs/statcomps/ssi_monthly/2006-11/index.html].

[6]   The basic benefit formula for SSDI benefits is similar to the benefit formula for Social Security Old Age and Survivors benefits. The worker's past annual covered earnings are indexed to reflect changes in national earnings levels. A formula which provides a higher replacement rate for low earners is then applied to these averaged earnings.

[7]   Social Security Administration, *OASDI Monthly Statistics, November 2006,* (Washington: GPO 2006), table 5, available on the website of the Social Security Administration at [http://www.ssa.gov/policy/docs/statcomps/oasdi_monthly/2006-11/index.html].

[8]   Social Security Administration, *Annual Statistical Report on the Social Security Disability Insurance Program, 2005,* (Washington: GPO 2006), table 19, available on the website of the Social Security Administration at [http://www.ssa.gov/policy/docs/statcomps/di_asr/ 2005/di_asr05.pdf].

[9]   While the majority of disability-related Social Security benefits are paid under SSDI, some individuals receive disability-related OASI benefits (e.g., disabled adult children of retirees, disabled widow(er)s and disabled adult children of deceased retirees).

[10] Social Security Administration, *SSI Monthly Statistics, November 2006,* (Washington: GPO 2006), table 7, available on the website of the Social Security Administration at [http://www.ssa.gov/policy/docs/statcomps/ssi_monthly/2006-11/index.html].

[11] SSI benefits are not available to residents of Puerto Rico, Guam, or the United States Virgin Islands. Residents of these jurisdictions are eligible to receive federal benefits from their commonwealth or territorial government under provisions of Title XIV and Title XVI of the Social Security Act. These benefits are administered by the Department of Health and Human Services.

[12] For additional information see CRS Report RL33374, Social Security Disability Insurance (SSDI) and Supplemental Security Income (SSI): The Disability Determination and Appeals Process, by Scott Szymendera.

[13] The medical listings can be found in the Social Security Administration publication *Disability Evaluation Under Social Security*, available at [http://www.ssa.gov/disability/professionals/bluebook/Entire-Publication1-2005.pdf]. This publication is commonly referred to as the *SSA Blue Book.* (Hereafter cited as *SSA Blue Book.*)

[14] Cases of children applying for SSI benefits are not subject to the work test but instead to a test of functional capacity.

[15] Data taken from the Social Security Administration Office of the Chief Actuary and is available on the website of the Social Security Administration at [http://www.ssa.gov/OACT/ProgData/effectiveRates.html].

[16] Data is taken from the "intermediate" assumptions of the Board of Trustees of the Federal Old-Age and Survivors Insurance and Federal Disability Insurance Trust Funds as published in table IV.B.3 of their 2006 *Annual Report,* available on the website of the Social Security Administration at [http://www.ssa.gov/OACT/TR/ TR06/index.html].

[17] Social Security Administration, *Fiscal Year 2007 Budget,* p. 6, available on the website of the Social Security Administration at [http://www.ssa.gov/budget/2007bud.pdf].

In: Social Security: New Issues and Developments ISBN: 978-1-60456-243-9
Editors: P. O. Deaven, W. H. Andrews, pp. 125-132 © 2008 Nova Science Publishers, Inc.

Chapter 6

POTENTIAL EFFECT OF MARRIAGE ON SUPPLEMENTAL SECURITY INCOME (SSI) ELIGIBILITY AND BENEFITS*

Scott Szymendera

ABSTRACT

Supplemental Security Income (SSI) is a major benefit program for low-income persons with disabilities and senior citizens. As a means tested program, SSI places income and resource limits on individuals and married couples for the purposes of determining their eligibility and level of benefits. To become and remain eligible to receive SSI benefits, single individuals may not have countable resources valued at more than $2,000 and married couples may not have countable resources valued at more than $3,000. Although a person's home and car are excluded from these calculations, most other assets owned by a person or married couple are counted and in most cases, the assets of both partners in a marriage are considered shared and equally available to both the husband and the wife.

A person's countable income must be below SSI program guidelines to qualify for benefits and a person's monthly benefit level is reduced by a portion of his or her earned and unearned income. The income of a person ineligible for SSI can be considered when calculating the benefit amount of that person's spouse. A complicated process of deeming is used to determine how much of the ineligible person's income is to be considered when calculating his or her spouse's monthly SSI benefits.

In some cases marriage may result in a person being denied SSI benefits or seeing his or her SSI benefit level reduced because of the increase in family income or assets that results from the marriage. This can occur if an SSI beneficiary marries another SSI beneficiary or a person not in the SSI program. This potential effect of marriage on the SSI eligibility and benefits of SSI beneficiaries has been called a "marriage penalty" by the National Council on Disability.

This chapter provides an overview of the potential effect of a marriage to another SSI recipient or an ineligible person on an individual's eligibility for and level of SSI benefits. Examples of cases in which a marriage can reduce a person's SSI benefits are

---

* Excerpted from CRS Report RL33675, dated May 2, 2007.

provided. To date, no legislation has been introduced in the 110th Congress that would change the way marriage can affect SSI eligibility and benefits.

This chapter provides an overview of the potential effects of marriage on Supplemental Security Income (SSI) eligibility and benefits. It includes an overview of the SSI program, information on the SSI resource limits, and a discussion of how the marriage of an SSI beneficiary to either another beneficiary or an ineligible person can affect his or her eligibility for benefits or monthly benefit level. In some cases, marriage may result in a person being denied SSI benefits or having his or her monthly SSI benefit level reduced. This situation has been called a "marriage penalty" by the National Council on Disability.[1]

SUPPLEMENTAL SECURITY INCOME (SSI)

Under the provisions of Title XVI of the Social Security Act, disabled individuals and persons who are 65 or older are entitled to benefits from the SSI program if they have income and assets that fall below program guidelines. SSI benefits are paid out of the general revenue of the United States and all participants receive the same basic monthly federal benefit. In most states, adults who collect SSI are automatically entitled to coverage under the Medicaid health insurance program.[2]

The basic monthly federal benefit amount for 2007 is $623 for a single person and $934 for a couple. This amount is supplemented by 44 states and the District of Columbia. Arizona, Georgia, Kansas, Mississippi, Tennessee, West Virginia, and the Commonwealth of the Northern Mariana Islands do not offer a state supplement.[3]

A participant in the SSI program receives the federal benefit amount, plus any state supplement, minus any countable income.[4]

**Table 1. Marital Status of U.S. Adult Population
and SSI Adult Recipients by Age
(in percent)**

	Over Age 18		Age 18-64		Over Age 65	
	U.S.	SSI	U.S.	SSI	U.S	SSI
Married	54.1	22.4	54.0	20.4	54.3	26.3
Widowed	6.4	20.2	1.8	7.5	30.1	43.9
Divorced or Separated	15.5	26.9	21.3	29.9	11.8	21.0
Never Married	24.0	30.6	27.9	42.2	3.9	8.7

Source: Congressional Research Service (CRS) table with data on U.S. population taken from the United States Census Bureau 2005 American Community Survey and data on SSI taken from Social Security Administration, *SSI Annual Statistical Report, 2004* (Washington: GPO, 2005), table 35.

Notes: Data on SSI is from the end of 2001. Numbers may not add up due to rounding. For additional information on the American Community Survey see the website of the United State Census Bureau at [http://www.census.gov/acs/www/index.html].

At the end of February 2007, nearly 7.3 million people received SSI benefits. In that month, these SSI beneficiaries each received an average federal cash benefit of $465.60 and the program paid out a total of over $3.5 billion in SSI benefits.[5] The average monthly benefit is lower than the federal benefit amount because a person's total monthly benefit may be lowered based on earnings and other income.

Nearly 70% of adult SSI recipients have been married at some point in their lives. Table 1 details the marital status of SSI recipients as compared to the overall population of the United States.

SSI Resource Limits

Individuals and couples must have limited assets or resources in order to qualify for SSI benefits.[6] Resources are defined by regulation as "cash or other liquid assets or any real or personal property that an individual (or spouse, if any) owns and could convert to cash to be used for his or her support and maintenance."[7] When a couple marries and pools their assets, they may find themselves with resources that render them ineligible for continued SSI benefits.

The countable resource limit for SSI eligibility is $2,000 for individuals and $3,000 for couples. These limits are set by law, are not indexed for inflation and have been at their current levels since 1989.[8] Not all resources are counted for SSI purposes. Excluded resources include an individual's home, a single car used for essential transportation and other assets specified by law and regulation.[9]

POTENTIAL IMPACT OF MARRIAGE ON SSI ELIGIBILITY AND BENEFITS

Marriage as Defined by the SSI Program

Federal regulations establish the definition of marriage for the purposes of determining SSI eligibility and calculating SSI benefits.[10] Two people are considered married for the purposes of the SSI program if one of the following conditions is present:

- The couple is legally married under the laws of the state in which they make their permanent home;
- The SSA has determined that either person is entitled to Social Security benefits as the spouse of the other person;[11] or
- The couple is living together in the same household and is leading people to believe that they are married.

Under the terms of the Defense of Marriage Act, P.L. 104-199, a married couple must consist of one man and one woman for the purposes of the SSI program.[12]

Marriage of an SSI Beneficiary to Another SSI Beneficiary

When two SSI beneficiaries marry, they are considered a beneficiary couple. As a result, they are entitled to a federal benefit of up to $904 per month and may have countable resources valued at up to $3,000. Their combined countable income is used to reduce their monthly benefit.

The marriage of two SSI beneficiaries can have a negative effect on their eligibility for benefits and their total amount of benefits. As a married couple, both beneficiaries are presumed to have access to the couple's shared income and resources. Compared with two single beneficiaries as single persons, a married couple has a lower resource limit, a lower maximum federal benefit, and a lower amount of excluded income as shown in table 2.

Table 2. Illustrative Comparison of SSI Income Exclusions and Benefits for Two Single Beneficiaries and a Married Couple

	Two Single Beneficiaries		Married
	Man	Woman	Couple
Monthly earned income	$200	$200	$400
Monthly maximum federal benefit	$603	$603	$904
Basic income exclusion	$85	$85	$85
Countable income (earned income minus exclusions)	$57.50	$57.50	$157.50
Total monthly SSI benefit (Maximum federal benefit minus countable income)	$545.50	$545.50	$746.50
Combined monthly benefits		$1,091	$746.50

Source: Congressional Research Service (CRS).

Resource Limitations

Single SSI beneficiaries can have countable resources valued at up to $2,000. Combined, two such single beneficiaries can have a total of up to $4,000 in countable resources and can exclude from their countable resources two cars and two houses. However, as a married couple, their maximum amount of resources is $3,000 and they may exclude from their countable resources one car and one house.

Maximum Federal Benefit

The maximum federal SSI benefit for 2006 is $603 per month for a single beneficiary and $904 per month for a married couple. Two unmarried beneficiaries could each receive up to $603 per month in benefits or a combined monthly benefit of up to $1,206. However, as a married couple, these beneficiaries can receive a maximum benefit of $904 per month.

Income Exclusions

A single SSI beneficiary is allowed to exclude $85 of income (the first $20 in monthly earnings and $65 in earned income on top of the first $20) as well as one-half of all earned income above $65 from the income used to reduce the monthly SSI benefit. Two single beneficiaries can each exclude the basic $85 for a combined exclusion of $170. However, a married couple is entitled to exclude only the basic $85 and one-half of their combined earnings over $65.

Marriage of an SSI Beneficiary to a Non-Beneficiary

The marriage of an SSI beneficiary to a person who does not receive SSI benefits can have a negative effect on the SSI beneficiary's eligibility and amount of benefits if the ineligible spouse brings significant income or assets to the family. Generally, the income and assets of both persons in a marriage are considered shared and equally available to either person, which can result in an increase in the beneficiary's countable income or resources after marriage.

Deeming of Income

When an SSI beneficiary marries a person who does not receive SSI benefits, a portion of the ineligible spouse's income is assigned, or deemed, to the SSI beneficiary and is counted as income for the purposes of determining benefit eligibility and the amount of monthly benefits. The procedure used to deem income from an ineligible person to his or her spouse who receives SSI benefits consists of several steps set by regulation and takes into account the overall size of the family.[13] The four steps in the income deeming process are included below and two examples of income deeming are provided in table 3 at the end of this chapter.

Step 1. Determining the Countable Income of the Ineligible Spouse

The first step in the deeming process is to determine the countable monthly income of the ineligible spouse by taking his or her total earned and unearned income and reducing it by a special limited set of income exclusions. Generally, most income other than federal social service benefits is counted.[14]

Step 2. Allocating Income for Ineligible Children and Sponsored Aliens

Once the countable income of the ineligible spouse has been established, this amount is further reduced to account for any ineligible children living in the household or any aliens that the ineligible spouse may be sponsoring.[15] For each child or sponsored alien, the countable income of the ineligible spouse is reduced by an amount equal to the difference between the monthly federal SSI benefit rate for a couple and the monthly federal SSI benefit rate for an individual.[16] For 2007, this amount is $311, the difference between the federal SSI benefit rate for a couple of $934 and the rate for an individual of $623.

Step 3. Determining SSI Eligibility

The final countable monthly income of the ineligible spouse is used to determine the continued SSI eligibility of the beneficiary. If the final countable income of the ineligible spouse is less than or equal to the difference between the monthly federal SSI benefit rate for a couple and the monthly federal SSI benefit rate for an individual ($311 for 2007), then no income is deemed to the beneficiary and the beneficiary is eligible to continue receiving SSI benefits as an individual.

If, however, the final countable income of the ineligible spouse is greater than the difference between the monthly federal SSI benefit rate for a couple and the monthly federal SSI benefit rate for an individual, then the beneficiary and his or her spouse are considered a couple and eligible to receive SSI benefits at the level for a couple.

Table 3. Examples of Income Deeming When an SSI Beneficiary Marries an Ineligible Spouse

	Example 1		Example 2	
Monthly income of beneficiary		$0		$0
Monthly income of ineligible spouse		$800		$2,000
Step 1. Countable income of ineligible spouse		$800		$2,000
Step 2. Allocations for two children	Countable income	$800	Countable income	$2,000
	Minus allocations of $311 for each child	$622	Minus allocations of $311 for each child	$622
	Final countable income	$178	Final countable income	$1,378
Step 3. Eligibility determination	Final countable income of $198 is LESS THAN $311 so beneficiary is treated as an INDIVIDUAL		Final countable income of $1,398 is MORE THAN $311 so beneficiary is treated as a COUPLE	
Step 4. Monthly benefit determination	Federal benefit for individual	$623	Federal benefit for couple	$934
	Minus countable income of beneficiary	$0	Minus countable income of couple	$0
			Income of beneficiary	
			Plus final countable income of ineligible spouse	$1,398
			Minus exclusions ($20, first $65 of all earned income, ½ of earned income above $65)	$741.50
			Couple's total countable income	$656.50
	Total monthly SSI benefit	$623	Total monthly SSI benefit	($934-$656.5) = $277.50
Combined monthly income and SSI benefit		*$1,423*		*$2,277.50*

Source: Congressional Research Service (CRS).

Step 4. Determining the SSI Benefit

If a married beneficiary is considered an individual after Step 3, then his or her monthly SSI benefit is equal to the federal benefit rate for an individual minus any of his or her countable income. The income of the ineligible spouse is not considered when determining the benefit amount in this case.

If, however, the married beneficiary and his or her spouse are considered a couple after Step 3, then their benefit is reduced by their combined countable income. The final countable income of the ineligible spouse is added to the total income of the beneficiary. This amount is then reduced by the standard income exclusions and the couple's monthly benefit is reduced by this final income amount.

Deeming of Resources

Unlike the rules governing the deeming of income from an ineligible spouse to an SSI beneficiary, the resource deeming rules are straightforward. Any resources owned by the ineligible spouse are deemed to the beneficiary. All of the resources of a married couple are considered to be available to the SSI beneficiary and are subject to the regular SSI resource limitations. If the beneficiary is considered a single beneficiary, then he or she may have countable resources valued at up to $2,000. If, after the deeming of income, he or she is considered part of a beneficiary couple, then the countable resource limit is $3,000. The only exception to this rule is that the pension plan of an ineligible spouse is not deemed to a beneficiary.

LEGISLATION INTRODUCED IN THE 110TH CONGRESS TO CHANGE THE WAY MARRIAGE AFFECTS THE SSI PROGRAM

To date, there have been no bills introduced in the 110th Congress that would directly change the way the marriage of an SSI beneficiary, either to another beneficiary or to a non-beneficiary, would affect the SSI eligibility and benefits of that beneficiary.

REFERENCES

[1]   National Council on Disability, The Social Security Administration's Efforts to Promote Employment for People with Disabilities: New Solutions for Old Problems (Washington: GPO, 2005), pp. 62-64.

[2]   Thirty-nine states, the District of Columbia, and the Commonwealth of the Northern Mariana Islands grant Medicaid eligibility to all adult SSI recipients, or have Medicaid eligibility rules that are the same as those of the SSI program. For more information, see [http://www.ssa.gov/work/ResourcesToolkit/Health/medicaid.html].

[3]   SSI benefits are not available to residents of Puerto Rico, Guam, or the United States Virgin Islands. Residents of these jurisdictions are eligible to receive federal benefits from their commonwealth or territorial government under provisions of Title XIV and Title XVI of the Social Security Act. These benefits are administered by the Department of Health and Human Services.

[4]   The first $20 of income in a month, the first $65 of earned income in a month, and one half of earned income above $65 in a month are not counted for the purposes of determining the SSI benefit level. For additional information on the SSI income rules, see CRS Report RS20294, SSI Income and Resource Limits: A Fact Sheet, by Scott Szymendera (hereafter cited as CRS Report RS20294).

[5]   Social Security Administration, SSI Monthly Statistics, February 2006, table 1. Available on the website of the Social Security Administration at [http://www.ssa.gov/policy/docs/ statcomps/ssi_monthly/2007-02/table01.pdf].

[6]   For additional information on the SSI resource rules, see CRS Report RS20294.

[7]   20 CFR § 416.1201.

[8]   42 USC § 1382(a).

[9]   A complete list of excluded resources can be found at 20 CFR §§ 416.1210- 416.1247.

[10] 20 CFR § 416.1806.

[11] For additional information on husband's and wife's benefits, see CRS Report RS22294, Social Security Survivors Benefits, by Kathleen Romig and Scott Szymendera.

[12] For additional information on the Defense of Marriage Act and its application to Social Security programs, see CRS Report RL31994, Same Sex Marriage: Legal Issues, by Alison M. Smith and CRS Report RS21897, The Effect of State-Legalized Same Sex Marriage on Social Security Benefits and Pensions, by Laura Haltzel and Patrick Purcell.

[13] 20 CFR § 416.1163.

[14] A complete list of exclusions can be found at 20 CFR § 416.1161.

[15] Children who are receiving SSI or other public income maintenance payments are not counted.

[16] This amount is reduced by the amount of any income of the child or sponsored alien.

In: Social Security: New Issues and Developments   ISBN: 978-1-60456-243-9
Editors: P. O. Deaven, W. H. Andrews, pp. 133-139   © 2008 Nova Science Publishers, Inc.

Chapter 7

THE SOCIAL SECURITY PROTECTION ACT OF 2003 (H.R. 743)*

Dawn Nuschler

ABSTRACT

On April 2, 2003, the House of Representatives passed H.R. 743 (the *Social Security Protection Act of 2003*, H.Rept. 108-46), as amended, by a vote of 396-28. A substitute amendment offered by Rep. Green of Texas was defeated by a 196-228 vote. One month earlier, H.R. 743 was considered by the House under suspension of the rules, and it failed to receive the two-thirds majority vote required for passage. H.R. 743 closely resembles H.R. 4070 from the 107th Congress. H.R. 4070, which passed the House unanimously and the Senate with amendment under unanimous consent, did not receive final passage before the 107th Congress adjourned. H.R. 743 is a bipartisan measure that would impose stricter standards on individuals and organizations serving as representative payees for Social Security and Supplemental Security Income (SSI) recipients; make non-governmental representative payees liable for "misused" funds and subject them to civil monetary penalties; tighten restrictions on attorneys representing Social Security and SSI disability claimants; limit assessments on attorney fee payments; prohibit fugitive felons from receiving Social Security benefits; modify the *"last day rule"* under the Government Pension Offset; and make other changes designed to reduce Social Security fraud and abuse. The Congressional Budget Office estimates that the measure would result in net savings of $655 million over 10 years.

On February 12, 2003, Rep. E. Clay Shaw, Chairman of the House Ways and Means Subcommittee on Social Security, introduced H.R. 743, the *Social Security Protection Act of 2003* (H.Rept. 108-46).[1] H.R. 743 closely resembles H.R. 4070 from the 107th Congress, which was passed by the House by a vote of 425-0 in June 2002. A substitute amendment to H.R. 4070 (S.Amdt. 4967) was passed by the Senate under unanimous consent in November 2002. The measure did not receive final action in the House before the 107th Congress adjourned.[2] On February 27, 2003, the House Ways and Means Subcommittee on Social Security held a hearing on the bill. On March 5, 2003, the House considered H.R. 743, as amended by the Chairman, under suspension of the rules (debate was limited to 40 minutes, floor amendments were not allowed and a two-thirds majority

---

* Excerpted from CRS Report RS21448, dated April 2, 2003.

vote was required for passage).[3] Following debate in which many Members expressed strong opposition to a provision that would modify the *"last day rule"* under the Government Pension Offset (described below), the measure failed by a vote of 249-180.[4]

On March 13, 2003, the House Ways and Means Committee held a markup on H.R. 743, as amended. Rep. Jefferson offered an amendment that would incorporate H.R. 887 into the bill. Under H.R. 887, sponsored by Rep. Jefferson and co-sponsored by 109 Members, individuals whose combined monthly income from a noncovered pension and a Social Security spousal benefit is $2,000 or less would be exempt from the Government Pension Offset (GPO). In addition, the Jefferson amendment would hold the Social Security trust funds harmless (i.e., the increased cost to the Social Security system as a result of the change would be paid from general revenues). At the markup, Rep. Jefferson stated that the proposal would cost an estimated $19 billion over 10 years.[5] The Jefferson amendment was defeated by a vote of 14-21. Rep. Stark offered an amendment that would reduce the GPO from two-thirds to one-third of the government pension.[6] As under the Jefferson amendment, the increased cost to the Social Security system would be paid from general revenues. The Stark amendment was defeated by a vote of 15-22. H.R. 743, as amended, was approved by the Committee by a vote of 35-2.

On April 2, 2003, the House considered H.R. 743, as amended, for a second time. The measure was considered under a rule (H.Res. 168, H.Rept. 108-54) that provided for one hour of debate on the measure and 40 minutes of debate on a substitute amendment by Rep. Green of Texas. The Green amendment would strike from the bill the provision that would modify the GPO *"last day rule"* (section 418, described below). It would make no other changes to the measure. The Green amendment failed by a vote of 196-228, mostly along party lines. A motion by Rep. Green to recommit the bill to the House Ways and Means Committee with instructions to report the measure back to the House with an amendment addressing the concerns of federal, state and local government employees with respect to the GPO also failed by a vote of 203-220. H.R. 743, as amended, was then passed by the House by a vote of 396-28. The major provisions of H.R. 743, amended, as passed by the House are described below. The Congressional Budget Office estimates that the measure would result in net savings of $655 million over 10 years (fiscal years 2004-2013).

MAJOR PROVISIONS OF H.R. 743, AMENDED, AS PASSED BY THE HOUSE

Representative Payees

The Social Security Administration (SSA) may designate a "representative payee" to accept monthly benefit payments on behalf of Social Security and Supplemental Security Income (SSI) recipients who are considered physically or mentally incapable of managing their own funds, or on behalf of children under age 18. In December 2001, an estimated 10.5% of Social Security recipients and 34.1% of SSI recipients had representative payees. In most cases, a family member or friend of the recipient serves as the representative payee. Other individuals and organizations that may serve as representative payees include members of community organizations; public agencies or non-profit institutions that have custody of the recipient; noncustodial federal institutions; and private, for-profit organizations licensed under state law that have custody of the recipient.[7]

SSA is required to reissue benefits misused by an individual or organizational representative payee if the Commissioner of Social Security (the Commissioner) finds that SSA negligently failed to investigate or monitor the payee. H.R. 743 would eliminate the requirement that reissuance be subject to a finding of negligence on the part of SSA. As a result, SSA would be required to reissue any payments misused by an organizational payee, or by an individual payee representing 15 or more recipients. Such payments would be reissued directly to the recipient or to an alternative representative payee. The "misuse of benefits" occurs when payments are used by the representative payee for purposes other than the "use and benefit" of the recipient. The bill would authorize the Commissioner to prescribe by regulation the meaning of the term "use and benefit."

Representative payees are not liable for misused funds. H.R. 743 would make individual payees and non-governmental organizational payees (those other than federal, state and local government agencies) liable for the reimbursement of misused funds. Such funds would be treated as overpayments to the representative payee (not the recipient), subjecting them to current overpayment recovery procedures in the Social Security Act.

Although an individual may not charge a fee for serving as a representative payee, certain organizations (such as Department of Veterans Affairs hospitals, nursing homes and nonprofit agencies) may charge a fee for serving in this capacity. The fee is based on a statutory formula and deducted from the recipient's benefit payment. H.R. 743 would require the organization to forfeit fee payments for any month for which the Commissioner or a court of jurisdiction finds that the organization misused all or part of a recipient's benefit.

The Commissioner may impose a civil monetary penalty and an assessment on persons who knowingly provide false information, or knowingly withhold information, to obtain Social Security benefits. The civil monetary penalty may be up to $5,000 for each violation; the assessment may be up to twice the amount of benefits wrongfully paid to the individual. H.R. 743 would clarify that such penalties may be imposed on persons who withhold information that they know, or should know, affects their eligibility status or benefit amount. It would require the Commissioner to issue a receipt acknowledging notification of changes in a recipient's work or earnings status until SSA has implemented a centralized computer file to record the date on which changes in work or earnings status are reported. In addition, the measure would impose the same penalties on representative payees who misuse benefits (a civil monetary penalty of up to $5,000 for each violation and an assessment of up to twice the amount of misused benefits).

Non-governmental fee-for-service organizational payees must be bonded *or* licensed, but they are not required to submit proof of such certification. H.R. 743 would require such representative payees to be bonded *and* licensed (if licensing is available in the state) and to submit proof of such certification annually (along with a copy of any independent audit performed on the organization since the previous certification). In addition to existing periodic onsite reviews of state institutions, H.R. 743 would require periodic onsite reviews of individual representative payees who serve 15 or more recipients; nongovernmental fee-for-service organizational payees; and any other agency that serves as a representative payee for 50 or more recipients. The bill would require the Commissioner to submit an annual report to Congress on the findings of such reviews, including problems identified and any action taken or planned to correct those problems.

Individuals are disqualified from serving as a representative payee if they have been convicted of fraudulent conduct involving Social Security programs. H.R. 743 would extend the restriction to individuals convicted of an offense under federal or state law that results in imprisonment for more than 1 year (unless the Commissioner determines that the individual's designation as a representative payee would be appropriate despite the conviction) and to individuals fleeing prosecution, custody, or confinement for a felony. The measure would require the Commissioner to prepare a report on the adequacy of existing procedures and reviews.

Representative payees are required to complete an annual accounting report describing how a recipient's benefits have been used. If misuse is suspected, a report may be requested by the Commissioner at any time. H.R. 743 would authorize the Commissioner to require a representative payee to collect the recipient's benefits in person at a local SSA office if he or she fails to submit annual accounting reports.

Claimant Representatives

Social Security and SSI disability claimants may choose to have an attorney or other qualified individual represent them in proceedings before SSA. The representative may charge a fee for his or her services, but the fee must be authorized by SSA under either the fee petition process or the fee agreement process. Under the fee petition process, the representative must file a fee petition with SSA after completing work on a claim (in addition, a copy must be sent to the claimant). SSA determines the amount of the fee, which is limited to 25% of past-due benefits awarded, based on factors including the complexity of the case and the type of services performed by the representative. Under the more simplified fee agreement process, the representative and the claimant must file a written fee agreement with SSA before a decision is made on the claim. In fee agreement cases, the representative's fee is limited to the lesser of 25% of past-due benefits awarded or $5,300.

If a Social Security claimant is awarded past-due benefits and his or her representative is an attorney, SSA withholds the attorney's fee from the benefit award and pays the attorney directly. If the representative is not an attorney, or the claim is for SSI benefits, SSA pays the total benefit award to the claimant, and the representative must collect his or her fee from the recipient. To cover the administrative costs associated with the direct fee payment process, SSA charges an assessment of up to 6.3% of the attorney's fee and deducts that amount from the attorney's fee payment.[8] H.R. 743 would cap the assessment on attorneys' fees at $75 (the cap would increase each year thereafter with the rate of inflation) and extend the attorney fee payment process to SSI claims. The extension of the attorney fee payment process to SSI claims would expire 5 years after implementation. In addition, the bill would require the General Accounting Office to conduct a study regarding fee withholding for *non-attorney* representatives.[9]

An attorney who is currently licensed to practice must be recognized by SSA as a claimant representative, even if he or she has been disbarred in another jurisdiction. H.R. 743 would authorize the Commissioner to refuse to recognize as an attorney representative (or disqualify if already recognized) an attorney who has been disbarred or suspended from *any* court or bar to which he or she was previously admitted to practice, or has been disqualified from participating in or appearing before any federal program or agency. H.R. 743 would authorize the Commissioner to refuse to recognize (or disqualify if already recognized) an attorney who has been disbarred or suspended from any court or bar to which he or she was previously admitted to practice as a *non-attorney* representative.

Social Security Benefits for Fugitive Felons

The Commissioner is authorized to withhold *SSI* benefits from fugitive felons.[10] In addition, upon written request, SSA is required to provide the current address, Social Security number and photograph of an SSI recipient in fugitive status to federal, state and local law enforcement officials to assist in the individual's apprehension. H.R. 743 would authorize the Commissioner to withhold *Social Security* benefits from fugitive felons and would require SSA to share information about such persons with law enforcement officials. In some cases, the Commissioner would be allowed, with good cause, to pay withheld Social Security benefits. Terms governing payment of withheld Social Security benefits would be prescribed by regulation.

Trial Work Period

Social Security disability recipients are entitled to a "trial work period" in which they may have earnings above a certain amount ($570 a month in 2003) for up to 9 months (which need not be consecutive) within a rolling 60-month period without any loss of benefits. Under H.R. 743, an individual who is convicted of fraudulently concealing work activity during a trial work period would not be entitled to receive benefits for trial work period months and would be liable for repayment of those benefits, as well as any other applicable penalties, fines or assessments.

Government Pension Offset

If an individual receives a government pension based on work that was not covered by Social Security, under a provision of current law called the Government Pension Offset, his or her Social Security spousal or survivor benefit is reduced by an amount equal to two-thirds of the government pension.[11] However, under the "last day rule," an individual is exempt from the GPO if he or she worked in a government job that was covered by Social Security on his or her *last day of employment.* H.R. 743 would require individuals to work in a government job that is covered by Social Security for the *last 60 calendar months of employment* to be exempt from the GPO.[12] (For more information, see General Accounting Office, "Social Security Administration: Revision to the Government Pension Offset Exemption Should Be Considered," Aug. 2002 (GAO-02-950).

Miscellaneous Provisions

H.R. 743 would make a number of other changes designed to reduce fraud and abuse within the Social Security program, such as requiring individuals and businesses to notify prospective customers that a product or service being offered for a fee is available directly from SSA free of charge. Other provisions would add Kentucky to the list of states authorized to have retirement systems that have either Social Security or non-Social Security-covered positions, and provide compensation to Social Security Advisory Board members. Finally, the measure would make several clarifying and technical amendments to the *Ticket to Work and Work Incentives Improvement Act of 1999* and other aspects of the program.

References

[1]   H.R. 743 is a bipartisan measure co-sponsored by Rep. Matsui, the Ranking Democrat on the Social Security Subcommittee and 30 other Members. On Feb. 25, 2003, Sen. Jim Bunning introduced a companion measure in the Senate (S. 439).

[2]   For information on H.R. 4070, see CRS Report RS21225, *Social Security Program Protection Act of 2002 (H.R. 4070)*, by Dawn Nuschler.

[3]   The bill did not go before the House Ways and Means Committee or the Subcommittee on Social Security for markup before consideration in the House on March 5, 2003.

[4]   The provision affecting the "last day rule" under the Government Pension Offset was not included in the version of H.R. 4070 that passed the House unanimously in the 107th Congress. It was included in the Senate-passed version of the bill.

[5]   The hold harmless provision is not included in H.R. 887. For more information, see CRS Report RS20148, *Social Security: The Government Pension Offset*, by Geoffrey Kollmann.

[6]   A reduction in the GPO to one-third of the government pension is included in Rep. Shaw's Social Security reform bill (H.R. 75, the *Social Security Guarantee Plus Act of 2003*).

[7]   For more information, refer to: SSA, Office of the Inspector General, "Organizational Representative Payee Program." Testimony by Inspector General James G. Huse, Jr. before the Senate Special Committee on Aging, May 2, 2000; and Testimony by Susan Daniels, Deputy Commissioner, Disability and Income Security Programs, before the House Committee on Ways and Means, Subcommittee on Social Security, May 4, 2000.

[8]   The assessment on attorney fees was established under the *Ticket to Work and Work Incentives Improvement Act of 1999* (P.L. 106-170) and set at 6.3% effective January 31, 2000. For each calendar year thereafter, the rate is set at the level (not to exceed 6.3%) needed to cover full administrative costs. In calendar years 2001-2003, the rate has remained 6.3%.

[9]   For more information on the attorney fee payment process, refer to: U.S. General Accounting Office (GAO), "Paying Attorneys Who Represent Disability Applicants," testimony by Barbara D. Bovbjerg before the House Ways and Means Subcommittee on Social Security, June 14, 2000; and "Systems Support Could Improve Processing

Attorney Fee Payments in the Disability Program," testimony by Barbara D. Bovbjerg before the House Ways and Means Subcommittee on Social Security, May 17, 2001.

[10] As defined under Section 1611(e)(4) of the Social Security Act, a fugitive felon is "an individual fleeing to avoid prosecution, or custody or confinement after conviction, under the laws of the place from which the person flees, for a crime, or an attempt to commit a crime, which is a felony under the laws of the place from which the person flees, or which, in the case of the state of New Jersey, is a high misdemeanor under the laws of such state; or violating a condition of probation or parole imposed under federal or state law."

[11] If an individual receives a pension based on work that was covered by Social Security, his or her Social Security spousal or survivor benefit is reduced by 100% of his or her Social Security benefit earned as a worker, under a feature of current law known as the "dual entitlement rule."

[12] Federal government workers who switched from the Civil Service Retirement System (which does not have a Social Security component) to the Federal Employees Retirement System (FERS) must have at least 5 years of service under FERS to be exempt from the GPO.

In: Social Security: New Issues and Developments   ISBN: 978-1-60456-243-9
Editors: P. O. Deaven, W. H. Andrews, pp. 141-146   © 2008 Nova Science Publishers, Inc.

Chapter 8

SOCIAL SECURITY: THE NOTCH ISSUE*

Kathleen Romig

ABSTRACT

Some Social Security beneficiaries who were born from 1917 to 1921 — the so-called *notch babies* — believe they are not receiving fair Social Security benefits.[1] The notch issue resulted from legislative changes to Social Security during the 1970s. The 1972 Amendments to the Social Security Act first established cost-of-living adjustments (COLAs) for Social Security benefits. This change was intended to adjust benefits for inflation automatically, but an error in the formula caused benefits to rise substantially faster than inflation. Congress corrected the error in the 1977 Amendments. However, benefits for beneficiaries born from 1910 to 1916 were calculated using the flawed formula, giving them unintended windfall benefits. The notch babies, born from 1917 to 1921, became eligible for benefits during the period in which the corrected formula was phased in. Some feel it is unfair that their benefits are lower than those who received the windfall benefits. The term "notch" comes from graphs of benefit levels over time; there is a v-shaped dip for those born from 1917 to 1921, during the transition to the corrected formula.

A number of legislative attempts have been made over the years to give notch babies additional benefits, but none have been successful. A congressionally mandated commission studied the issue and concluded in its 1994 report that "benefits paid to those in the 'Notch' years are equitable, and no remedial legislation is in order."

ORIGINS OF THE NOTCH

The 1972 Amendments

Congress approved legislation in 1972 to adjust Social Security benefits for inflation automatically (P.L. 92-336). However, the formula for calculating the new cost-of-living adjustment (COLA) was flawed. Although intended to provide inflation adjustments only to

---

* Excerpted from CRS Report RS22678, dated June 13, 2007.

people already receiving benefits, each increase for current beneficiaries also raised the initial benefits of future beneficiaries. The formula assumed that wages would continue to rise faster than prices, as they had in the past. However, the high inflation and unemployment in the 1970s resulted in higher-than-intended increases for beneficiaries affected by the new formula, and lower-than-expected revenues for Social Security.[2] If the erroneous formula had not been changed, future beneficiaries could have received initial benefits that exceeded their pre-retirement earnings — higher than Congress intended and higher than payroll taxes could finance.[3]

The 1977 Amendments

As part of the 1977 Amendments (P.L. 95-216), Congress corrected the error in the COLA formula in the 1972 Amendments by creating a new formula in which initial benefit levels are indexed to wages, then increased by inflation after the initial year. Without the 1977 Amendments, the system would have become insolvent within five years.[4] The correction to the COLA formula resulted in different treatment for all Social Security beneficiaries depending on year of birth, as described in the following section.[5]

BENEFIT LEVELS BEFORE, DURING, AND AFTER THE NOTCH

Beneficiaries Born from 1910 to 1916

The erroneous COLA formula created by the 1972 Amendments affected people who turned 62 in 1972 or later — that is, individuals born in 1910 and later. This is because the formula used to calculate Social Security retirement benefits is based on the year an individual reaches the earliest age of eligibility, which is age 62. When the error in the benefit formula was corrected in the 1977 Amendments, benefits for people who were already eligible for retirement benefits were left unchanged. As a result, beneficiaries born between 1910 and 1916 — the seven years prior to the notch — were allowed to receive unintentional windfall benefits for the rest of their lives.

Beneficiaries Born from 1917 to 1921

The 1977 Amendments corrected the error in the Social Security benefit formula, starting with individuals born in 1917. As a result, the benefits of people who were born during the notch years are lower than those of the beneficiaries who came just before them. To ease the transition to the new, corrected formula, Congress phased in the change for people born from 1917 through 1921 — the notch babies.[6] Figure 1 shows inflation-adjusted initial monthly benefit amounts for individuals born from 1900 to 1965. The notch babies' birth years are shown in yellow. The term "notch" originated from graphs such as this one, where the lines representing the benefit levels of notch babies dip below the lines representing the benefit levels of individuals born immediately before and soon after.

Many notch babies actually receive higher real benefits than people who were born after they were, all else equal. For example, people born in 1917 receive significantly higher average monthly benefits than people born in 1922 (the first year the correct formula was fully phased in). As shown in figure 1, an average wage earner born in 1917 would receive a monthly benefit of $1,166 (in 2007 dollars), while an average wage earner born in 1922 would receive a monthly benefit of $1,080.

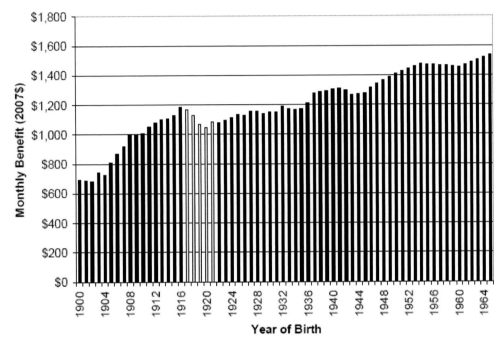

Source: 2007 Social Security *Trustees Report*, table VI.F10.
Note: The lines representing the notch period (1917-1921) are yellow. Average wage earners are assumed to have earnings equal to SSA's Average Wage Index (AWI) each year (about $40,000 in 2007).
Figure 1. Initial Benefit Amounts for Average Wage Earners Retiring at Age 65 in 2007 Dollars.

In addition, most notch babies have significantly higher replacement rates than people born after they were, all else equal. A *replacement rate* is one way of measuring the adequacy of a person's post-retirement income; it is a comparison between a person's income before and after retirement. This chapter calculates replacement rates in the same way as the Social Security Administration (SSA) actuaries, which is to show the proportion of beneficiaries' average indexed earnings replaced by their initial Social Security benefits. In 2007, the estimated replacement rate for an average wage earner retiring at age 65 is 40%.

In drafting the 1972 Amendments, Congress intended to maintain replacement rates at roughly 40%, but the double-indexing error caused replacement rates to rise above 50% before the error was fixed, as shown in figure 2 below. The notch babies' replacement rates are higher than most beneficiaries born after they were — particularly in comparison to current and future beneficiaries, whose replacement rates are declining as the full retirement age increases.

Beneficiaries Born after 1921

Benefits for people born in 1922 and later are calculated using the new, corrected formula established by the 1977 Amendments. This formula is currently being used to calculate the annual COLA.

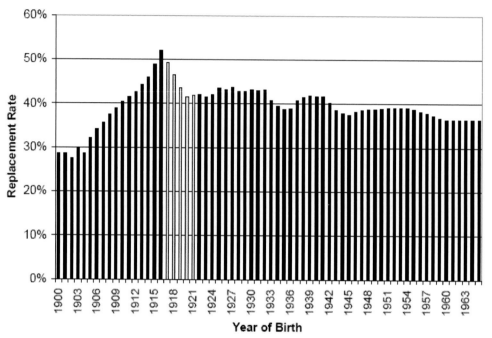

Source: 2007 Social Security *Trustees Report*, table VI.F10.

Note: The lines representing the notch period (1917-1921) are yellow. Average wage earners are assumed to have earnings equal to SSA's Average Wage Index (AWI) each year (about $40,000 in 2007).

Figure 2. Replacement Rates for Average Wage Earners Retiring at Age 65.

COMMISSION ON THE SOCIAL SECURITY NOTCH ISSUE

In 1992, Congress voted to establish a 12-member commission to study the notch issue. The Commission on the Social Security "Notch" Issue released its report on December 29, 1994.[7] Its principal conclusion was that the "benefits paid to those in the 'Notch' years are equitable, and no remedial legislation is in order." Its report states that "the uneven treatment between those in the 'Notch' years and those just before them was magnified by the decision of Congress to fully grandfather" people born before 1917 under the old law. It further states that "in retrospect" Congress "probably should have" limited the benefits of those whose benefits were calculated using the erroneous formula in the 1972 Amendments, but that it was too late to do so given their advanced age.

ADVOCACY GROUP ACTIVITY

Among advocacy groups, support for legislation to increase benefits for notch babies has been limited. The lead proponent of such legislation is the TREA Senior Citizens League (TSCL). TSCL argues that the transitional benefit formula affecting notch babies was flawed. Some Members have complained that TSCL has misled seniors about the issue in mailings that solicit money.[8] A few veterans' groups and grassroots notch groups also have supported notch legislation.

Most other organizations representing older Americans, led by AARP, have opposed notch legislation. The AFL-CIO, the National Association of Manufacturers, and the National Taxpayers Union also have come out in opposition, as did the Carter, Reagan, and George H. W. Bush Administrations. The Clinton Administration took no position, and the George W. Bush Administration has also taken no position.

LEGISLATIVE ACTIVITY

Many bills to increase benefits for notch babies have been introduced in Congress, but there has been little legislative action on them. Various attempts were made in past Congresses to gain support for discharge petitions to force the House Ways and Means Committee to report out a bill, but the sponsors were unable to get enough signatures. However, notch legislation did reach the Senate floor a number of times.

Bills Introduced in 110th Congress

Three bills have been introduced in the 110th Congress that would affect notch babies. No official cost estimates for these bills are available.

- H.R. 368, introduced by Representative Ralph M. Hall, would provide additional benefit increases to retired workers born from 1917 to 1926, which would also increase benefits for their dependents and survivors. The amount of the increase would range from 5% to 55%, depending on birth year. Eligible beneficiaries could also elect to receive lump sum payments totaling $5,000.
- H.R. 288, introduced by Representative Jo Ann Emerson, would provide additional benefit increases to retired workers born from 1917 to 1926, which would also increase benefits for their dependents and survivors. The increase would range from 10% to 60%, depending on birth year.
- H.R. 287, also introduced by Representative Emerson, would allow an income tax credit equal to Medicare Part B premiums paid by retired workers born from 1917 to1926 (or their surviving spouses).

REFERENCES

[1]   The Social Security Administration (SSA) and a 1994 commission on the notch issue define the notch period as 1917 to 1921, though some advocates define the period as 1917 to 1926.

[2]   For example, annual inflation averaged over 7% during the 1972-1977 period, compared to less than 3% from 2002-2007. (U.S. Department of Labor, Bureau of Labor Statistics, Consumer Price Index-All Urban Consumers (CPI-U) 1913 to present, at [ftp://ftp.bls.gov/pub/special.requests/ cpi/cpiai.txt].)

[3]   1977Annual Report of the Board of Trustees of the Federal Old-Age and Survivors Insurance and Disability Insurance Trust Funds, May 10, 1977. (1977 Trustees Report.)

[4]   1977 Trustees Report.

[5]   See also Social Security Administration, *The "Notch" Provision*, SSA Publication No. 05-10042, January 2004, at [http://www.ssa.gov/pubs/10042.pdf].

[6]   As of December 2005, about 2.6 million — less than 9% — of Social Security retired worker beneficiaries were born between 1917 and 1921, and thus are considered notch babies. (SSA, *Annual Statistical Supplement* 2006, table 5A, May 2007, at [http://www.ssa.gov/policy/docs/ statcomps/supplement/2006/5a.pdf].)

[7]   The Commission on the Social Security "Notch" Issue, *Final Report on the Social Security "Notch" Issue*, December 31, 1994, at [http://www.ssa.gov/history/ notchbase.html].

[8]   See transcript of hearing, "Misleading Mailings Targeted to Seniors" before the Subcommittee on Social Security of the Committee on Ways and Means, Serial 107-44, July 26, 2001, at [http://waysandmeans.house.gov/legacy/socsec/107cong/7-26-01/107-44final.htm].

INDEX

H

I

J

K